THE TWELVE

OLYMPIANS

CHARLES SELTMAN

LITT.D., FORMERLY FELLOW
OF QUEENS' COLLEGE AND
LECTURER IN CLASSICAL ARCHÆOLOGY
IN THE UNIVERSITY OF CAMBRIDGE

THOMAS Y. CROWELL COMPANY

ESTABLISHED 1834   NEW YORK

TO

PAN AND THE NYMPHS

*The author's thanks are due
to the following for permitting quotations:*

George G. Harrap & Co. Ltd. (H. B. Cotterill's *Odyssey*);
Mr F. L. Lucas and J. M. Dent & Co. Ltd. ('Hymn to
Aphrodite' in *Greek Poetry for Everyman*); Professor
W. K. C. Guthrie and Methuen & Co. Ltd. (*The Greeks
and their Gods*); Dr E. V. Rieu and Penguin Books Ltd.
(*Odyssey* and *Iliad*); the Editors of the Loeb Classical
Library (H. G. Evelyn-White's *Hesiod and Homeric Hymns*
and A. W. Mair's *Callimachus*), published by Wm. Heine-
mann Ltd.; Mr J. E. Powell and the Clarendon Press
(*Herodotus*); Mr D. W. Lucas, Mr F. J. A. Cruso, and the
Cambridge Greek Play Committee (*Euripides' Bacchæ* and
Aristophanes' Frogs); Mr R. C. Trevelyan and Allen &
Unwin Ltd. (*Translations from Greek Poetry*); and the Editor
of *History Today* for allowing the author to quote *in extenso*
from some of his own articles.

PREFACE

Four years have passed since the present work was produced by Pan Books Limited under the title *The Twelve Olympians*, and the friendly reception given it has induced me to agree to this fresh edition.

The gratitude to certain scholars and helpers which I expressed in the earlier version of this book is as strong as it ever was, and I should now like to add to theirs yet another pair of distinguished names: Professor Martin P. Nilsson, and Professor H. J. Rose, who have suggested a number of minor changes in the text. Alterations made in certain details about the Hittites are due to help given me by Mr Ronald Crossland.

My own interest in the goddesses and gods of the Greeks goes back to an early childhood part-spent in frequent wandering and day-dreaming among the sun-baked ruins of Pompeii, and to much instruction in ancient lore. Because of a life spent with a variety of religious experiences – wherein both agnosticism and mysticism once played their parts – I felt moved to write Chapter I, entitled 'The Beliefs of the Greeks', which must not be misunderstood. It is not a proclamation of my own personal views – which are touched upon in the Epilogue – but an attempt to learn the facts about a religious climate that differs from ours. I am endeavouring, while I seek to understand the old beliefs, to keep my mind detached from those pieties of childhood which are engendered in the nursery and proclaimed in the Litany. But I in no way wish to derogate from the official and recognized faiths of the Western World, rather only to indicate – with such scientific impartiality as it may be possible to attain – the differences between ancient and modern modes of approach to godhead; and also to point out that a Greek would have raised eyebrows of surprise at a variety of prevalent views, practices, and ways of religious life. Yet these require consideration in order to contrast them with ancient Greek views, practices, and ways of religious life, and in order to account for the weakness of a cultured, fancy-free paganism unconstrained by and unobedient to sanctified persons or writings. It is not possible to understand ancient myth, cult, and faith until we have been made aware that these things were vulnerable not because they were, like some of their modern equivalents, absurd, but because they were too fragile and too fine.

Cambridge, 1956   C.S.

TO

PAN AND THE NYMPHS

CONTENTS

A map of Greece appears on pages 24–5

ILLUSTRATIONS

The photographs have been kindly supplied by Directors and Curators of the respective museums; one with the portrait of Alexander, Plate XIV, was given me by Professor Bernard Ashmole. Plate VI (the statue) is by permission of 'Atlantis', Zurich, and Plate I by permission of Mr Paul Boissonas, Geneva.

A SHORT BIBLIOGRAPHY

Some abbreviations used:

AAC	H. BOSSERT, *Art of Ancient Crete*, 1937
AGA	CHARLES SELTMAN, *Approach to Greek Art*, 1948
AJA	*American Journal of Archæology*
CAH	*Cambridge Ancient History*
HESP	*Hesperia*
JHS	*Journal of the Hellenic Society*
NC	*Numismatic Chronicle*
OCD	*Oxford Classical Dictionary*
RE	*Real-Encyclopaedie*

Some books and articles relevant to the subject:

COOK, A. B., *Zeus*, 3 vols., 1914–1940

GRAVES, ROBERT, *The Greek Myths*, 2 vols., 1955 (contains many debatable interpretations)

GUTHRIE, W. K. C., *The Greeks and their Gods*, 1950

MURRAY, GILBERT, *Five Stages of Greek Religion*, 1925

NILSSON, M. P., *Minoan-Mycenæan Religion*, 2nd edition, 1950

ROSE, H. J., *Handbook of Greek Mythology*, 1928

SAVILL, AGNES, *Alexander the Great and his Times*, 1955

TARN, W. W., *Alexander the Great*, 1948

and note especially:

CHITTENDEN, J., 'The Master of Animals' in *HESP*, 1947, and 'Diaktoros Argeiphontes' in *AJA*, 1948

GUETERBOCK, H. G., 'Hurrian Kumarbi Myths'; 'Forerunners of Hesiod', in *AJA*, 1948, and *The Song of Ullikummis*, 1952

Translations (recent):

LUCAS, F. L., *Greek Poetry for Everyman*, 1951

RIEU, E. V., *Homer, The Odyssey*, 1946

RIEU, E. V., *Homer, The Iliad*, 1950

POWELL, J. E., *Herodotus*, 2 vols., 1949

THE PRINCIPAL GREEK DEITIES

with their Roman equivalents

The Twelve Olympians: *Special Concern*

ZEUS	Jupiter	sky
HERA	Juno	marriage
POSEIDON	Neptune	sea
DEMETER	Ceres	corn
APOLLON	Apollo	law
ARTEMIS	Diana	hunting
HERMES	Mercury	commerce
ATHENE	Minerva	learning
HEPHAISTOS	Vulcan	handicrafts
APHRODITE	Venus	procreation
ARES	Mars	war
DIONYSOS	Bacchus	wine

Other Important Deities:

HESTIA	Vesta	hearth
EROS	Amor	love
HELIOS	Sol	sun
SELENE	Luna	moon
PAN	Pan	flocks
PERSEPHONE	Proserpina	springtime
HADES	Pluto	underworld

Remoter Gods, more vaguely remembered:

GE	Tellus	earth
KRONOS	Saturn	father of Zeus
RHEA	Ops	mother of Zeus
OURANOS	Uranus	father of Kronos

THE engaging and wayward gods of Greece, being the concepts of a humane and fastidious people, were not cold, distant, astral gods. Even Helios and Selene, the Sun and Moon, received very little cultus among the Greeks and were not Olympians, because it was observed that the heavenly bodies moved in their own courses and were indifferent to – perhaps ignorant of – men. But the Olympian gods concerned themselves intimately with mankind, to help, to encourage the good and fine, and to punish folly and vainglorious behaviour. They were like men, though endowed with vast power, energy, and mobility; yet they were imperfect, comprehensible, and finite. They had sex, but not only one sex. These Olympians were mighty, but not almighty; they were probably eternal, but not of necessity all twelve co-eternal. A Greek might have asserted that the Twelve were One, and that the One was Twelve; but this would have seemed an academic point, the asseveration or rebuttal of which could not have attracted a charge of heresy – for no such thing as heresy existed.

The clearest token of the part-human character of the divinities was their association with a partly terrestrial home, or rather head-quarters: Mount Olympus, that enormous *massif* which separates Thessaly from Macedonia. It seems that this persistent association was due to the unusual splendour of the physical phenomena arising in that Greek climate among those mountains beside that ever-present sea. I have come round the spur of a mountain in North-east Peloponnesus to find myself facing a full moon so vastly magnified as to cause a gasp of astonishment, for it seemed four or five times the diameter of a big English harvest moon. One knew that the iridescent dust of Athens and all Attica was rising from the hot earth into a cold sky and producing a fantasy of magnification; but the eye did see the huge moon. Again, I have left Itea, the port of Delphi, before dawn in a small lateen-rigged fishing-boat, to cross the Gulf of Corinth for Achæa. We were half-way across when the sun came up with a jerk, over the isthmus far to the east, slid into an inky cloud-bank which turned imperial purple edged with cardinal red; and, as the sun came out above the bank, such massed and solid colours were given to the eye as pass description, while the sea itself had been changing from lead to a wine-dark tone, to a turquoise blue. To the north the vast snow-capped dome of Parnassus glowed coldly, and to the south-east the icy cone of Mount Kyllene stood against a deeper blueing sky.

In South-western Peloponnesus Mount Ithome rises to over 2,600 feet, and from its summit one may often clearly see Cephalonia; or from the top of Attic Pentelicon's 3,600 feet. Melos is visible to the south; and in both cases the distance is over one hundred miles. Such phenomena in quantity, with colour, solid colour everywhere, are the unique possession of Greece today, as in ancient times. And they meant even more to the brilliant, alert minds of the Greeks than they do to us; for we can find the physical explanation of those visible splendours in Nature; but the Greeks knew these as visions from the realm of the gods. And Olympus itself was – and is today – producing its own strange divine-seeming phenomena.

Viewed from the wide plain of Thessaly against a northern sky, the mountain has magnificence. Viewed from the Jugoslav frontier and the wide valley of the Vardar against a southern sky, the huge mass is even more impressive. But many will agree that the grandest effect of all is obtained when Olympus is seen from some ancient site in the Macedonian peninsula named Chalcidice, because from there one sees the snow-capped ten thousand feet rising straight out of the sea, fifty miles away across the long, deep Gulf of Salonica.

Varied atmospheric effects occur, and a description of them can be helped by simple diagrams. Fig. A symbolises Olympus completely free of cloud, a rare event which I have observed twice from the north, and on both occasions shortly before sunrise after a cold, clear night. Fig. B symbolises the ten-thousand-foot mountain cut by a heavy layer of cloud. Below the cloud is rain or grey weather, above it glowing sunlight. Apart from times when the whole mass is hidden in mist, this is one of the most usual aspects

of Olympus, and there is abundant evidence[1] to show that the
Greeks interpreted this phenomenon after a special fashion which
really conditioned the whole of their conception of the Olympian

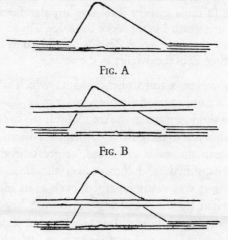

FIG. A

FIG. B

FIG. C

gods. That which lay below the long cloud-layer was called *aer*;
that which was above the clouds and into which the summit of
Olympus protruded was called *aither*. It is not enough to use the
English derivatives 'air' and 'ether', for the original Greek words
had other connotations. Now, *aer* with its moisture, cloud and
mist is what mortals dwell in; the gods, however, dwell over the
cloud in *aither*; and within that vast brightness they move freely
and fast. This Greek concept has been most admirably expounded
by Guthrie, whose words must be quoted:

The distinction was relative rather than absolute, but it remained as
real as the distinction between dark and bright, and, I think we may
say, between mortal and immortal. It remained also as a local distinction. Living in England we might be pardoned for supposing that the
soft atmosphere in which we move, at times thickening into mist or
cloud, or dissolving about us in rain, constituted the whole depth of
the sky. Not so the Greek. In his climate it was possible to see beyond
these impure vapours, and what he saw as he looked up into the daz-
zling vault of a clear Mediterranean sky was so striking that he felt as if

[1] Cook, *Zeus*, I, p. 101; Guthrie, *The Greeks and their Gods*, pp. 207 ff.

he was seeing into something generically different from the air and vapours which hang around the earth. This it was which he named the brilliant, or blazing, element *aither*. To discover therefore whether the summit of Olympus pertained for the Greeks to earth or heaven we have to decide (if the discovery is to have any significance) whether they regarded it as situated in the *aer* or the *aither*. The answer, beyond a doubt, is that it was in the *aither*. Zeus, who holds court on Olympus, is at the same time Zeus the dweller in the *aither*.[1]

There is, however, a third phenomenon, which is symbolised by Fig. C. I have only personally observed it once, on a late spring evening about sundown when looking west from the acropolis of ancient Olynthus across the gulf. Innumerable billions of dust particles wafted into the *aither* produced, at great height, a strong 'screen' that magnified; and thus – over the cloud-layer – the mountain summit was vastly enlarged, even as its snow-cap was being illuminated by the westering sun setting beyond it. Not only did it seem several thousand feet higher, but it gave the illusion of being far too big to fit on to its base, which rose from solid earth to the cloud-belt. How many a Greek and Macedonian seeing such a vision must have felt that he had looked if only briefly upon the dwelling of the Olympian gods!

Thus and thus the mountain appears from below; but how does it seem to those few who have made the ascent? Not many have climbed it, for, until after the Balkan War of 1912, brigandage was rife in the whole region. The summit (Plate I, facing page 16) was photographed by F. Boissonnas in 1920, and his picture shows the 'Throne of Zeus' and 'Mytika', the two highest peaks. A fine description of the view from the summit was provided by Urquhart, who climbed the mountain in 1830:[2]

I spent no more than an hour at this giddy height, where the craving of my eyes would not have been satisfied under a week. I seemed to stand perpendicularly over the sea, at the height of 10,000 feet. Salonica was quite distinguishable, lying north-east; Larissa appeared under my very feet. The whole horizon from north to south-west was occupied by mountains, hanging on, as it were, to Olympus. This is the range

[1] Guthrie, *op. cit.*

[2] D. Urquhart, *The Spirit of the East*, 1838, I, pp. 398 ff., quoted by Cook, *Zeus*, ii, p. 905.

MOUNT OLYMPUS, Abode of the Gods, an enormous *massif* which separates Thessaly from Macedonia. The farther summit is known as 'the throne of Zeus'.

PLATE I

ZEUS, the Cloud-Gatherer. The thunderbolt once in his right hand is his most alarming attribute. Bronze, 7 feet high, made about 460 B.C. Found in the sea near Cape Artemision in 1926.

Silver Coin of Olympia with head of Zeus laureate, struck about 420 B.C.

Silver coin with head of Zeus having the features of Antiochus IV God Manifest, King of Syria. Struck in Antioch in 167 B.C.

PLATE II

that runs westward along the north of Thessaly, ending in the Pindus. The line of bearing of these heaved-up strata seems to correspond with that of the Pindus, that is, to run north and south, and they presented their escarpment to Olympus. Ossa, which lay like a hillock beneath, stretched away at right-angles to the south; and, in the interval, spread far, far in the red distance, the level lands of Thessaly, under that peculiar dusty mist which makes nature look like a gigantic imitation of an unnatural effect produced on the scene of a theatre. When I first reached the summit and looked over the warm plains of Thessaly, this haze was of a pale yellow hue. It deepened gradually, and became red, then brown, while similar tints, far more vivid, were reproduced higher in the sky. But, when I turned round to the east, up which the vast shadows of night were travelling, the cold ocean looked like a plain of lead; the shadow of the mighty mass of Olympus was projected twenty miles along its surface; and I stood on the very edge.

Imagination in the Homeric age pictured each deity as owner of a separate house, which was a superlatively designed and furnished royal residence. But as the earthly palace changed – with the fading of kingship in Greece – into a temple, so on Olympus the divine mansions, invisible to mortal eyes, were thought of as mighty temples in the *aither*. Men built famous houses on earth for the gods so that, when they sped like lightning through *aither* and floated down in *aer*, they might find a worthy lodging among men and bestow their blessings. For the Spirit that is Zeus there was a habitation at Olympia or in the Olympieion at Athens, for Hera there were Argos and Samos, for Athene there were the Parthenon in Athens and smaller houses on many citadels. Apollo could dwell at Delphi or Delos or beside Miletus; Artemis had her splendid house at Ephesus and lesser ones elsewhere; Aphrodite had lodgings on Acrocorinthus and Eryx, at Ægina and Cnidus; while Hephaistos had one fine building in Athens, though elsewhere he dwelt in a simple gas-jet. Poseidon found welcome in great temples at Sunium and Poseidonia; Demeter in the House of Initiation at Eleusis, or her dwelling at Megalopolis. Only the restless gods – the good Hermes and the bad Ares – had in general small insignificant shrines, because they were for ever on the move. And the latest of the dwellers on Olympus, Dionysos, could find lodging in every theatre throughout Hellas.

The Athenians of the Court of Areopagus who examined the claims of Paul could agree with many of his views, especially that Divinity did not dwell in temples made with hands. But even as the devout experience in cathedral and church an Immanence as of a Real Presence, so the ancient Greeks might feel a Presence within some great and holy temple. The Greeks were not idolaters,[1] for the image was in the shrine to suggest divinity but not to receive direct worship; and if the image was of high aesthetic merit, that was only because the Greeks happened to possess an unusual amount of sensibility for what was fine.

Olympus was for long imagined by the average man and woman to be the headquarters of gods wayward and enigmatic; bound by no human codes of conduct – for that, indeed, would be absurd among gods – yet, with few exceptions, benevolent to men, courteous, kind, and civilised; divine Beings whose divinity was tempered by humanity. And so for a few centuries one European people devised a genial theology called pagan, enlivened by carefree humour and unexampled in that it assumed the existence of a company of the gods who understood the foolish as well as the splendid qualities that are constitutional to Creation's most complicated mammalian masterpiece.

If, however, one's thoughts may stray for a moment from the sublime to the commonplace, it is possible to look on Olympian Society as the most exalted idea ever imagined for the Universe of an exclusive Club. Full membership, only for Divinities, was confined to Twelve, and one lady Goddess retired to make way for the admission of an essential God. None of the once-mortal 'lower orders' could gain full admission, but on a few occasions, one here, one there, achieved honorary membership and was permitted to join the Great Gods. The story of Olympus is incomplete without some acquaintance with these honorary members, more than one of whom introduced something like comedy – even buffoonery – among the high Gods. That, however, was very much in the Greek spirit. Chapters which follow are given, one each, to each of the great Olympians, and after them comes a chapter devoted to the study of certain blessed mortals who

[1] See p. 47 below.

achieved apotheosis, or canonisation, even though their saintliness was often seasoned with truculence. These great and famous men and women were 'assumed' into the ethereal glory of the Holy City of the Gods, while on earth altars were set up and temples consecrated to them, even as new ecclesiastical buildings today are dedicated to Saints. Yet it would appear that available accommodation on Olympus was noticeably more limited than in the New Jerusalem, and so elevation was a rare event.

I. THE BELIEFS OF THE GREEKS

GREECE, the eastern outpost of civilised Europe, vital in our own day, a country still great despite its small size – *that* we can envisage. And the Greeks we have met who often surprise us because in contrast to some Europeans, their attitude to life seems very much like our own – *these* are real. So is ancient Greece in a way, because always there are the names that seem a part of our own heritage: Homer and Sophocles, Pericles and Plato, Aristotle and Alexander, Athens, Sparta, and Corinth. There exists no kind of barrier, intellectual or emotional or spiritual, to separate us from the land and its people. But once we begin to try to understand something about the gods and about the beliefs held in ancient Greece, then barriers of spirit, emotion, and intellect close down to hold us back. We must pay toll to pass through, divesting ourselves of some of our ancient prejudices and inhibitions, in order to enter into an enchanted realm where we shall discover that Zeus and Apollo, Hermes and Aphrodite, were of a truth utterly real to living intelligent people who were curiously like ourselves.

Like ourselves in many ways; and also very different; but they differed from us in the realm of Custom and Conduct rather than in the realm of Values and Virtue. Generally we may be more like those Greeks than like our own mediæval ancestors, for we think more like the Greeks and live more like them. Yet, as far as religious and social Custom and Conduct are concerned, we are more like timorous sinners in mediæval Europe, and more like our own grandparents. The inhabitants of Great Britain and of North America have, until fairly recent times, been very religious people, and large numbers still are; for one must count in not only the independent spirits who desire to be masters of their fates and captains of their souls, but also those who surrender to any Church that claims a divinely guaranteed mission. In addition to these there are people who still pay a kind of mental lip-service to some form of authoritarian faith, and whose attitude savours of adherence less to dogma than to expediency.

With such folk it is a case of

> . . . always keep a-hold of nurse
> for fear of meeting something worse.

'Nurse', of course, may be a good thing; but professionally she must hinder our initiative and curb our free thought, for she is an expert on Custom and Conduct, but no judge of either Values or Virtue. In fact, anyone who wants to know about Greek religion and about the goddesses and gods of the Greeks must decide to slip away for a while from 'Nurse'.

The Renaissance too – a kind of 'Schoolmarm' with much knowledge and more enthusiasm about the ancient Greeks – had likewise better be forgotten if one wants to comprehend Greek religion. For the Renaissance – through the work of Raphael, Rubens, and many another genius – has painted a vision of robust and nearly naked figures, heroic in dimension, meant to depict pagan gods. Nevertheless, such are not the gods and goddesses of the Greeks. They are not symbols of Greek religion – of the Greeks' living belief in the Divine.

Supposing a man to have a free and enquiring spirit, then he will observe and note the facts about the religion of the Greeks with the same degree of interest which may be given to other phenomena of the human kind. If, on the other hand, he is an adherent of one of the faiths that have stemmed from Mediterranean regions – Jewish, Orthodox Greek, Roman Catholic, Moslem, or Protestant of the North – then a little adjustment of mind, though not of belief, is needed for a better understanding. Those of the strictly monotheistic living faiths will be the most shocked at Greek polytheism and at the depiction of divinities in the guise of naked human beings. For believers within the Christian groups these phenomena are actually less shocking; for while 'Nurse' maintains a dogma of monotheism, she holds to several aspects of divinity and believes in the Prince of Darkness. Meanwhile, our 'Schoolmarm' has told us that 'goodness is beauty; beauty, goodness'. *Ergo* beautiful gods and goddesses are good. The aspects of Greek religious belief and practice that are really strange to us are other than these, and they arise from the fact that Mediterranean paganism was not a robust growth; therefore one observes the absence of certain elements which have enabled more forceful faiths to stay the course. Let us, accordingly, consider the strange deficiencies in Greek religion.

(1) *Among the ancient Greeks there was no class or caste of priests.*[1] This one fact by itself is of such outstanding importance that it really controls all that is to follow. Further, it happens to be an almost unique state of affairs. The permanent, and often hereditary, priestly castes in Babylonia, Egypt, Persia, Syria, and the various Anatolian regions, as well as Druid-priests among the Celts of Central and Western Europe, wielded immense power. Any man who held ideas which clashed with the traditional, accepted, and therefore holy decrees and dogmas of the priesthood, expressed his heterodoxy at his peril. After the return of the Jews from the Babylonian captivity a priesthood of authority gradually won unchallenged dominion in Judæa and became the ruling class, though in this case, for special reasons, it was at first different from the priesthood of a state religion.[2]

All over the world, except in Greece and Italy, these conditions prevailed, and it was because ancient Rome possessed – like Greece – no class or caste of priests that the Græco-Roman civilisation grew into a single and inseparable organisation which, while it lasted, allowed to mankind so extensive a freedom of thought and deed. There were priests; for sacrifices had to be made, festivals kept, prayers uttered, rites observed; and for the goddesses there were priestesses. But all these were just ordinary laymen with normal lives to lead within their communities, with responsibilities and employments like other folk, families to raise and duties to the State. Only upon solemn feast-days and holy-days did they dress them up in robes and wreaths to do their acts. The father of a Greek family, like the *paterfamilias* in Rome, was chief priest within his own house; and some prominent magistrate or local ruler was chief priest of the City and the State. Sometimes the office ran in certain families, sometimes it was elective, generally it

[1] *OCD*, p. 729.

[2] For a recent account of this matter see H. St J. Hart, *A Foreword to the Old Testament*, 1951, Chapter V.

involved expenditure on your part instead of income; but it was an honour and a token that your fellows thought well of you. In one respect the Jewish priesthood had a resemblance to those of the Greeks and the Romans, for the Hebrew priests were expected to lead a normal life like ordinary men, to marry and raise a family, to have a profession or a trade; nevertheless, they were all of one caste and clan.

(2) *Humility and obedience were never Greek virtues.* If these are 'virtues' there must first exist self-assured men who shall exact them; but since no cleavage was known between priests and laymen, and since priests were only laymen engaged part-time on a special job and therefore lacking in authority, they never demanded of their fellow-citizens self-abasement or unquestioning humble submission. 'Trust Nurse', 'Mother knows best', 'Father is always right' – such precepts did not enter, even remotely, into the Greeks' scheme, because in matters affecting his religion the Greek had reached maturity at an early stage. And by humility in this context is meant the kind of abjectness of an enslaved chieftain trodden upon by a Persian King of Kings, or of a spaniel rolling in agonies of self-abasement at its master's feet. This the Greeks deplored as *proskynesis*, a 'prostrating'. There is a different kind of 'humility' which is neither demeaning nor degrading, termed *aidōs* ('respect', 'reverence', or 'regard') by the Greeks, which is the kind of 'humility' required by philosopher, scientist, and scholar in search of knowledge, yet this kind is not an accompaniment of blind obedience.

(3) *Greek religion had no dogma.* An amateur priesthood like theirs had no cause to claim either unique validity for its own rites and beliefs or a unique reality for its god or its divine family. Such claims would have been at variance with the normal attitude of the Greeks, who were ready to accept foreign gods or goddesses, to worship them after the proper fashion due to them, to honour them as guests, and finally to give them 'papers of naturalisation'. Religious particularism was not a possibility for civilised Greeks.

(4) Arising from the last point, *there were no missions.* Within their own religious framework certain men, being deeply devoted

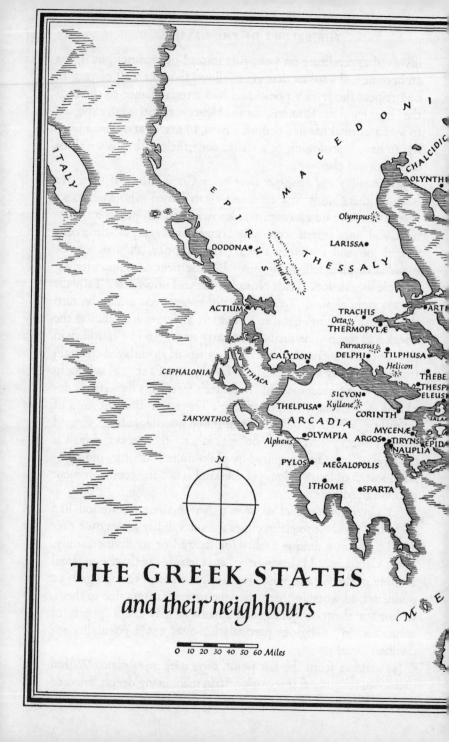

THE GREEK STATES
and their neighbours

0 10 20 30 40 50 60 Miles

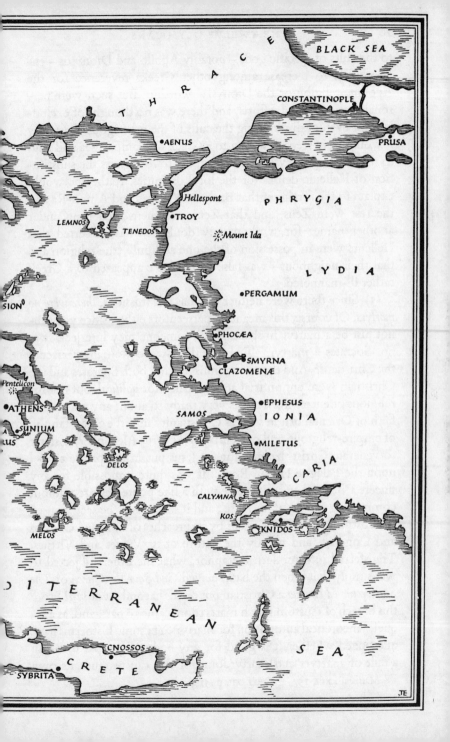

BLACK SEA

THRACE

CONSTANTINOPLE

PRUSA

AENUS

PHRYGIA

Hellespont

LEMNOS

TROY

TENEDOS

Mount Ida

LYDIA

PERGAMUM

SION°

PHOCÆA

SMYRNA
CLAZOMENÆ

Pentelicon

ATHENS

SAMOS

EPHESUS

IONIA

A

SUNIUM

RUS

MILETUS

CARIA

DELOS

CALYMNA

KOS

MELOS

KNIDOS

DITERRANEAN

SEA

CNOSSOS

SYBRITA

CRETE

JE

to the cults of specific gods – notably Apollo and Dionysos – endeavoured to increase among other Greeks reverence for the Apolline religion or the Dionysiac worship. But such were personal, not organised, efforts, and there was no thought of excluding nor even of diminishing the cults of the other gods. Certainly it would have seemed wrong to a Greek to 'compass sea and land to make one proselyte',[1] or to propose to foreigners the substitution of Hellenic deities for the local divinities. Rather he would explain to the foreigner that Baal and Yahweh and Amon-Ra and the rest were Zeus, and that Zeus was them each time under another name; for, without any doubt, to have asserted that Hellenes were in possession of the one and only true religion and that their neighbour's was false would have appeared to a Greek rather ill-mannered.

(5) Since there were neither dogmas nor missions, *there were no martyrs*. Of course, this meant no persecutors either, since you cannot just be a martyr in space. 'But', someone may interject, 'was not Socrates a martyr?' 'Did not the Graeco-Romans persecute the Christians?' And the answer must be that both Socrates and the Christians were put on trial and punished for *political*, but not for religious offences.[2] Rome was very ready to adopt any reasonable faith of Oriental origin such as Christianity into the great 'family' of empire-religions, and one emperor, Severus Alexander, wishing to venerate Christ, had a statue of Jesus put in the palace chapel upon the Palatine Hill in Rome. It was quite impossible for any sincere Christian to reciprocate with a like polite gesture without committing the sin of a 'lapse', and it seems that the sect aroused the hostility of normal citizens by its breaches of accepted Custom and Conduct, and not by the nature of its Values and Virtues. Transferred into modern metaphor, what the others objected to was simply that when the band played *God Save the Queen* or *The Star-spangled Banner* a Christian put on his hat and sat down! From this breach of Custom much martyrdom came to pass, and, as a sequel, a theoretical admiration for martyrs. Yet some historians have questioned whether it is good for any body of people to begin a cult of martyrs and martyrdom, for this can produce its own

[1] *Matthew* XXIII, 15.   [2] *CAH*, XII, p. 517.

opposite – a cult of persecutors and persecution. Later generations may derive a certain pleasure from a record of the supposed sufferings of forebears; and thus suffering itself becomes a virtue which confers a lurid glamour alike on the tortured and the torturer, who may even become popular figures in the cinema. The girl beaten-up in the film is only the modern substitute for the virgin-martyr, over whom the hagiographer once delighted to linger.

(6) *There was no Sacred Book.* Someone in search of an epigram once called Homer 'the Bible of the Greeks' – a most misleading remark. A fifth-century Greek, because he respected tradition, was apt occasionally to seek authority for his beliefs and actions in the Homeric poems. But these writings never had for him that enormous authority which was attached to a 'Book' that was inspired, like the Old Testament, the Bible, and the Koran. The religion of the Greeks was nourished on local legends, ancient tradition, bits of ritual half-remembered for interpretation, hymns of praise, epigrams, old-wives' tales, explanatory anecdotes – all of these so desperately contradictory of one another as to give cause for nothing but quiet speculation or gentle amusement to the Greeks themselves. There was no holy, indisputable, God-dictated Book to which you could refer back to obtain a final ruling. One remarkable result of this lack was that to the end Greek religion remained utterly without controversies, since there were no heresies, for the simple reason that all opinions about the gods were equally tenable. In fact, no Book, no Heretics!

(7) *There was very little preoccupation with sin*, and, of course, *no* doctrine of the Fall of Man from innocence into sin, coupled with the later view that mankind starts from infancy in a state of wickedness. The Greek word *hamartia*, often translated as 'sin', really meant 'failure', 'fault', or 'error of judgment', and distinction would be made between: (*a*) such error or folly – your own affair; (*b*) the failure of duty to men – a tort; (*c*) offence against the State – crime; and (*d*) offence against a god – sin. In normal Greek mythology there were only five sinners condemned to eternal torment: Ixion, who assaulted Hera – 'an infringement', this has been called, 'of Zeus' prerogative';[1] Tityos, who assaulted

[1] Guthrie, *The Greeks and their Gods*, p. 121.

Leto, mother of Apollo and Artemis; Tantalos, who made himself immortal by stealing the Food of the Gods; Sisyphos, who gave away the secret of one of Zeus' private intrigues. The fifth sinner was Prometheus, who tried to pass on to mortals powers which should be reserved for gods; but he was ultimately pardoned. Clearly the only sin was to commit a personal offence against a divinity. As for guilt, like the guilt of Œdipus or of Orestes, that was altogether a different matter; it had been put upon you by a Fate beyond the gods, and there was nothing for it but to be purified by a god. It was dire misfortune, but no fault of yours.

The Greeks are now discovered to have had a religious system which was deficient in a number of things: no priestly caste, no unquestioning obedience, neither dogma nor missions, no martyrs, no Sacred Book, and very little concern about sin. Yet all or most of these are found to be present in religions of authority which have commanded the adherence of mankind; and the elements of gentleness, humour, regardfulness, as well as the love of knowledge, a free spirit of enquiry, and natural toleration, which all distinguished the Greek way, would put it at a disadvantage in the face of any well-organised and forceful faith. But far more significant for mankind than anything as yet mentioned is the difference between Greek and most subsequent religious thought and practice concerned with the attitude to sex. Here we may place together Hebrew, Greek, and Roman attitudes as of one group, and the mediæval – Eastern and Western – attitude as of the other. Mediæval religion, by respecting in theory priest and monk and nun above other mortals, partly because they professed celibacy and chastity, brought sex right into the forefront of mental and spiritual stress, instead of regarding it as but a normal function in its proper place. Men may at times feel that they strengthen some weakness of will by certain vows of abstinence, like the sons of Jonadab, son of Rechab, who refused strong drink; or the Jews or Hindus, who abstain from the flesh of pig or cow. But a Greek like Herodotus would have viewed with surprise any stranger who deprived himself of such a god-given function as speech by a vow of silence, and with astonishment any barbarian who abstained totally from what is, albeit spasmodically, the strongest of all emotions and urges – hunger alone excepted – in order to suffer as a vicarious sacrifice for the sinfulness of mankind. A Greek philosopher would have observed that so intemperate a practice might change for the worse not only the lives of individual men and women, but the trend of history. We, in our day, looking back, can see that this concentration for over a millennium upon sex as so great a concern of religion is responsible for the modern world's preoccupation with the subject. By contrast, Greek thought, religion, art, and custom treated sex merely as an incidental function of humanity, as something unembarrassing and healthy in moderation.

The almost casual attitude of the Greeks to sex requires stressing, because we are apt to misinterpret the nudity of gods, heroes, and mortals in art as an interest in things sexual. I venture to quote what, in another context, I wrote a number of years ago on this topic. We can be

misled by our own heritage of prudery, which the Greeks lacked. Just as we can look at a naked dog or horse without instantly thinking of the kennels or stud, so the normal Greek could see the naked human figure without sex-obsession. His emotion could be stirred by the fineness of a fine form for its own sake, whether animal or human, and his art was no less competent to make a bronze horse than a bronze athlete.[1]

The Greeks were not, as their opponents pretended, a nation of whole-time debauchees, but a lot of hard-working, friendly, human beings with much the same kind of follies and virtues as are ours today.

Greek goddesses and gods are, in reality, still relevant now, for some of them came through the Dark and Middle Ages as Planets; and although a renegade Athenian mystic named Clement – later of Alexandria – did his best to smear the older faith, his achievement fell short of his hopes because he had a mind over-fond of pornography. When the temples of the gods were closed and their altars and statues broken, men still continued to venerate them, for they rose into the firmament to become the darlings of astrologers and magicians. Mediæval and many later men have believed

[1] AGA, p. 29.

their destinies to be ruled by the god-planets, Venus and Jupiter, Mars and Mercury, Neptune and Saturn. The very days of our week are in most European languages named after Helios, Selene, Ares, Hermes, Zeus, Aphrodite, and Kronos under their Latin or Nordic titles. Then poets and painters of the Renaissance brought them all back to earth again; and if, here too, we know them rather better by their Latin than by their Greek names, that is but a minor detail. It is pleasant to reflect that as Concepts, Beings, Symbols – both of God made man and of man made God – they have not yet left us; nor we them.

II. HERA

LONG before the Hellenes – that is, the real Greeks – came down from the North to occupy and give its name to Hellas, and to spread into the islands and many coasts of the sea, quite different people inhabited those regions. They were people to whom we now give the names of Minoans and early Helladics, and they were men of the Mediterranean race; while the Hellenes – or Greeks – were of Indo-European stock, speaking a language totally different from that of their predecessors. The Greeks subjugated these people, but did not exterminate them, exactly as the Angles and Saxons did not kill off the Britons. Moreover, in many cases the chieftains and princes of the Greeks married the young concubines or daughters of the local warriors whom they had slain in battle.

That older race had customs and codes of conduct very different from those of the incoming Greek stock; for while the older was based on matriarchy and polyandry, the younger was patriarchal and monogamous, even as we claim to be in our own day. Among the Mediterraneans, as a general rule, society was built round the woman, even on the highest levels, where descent was in the female line. A man became king or chieftain only by a formal 'marriage', and his daughter – not his son – succeeded; so that the next king or chieftain was the youth who married his daughter. It is improbable that any woman was restricted as to the number of lovers she might choose, and marital jealousy can scarcely have existed. For this reason these people imagined a similar, though glorified, state of affairs for their gods.

The Great Goddess was always supreme, and the many names by which she was called were but a variety of titles given to her in diverse places. She had no regular 'husband', but her mate – her young lover – died, or was killed, every autumn, and was glorified in resurrection every spring, coming back to the goddess; even as a new gallant may have been taken into favour every year to mate with an earthly queen. The lover of the goddess was a lover-god who was known by a variety of names or titles – even as she was.

Sometimes imagination pictured the miraculous appearance of the divine progenitor as visiting her in bird form. When they hailed her as Europa they said her lover appeared as an eagle; when they saluted her as Leda, they declared that her mate was disguised as a swan; when they gave their goddess the name Theleia or Lamia or Io, they averred that her lover arrived as a vulture or hoopoe or woodpecker; when they glorified her by the simple title of 'Lady' – or Hera in Greek – they alleged that her admirer came as a cuckoo. Indeed, bird-epiphanies have always been popular in Mediterranean lands.

Until the Northerners arrived, religion and custom were dominated by the female principle, and men were but the servers of women in the chase and the fields, in love and war. Therefore only the Goddess was supreme, though under many names.

At this point it has become apparent that the Northerners – the Greeks – coming down between about 2000 and 1300 B.C.[1] in a series of invading waves, came into contact with a group of customs and conduct-codes which must have startled *them* to a much greater degree than any contemplation of Greek paganism can possibly startle *us* now! It was all so wildly different from their simpler 'sky' religion; and, although in the early stages the details of this are not easy to put together, it seems that they in their turn imagined a divine family in the heavens which reflected the pattern of their own domestic life, exactly as the Mediterranean beliefs about the great 'Goddess of many Titles' reflected the pattern of the Minoan and kindred social orders.

The patrilineal incoming Greeks had their supreme God – Zeus – who was the Sky and the All-Father, and who had a family. This meant a wife, a daughter, and a sister of his – a kind of old maid who lived with the family. If there were others they got lost or went astray on the way south; but we shall encounter some of the family later; yet, because they were not strong divine personalities, they tended to get absorbed into other divine concepts – all except the Old Maid. On the other hand, Zeus, god of sky and weather, wielder of the thunder, flasher of lightning, was in the true sense terrific; and he remained the dominant God

[1] H. Bossert, *AAC*, pp. 10 ff.

HERA, goddess of marriage and the home. Bronze statuette 5.4 inches high, made about 540 B.C.

ARTEMIS the Huntress, 'Mistress of Animals'. Bronze, about 9½ inches high, made about 500 B.C. Found near Olympia.

(LEFT) *Silver coin* of Olympia with the head of Hera crowned, struck about 380 B.C.

Silver coin of the Achæan League with the head of Artemis, struck about 366 B.C.

PLATE III

ATHENE, goddess of skill in learning or in art. Bronze, about 6 inches high, showing her letting fly an owl. Made about 460 B.C., and acquired in Athens by the 7th Earl of Elgin early in the nineteenth century.

(LEFT) *Silver coin* of Athens with the head of Athene, struck about 520 B.C.

Corinthian silver coin, struck in Ambracia, with the head of Athene, *c.* 440 B.C.

PLATE IV

Almighty and Eternal for as long as Greek religion endured.

For all their assurance about the rightness of their worship of the divine family, the Greeks, who came down from the North and were frequently united to women of the Mediterranean race, were already very tolerant people. The last thing that they would have contemplated would have been the suppression of an older faith, almost shocking though it may have appeared with its goddess-centred cults. Toleration generally calls for some sort of compromise. 'We', said the Greek chieftains – so I imagine it – 'we act thus and thus; and having left our first wives behind, we marry the young women of the land, the dainty, olive-skinned, dark-haired daughters of the South, who enchant us. Zeus, the Almighty, surely acts likewise and weds the Great Goddess whom our new wives adore.'

And thus it came to pass, 'according to the gospel', that Zeus did marry her. The region in which a first encounter occurred was the country of Argos in the north-eastern part of Peloponnesus, and at a great holy place, later called 'the Heraion', which is Greek for 'Sanctuary of Our Lady'. Perhaps the Greeks never learnt the secret name of her, and perhaps the folk of the older stock would not tell; and that is why she became known as Hera – 'Lady' in Greek – feminine of Hero, 'Lord'. What occurred was the domestication of a once-free polyandrous and independent goddess, and it is a fair assumption that this corresponded to what was going on among Greek princes with wives of the earlier race.

Much later the Greeks, whose sense of humour always mixed thoroughly into their religion, said that Zeus wooed Hera for three hundred years before he married her. However, this may in a fashion represent the time it took for the Zeus-religion and the Hera-religion to achieve 'canonical' unity. Once they had done this a kind of gospel, or myth, about Hera could grow up; and this deserves some consideration.

It begins with a repulsive story which is now known to be neither Greek nor Minoan-pre-Greek, but to have derived from quite another source. In the central region of Asia Minor a civilisation now known as Hittite flourished about 1600-1200 B.C. Its more advanced features were derived from Mesopotamia. Tablets in the language of the Hittites and that of the Hurrians (contemporaries in North Syria) contain stories, some of which got into Greek myth; but this is a tale of murder and cannibalism in a struggle for supremacy among Near Eastern gods. Parts of the story may well go back to Mesopotamia of the third millennium. Presumably the tales were passed on from Hurrians to Phœnicians.[1] Cyprus – part Greek, part Phœnician about 800 B.C. – contained plenty of people speaking both languages, and any interested Cypriot trader or seaman might have passed on the legends to numerous Greeks, including Hesiod, whose family – somewhere between 800 and 750 B.C. – migrated from North-west Asia Minor to Bœotia, where he composed his *Theogony*, or 'Birth of the Gods', flinging into his 'stockpot' any bits of offal he could collect.

When we come to consider the myth of Aphrodite we shall have more to say about this group of Hittite theological yarns, which are actually a very recent archæological discovery. For the moment we can only deplore the bad taste of the Bœotian farmer-poet, Hesiod, for using rubbish.

Hera, so he said, was the sister of Zeus, who had older sisters and brothers, Hestia, Demeter, Poseidon, and Hades, all being the children of Kronos and Rhea. 'Fate' had foretold that Kronos would be dispossessed by one of his children, who would cast him from the Throne of the Almighty and succeed him; therefore Kronos, compelling Rhea to hand over each child as it was born, swallowed it whole. By the time the sixth child appeared, Rhea, being a little discouraged, resorted to a stratagem and gave Kronos a stone wrapped in a blanket to swallow. The live infant – Hesiod says he was Zeus – was clandestinely reared, and, having grown up at a great speed, attacked his father Kronos, obliging him to regurgitate the undigested older children, one of whom was Hera. She, after prolonged courtship, married Zeus. This was the *hieros gamos*, the 'Holy Marriage', commemorated annually at Argos, her chief sanctuary, and at her other important sanctuary in Samos as well as in several other Greek cities and states. By the union of Zeus

[1] H. G. Güterbock in *AJA*, 1948, pp. 123 ff. See also A. Goetze in *Ancient Near Eastern Texts relating to the Old Testament* (Princeton), 1950, pp. 120 ff.

and Hera marriage was, for the first time in Greece, sanctioned by divine example, became more than a tribal custom, and was dignified as a rite – indeed, almost sanctified as a sacrament.

Devotees remembered certain things about the Lady Hera that dated back to her pre-Greek days when her life was untrammelled by a sky-god husband. Of such was the story that by bathing in the spring Kanathos at Nauplia she annually renewed her virginity, for the concept of the Virgin Mother has always been acceptable in Southern Europe. Hephaistos was her son, virgin-born without union with Zeus, but she was not very fond of him. Nor was her marriage very fruitful, though some said Ares, god of war, and Hebe, goddess of youth, were their children.

Hera was a competitor against Athene and Aphrodite for the golden apple which was to be awarded to the loveliest, young Paris being the judge. But it was no part of the Greek story that the three goddesses showed themselves naked to Paris, as in the famous painting by Rubens in the National Gallery in London. That detail is a late invention of the atheist cynic Lucian, who was born about A.D. 120, in the days of the Roman Empire. Hera was always on good terms with Athene, but certainly not with Aphrodite, and in the Trojan War the two former helped the Greeks, while the latter abetted the Trojans. Her myth, in fact, was short; and very properly, since the Lady who is to be the pattern and exemplar for all good married women should lead a life of virtuous obscurity, the past forgiven because it is forgotten – or almost.

The reflections which occur about Hera are simple. After the fusion of the Northern and Mediterranean races she was established above all as the goddess of marriage, married life, and the home. Some long time before 600 B.C. it had become clear to most of the Greeks that marriage – not love, which need have nothing whatever to do with it – was the greatest stabiliser of their social order. Concerned mainly with the humdrum life of women in the home, Hera was not the kind of goddess to move poets to enchanting hymns such as were written for other deities. In art she is normally represented as the Queenly Bride, diademed, a veil over her head, discreetly draped, and with a sceptre in her hand. No remarkable early or classical statue of her happens to have survived, but there are pleasing pictures of her on many Athenian vases, and there is an enchanting bronze statuette in the Fitzwilliam Museum in Cambridge (Plate III, facing page 32). She wears a glove-like Doric *peplos* and a crown-like *kalathos* upon her head. The gentle smile on the little face is appealing.

It is worth remembering too that the cult of the Great Goddess which grew into the Greek worship of Hera is evidence that the idea of personal divinity has been in the minds of men and women since an age very remote indeed, long before the concept of Zeus, the Personified Sky, began to be imagined. Deity at first was female; and her male consort or consorts played only the minor roles of servitors.

III. ZEUS

ZEUS is the Sky and Weather, and he dwells in the sky. Long ago Homer said, 'The portion of Zeus is the broad heaven in brightness and in cloud'; and within the great age of Greek civilisation from 600 B.C. onward Zeus is constantly conceived either as the sky itself or as the Being who lives in the sky, whence comes the weather. Yet when he descends upon the world he rests on the very highest point of Greek earth that rises up towards the sky, and therefore it is upon the glittering summit of Olympus – rising out of the sea to near ten thousand feet – that he and the other gods dwell. He is the 'cloud-gatherer' who sends rain, lightning, thunder, and the bolt that blasts and destroys. The thunderbolt is his grandest and most frightening attribute. Then, as human thought, reflection, and philosophy grow, it gradually appears that Zeus is a Life Force expressing himself in matter and evolving organisms in pursuance of his own purpose, whence there develops a philosophy and a religion of optimism calling men to co-operate with God. And out of this arises the greater concept of pure, eternal all-embracing Divinity – which is Zeus. One Greek poet wrote of Zeus, 'In Him we live and move and have our being'; and another in a hymn to Zeus said, 'For we also are Thine offspring'. These are the quotations[1] that Paul himself used, drawing on Greek sources to explain to Greeks his Christian conception of Almighty God.

The Greeks came down into Hellas in two main groups between 2000 and 1300 B.C., though each of these probably filtered down fairly slowly over periods of years. The first we call the Minyan group of Greeks, the second the Achæan. The name of Zeus is associated most definitely with the latter, but he had actually arrived already as the chief god of the former or Minyan group. The Great Goddess of the pre-Hellenic folk had possessed, as we saw, one nature, but many different names. Zeus possessed one name, but there were many variants. The 'first' Zeus, who came with the Minyan group, was called Dān, and his wife was

[1] *Acts*, xvii, 28.

Dā; there are local variants between the 'first' and the 'second' Zeus in which he appears as Zān. The genitive case may be either 'Dios' or 'Zēnos', the accusative either 'Dia' or 'Zēna'. So the Greeks had a varied repertoire of names, but *all* the emphasis was on the 'Da' or 'Di' sounds. The wife who came down with the 'second' or Achæan Zeus was named Diōne.

It is here that one may in passing observe a remarkable Italian parallel; for another Indo-European group of people, later called the Latins, moved into Italy with gods of very similar names. 'Diu-pater' and his wife 'Diu-no', who became known as 'Jupiter' and 'Juno', were, without any doubt, deities of the same origin.

But, one may ask, what happened to 'Dān' and 'Dā', who came down with the first Greek group from about 2000 B.C. onwards? Titles were attached to them, and Dān was addressed as Potei-Dān – the first word meaning Master – and so became Poteidān, the regular early form of Poseidon. His wife, beginning to take to herself some of the characteristics of the Great Goddess of the pre-Hellenic folk, began to be known as 'Mother Dā', or – so it seems – 'Dā Mater', and thus became in classical Greek days the famous Demeter.[1]

When five or six hundred years later the second group, the Achæan Greeks, came down with Sky-god Zeus, they, of course, failed to observe the identity of their god with the Poteidān of the Minyan Greeks, whom they now made their subjects. 'He is the elder brother of our Zeus', they said, 'but he cannot be the sky, for that is Zeus: let him therefore be the sea. This is most suitable, for you Minyans are obviously splendid sailors, which we are not.' Therefore Dān, the proto-Zeus, quietly assumed, as Poseidon, dominion of the sea.

This episode gives no cause for surprise, because divine identity is not always apparent on the surface. A learned theologian from Tibet or Afghanistan, paying a visit to England in order to study our religious customs, might enter first a small building the incumbent of which was an Anglo-Catholic, and then a Four Square conventicle having no stipendiary minister. In the ancient

[1] That is one view. But it remains hypothetical and other explanations have been advanced.

parish church he might smell the inebriating Oriental perfume of incense and see a crucifix upon the altar, a light burning before a reserved Host, and an image of Our Lady in one aisle. In the other place – the defiant chapel of the Plymouth Brethren, pulpited and pewed in pitch-pine – the enquiring Asiatic would discover the hard, clean smell of scrubbing-soap, and would see nothing set apart as holy except for one Great Book upon the desk, and it would be hard for him to believe that both buildings were devoted to the cultus of the same God.

In the early days before the Greeks began to move into Greece, Zeus, like Elohim in the Old Testament, had a family; but whereas Elohim's was mostly masculine,[1] Zeus was companioned mainly by female dependants – a wife, a maiden sister, and a daughter. As his worshippers came south they acquired a great shrine at Dodona in Epirus; and this was as far as Diōne, his first wife, got; for her worship was almost unknown, or only insignificant, farther south. But Zeus moved on to meet at Argos the Great Goddess whom they now named Hera, or 'Our Lady', and ultimately – as already recounted – to marry her. It was this wedding which greatly altered his character for a very long while, for people began to attach to Zeus, the husband of Hera, all too many of the stories and myths which had appertained to the many consorts and lovers whom the Great Goddess had had in remoter days. It was an admirable rehabilitation of the now-reformed goddess of married life and the sanctity of the home to be able to say, 'Ah yes, but those adventures she is alleged to have had with this lover and that, disguised betimes as this bird or that, why – don't you see? – it was really Zeus! Don't forget that he was courting her for three hundred years.' Thus, to save the good name of his consort, a reputation for meaningless and morbid ornitho-morphology was foisted upon Zeus, who at the same time began to figure as a fickle – though philoprogenitive – gallant of a god. In the latter role he naturally resembled his worshippers, for princely Greek Achæans already possessed many of the customs and privileges which one associates with the feudality of Northern Europe in the Middle Ages.

[1] *Genesis*, VI, 2-4; *Job*, I, 6-12 and II, 1-6.

Zeus virtually left his Northern wife, Diōne, at Dodona, but his daughter came with him – a Valkyrie-like goddess perhaps, a virgin warrior – who became of immense importance in Greek religion and history. After a while this girl goddess became identified with an older, pre-Hellenic warrior-goddess generally known as Athene; and a later chapter must tell of this. But when the Greek girl-warrior, daughter of Zeus, came south she may have been spoken of generally simply as *Pallax* – meaning 'the Maid' – which more often took the form of 'Pallas'. The third female dependant of Zeus was Hestia, goddess of the hearth. It must not be forgotten that in those remote days the maintenance of the household fire was of great importance, for if it once went out a rekindling was rather complicated. Each household was, therefore, fussy about the house fire, and an unmarried daughter, sister, or aunt was the proper person to be put in charge of it. There was something sacred about that fire in the home; and the little township or big city kept the town or city hearth going as a community-hearth. All such fires were sacred to Hestia, goddess of hearths, for it was she herself who tended the fire of the family of gods upon Olympus. In fact, Hestia was inconspicuous but exceedingly important; and she was both originally and in reality one of the 'Twelve Olympians'. Yet she was, by virtue of her office and employment, the one and only stay-at-home. When the other gods went out, this gentle Cinderella, this restful 'sitter-in', remained behind. And when the last of the great gods appeared on the scene – Dionysos, son of Zeus most high – someone had to make way. So Dionysos became, as it were, a member of the official list of the Twelve, and Aunt Hestia stepped down; though of course she continued to live on Olympus because of that divine hearth.

It has already been observed that just as these 'Dios' and 'Diōne' divinities came down to Greece, kindred Indo-Europeans moving into Italy took with them their gods, Diu-pater (Jupiter) and Diu-nō (Juno). There, in some of the central Italian lands, it became customary to set up in some townships a Capitol, 'head- or chief-temple', for the worship of three particular gods, Jupiter, his consort Juno, and his daughter Minerva – a warrior-maid like the child of Zeus. They were invariably grouped together; and in sight of their chief shrine in Rome itself was the celebrated Temple of Vesta with the eternal fire upon the City's hearth. Vesta was in name, as in fact and function, identical with the Greek Hestia. From the Italian end, the Sky-god is observed to arrive with wife, daughter, and sister, but with no other obvious divine relative. In Greece it is much the same with a like set of female dependants. Was there a son? Conceivably there was a Northern 'Apollon' whose personality and cult were fused with those of an East Greek Apolline god. Yet it is not possible to say more than this: half the Apollo-concept, including his role as son of Zeus, may have come down from the North to get mingled with another kindred cult.

ZEUS was, ZEUS is, ZEUS shall be,

men sang in the Hymn at Dodona, and it is time to return to consider him in three consecutive aspects: Zeus the Despot, Zeus the Creator, and Zeus the Eternal God.

I. *Zeus the Despot.* That is his nature in the Homeric epics, for he is the god of the kings and chieftains of Homeric society, and his actions and thoughts correspond, on a higher level, to theirs. Indeed, the gods of high Olympus, the princes and leaders of the people, the commonalty and the serfs, formed together one compact society 'organised on a basis of strongly-marked class-distinctions'.[1] The gods and the princes were the upper class, the rest the lower; and princes claimed descent from gods – from Potei-Dān (Poseidon) in the very ancient families, and from Zeus in the more powerful Achæan families. That is why they were bracketed with gods rather than with common men, and that is why they gloried in tales of some ancestress loved by Zeus and honoured above her sisters by the receipt of his favour, a mortal princess who bare a 'son of god', a Hero, from whom they traced descent. There could be no possible stigma in this, since there was no stain upon a mortal man of rank who took a girl of the people, and nothing but high regard for the lucky girl whom he singled out; nor was there any taint in bastardy.

Since, however, there were no 'higher gods' above and beyond the Olympians, it was evident that the immortals were less subject

[1] Guthrie, *The Greeks and their Gods*, p. 118.

to restraint and at times more violent than mortals would be; and it has rightly been pointed out that in the Homeric poems mortals like Diomede or Ajax sometimes show more of nobility and generosity than does Zeus. The very same thing is found in early tales about Yahweh, the God of Israel, for Abraham in his attempts to intercede for the men of Sodom and Gomorrah sought mercy from the Inexorable,[1] and Moses with true nobility restrained Yahweh from the total slaughter of Israel by reminding Him that He was long-suffering and of great mercy, forgiving iniquity and transgression.[2]

If Zeus the Despot could be wayward in his dealings with men, he could act tyrannically to the other gods over whom he took absolute precedence. But the goddesses could and did wheedle him, exactly as noble ladies were able to 'manage' their lords. Nothing can better illustrate this than the superb passage in the fourteenth book of Homer's *Iliad* which tells how Hera – full of guile because of an ulterior motive – aroused with daintily sensual skill her lord and husband's desire for her, and, having satisfied it, lulled him gently to sleep. One may picture the Hera of this enchanting story smiling like the little goddess shown in Plate III facing page 32.

Hera went in and closed the polished doors behind her. She began by removing every stain from her comely body with ambrosia, and anointing herself with the delicious and imperishable olive-oil she uses. It was perfumed and had only to be stirred in the Palace of the Bronze Floor for its scent to spread through heaven and earth. With this she rubbed her lovely skin; and then she combed her hair, and with her own hands set her shining locks and let them fall in their divine beauty from her immortal head. Next she put on a fragrant robe of delicate material that Athene with her skilful hands had made for her and lavishly embroidered. She fastened it over her breast with golden clasps and, at her waist, with a girdle from which a hundred tassels hung. In the pierced lobes of her ears she fixed two ear-rings, each a thing of lambent beauty with its cluster of three drops. She covered her head with a beautiful new head-dress which was as bright as the sun; and, last of all, the Lady goddess bound a fine pair of sandals on her shimmering feet.

[1] *Genesis*, XVIII, 20 ff.   [2] *Numbers*, XIV, 11 ff.

Presently she drew near to the highest crest of lofty Mount
Ida near Troy, where Zeus was resting, and he saw her

and at the first look his heart was captured by desire as in the days when
they had first enjoyed each other's love and gone to bed together without their parents' knowledge. He rose to meet her and said: 'Hera, what
business brings you here from Olympus? And why no horses and no
chariot to drive in? . . . Today let us enjoy the delights of love. Never
has such desire, for goddess or woman, flooded and overwhelmed my
heart; not even when I loved Ixion's wife, who bore Peirithous to rival
the gods in wisdom; or Danaë of the slim ankles, the daughter of
Acrisius, who gave birth to Perseus, the greatest hero of his time; or the
far-famed daughter of Phœnix, who bore me Minos, and the god-like
Rhadamanthus; or Semele, or Alcmene in Thebes, whose son was the
lion-hearted Herakles, while Semele bore Dionysos to give pleasure to
mankind; or Demeter, Queen of the Lovely Locks, or the incompar-
able Leto; or when I fell in love with you yourself – never have I felt
such love, such sweet desire, as fills me now for you.'

'Dread Son of Kronos, you amaze me,' said the Lady Hera, still dissembling. 'Suppose we do as you wish and lie down in each other's
arms on the heights of Ida, where there is no privacy whatever, what
will happen if one of the eternal gods sees us asleep together and runs
off to tell the rest?' . . . 'Here,' said Zeus the Cloud-compeller, 'you
need not be afraid that any god or man will see us. I shall hide you in a
golden cloud too thick for that. Even the Sun, whose rays provide him
with the keenest sight in all the world, will not see us through the mist.'

As he spoke, the Son of Kronos took his Wife in his arms; and the
gracious earth sent up fresh grass beneath them, dewy lotus and crocuses, and a soft crowded bed of hyacinths to lift them off the ground.
In this they lay, covered by a beautiful golden cloud, from which a rain
of glistening dewdrops fell.[1]

This story, which Sir Walter Leaf once described[2] as 'radiant
with humour, grace and healthful sensuousness', is one of the only
two amorous episodes in all the forty-eight books of Homer. The
other one will be recounted later. It happens, however, to illustrate
two phenomena. Firstly, Hera is far from taking umbrage at her
lord's recital of seven other love-affairs, but complimented – even
perhaps enchanted – that Zeus finds her more bewitching now

[1] Translation by E. V. Rieu.   [2] W. Leaf, *Iliad*, II, p. 53.

than in the early days of their pre-marital amours. Secondly, the story depicts a code and custom of Homeric princely society; for then, and later, the Greeks were a monogamous people, believing in having one lawful wife, but tolerant of outside relationships, and attaching no stigma to the children born of such. A situation which gave to Zeus one wife and numerous mistresses was one which later story-tellers and poets happily developed, but it had no connection with anything but literature,[1] and it did not enter into the Zeus-ward thoughts of the truly devout.

Anyhow, having reflected on the loves of Zeus and Hera on Mount Ida, one may recall part of a kindred poem set down several centuries later in the Hebrew *Song of Songs*[2] about love on other mountain-tops – Lebanon and Hermon.

> Thou art all fair, my love:
> There is no spot in thee
> Come with me from Lebanon, my spouse,
> With me from Lebanon:
> Look from the top of Amana,
> From the top of Shenir and Hermon,
> From the lions' dens,
> From the mountains of the leopards.
> Thou hast ravished my heart, my sister, my spouse;
> Thou hast ravished my heart with one of thine eyes,
> With one chain of thy neck.

Zeus the Despot was certainly a lordly god, and the approval of his devotees was in true accord with the civilisation and society to which they belonged. But in due time he seemed to assume a different aspect; the guise of

II. *Zeus the Creator.* This conception began to imply the recognition of a god who loves mankind – a humanist god. But linked with such a conception as this was a general tendency towards admiration for the human species, not only for its mental but also for its physical worth. And this tendency came into operation in a remarkable manner; for at the sanctuary of Olympia first – and afterwards at other famous sanctuaries – something without any real parallel in the world's history occurred. The institution of

[1] See Guthrie, *op. cit.*, p. 55.   [2] *Song of Solomon*, IV, 7 ff.

organised athletics as an act of worship towards Zeus, and of the body trained to perfection as a thing dedicated to God, was a new and most startling concept in the history of mankind. But it was the necessary prelude to the birth of humanism.

As we date from the 'year of Grace', as the Romans dated from 'the Foundation of the City', so the Greeks dated from 'the First Olympiad', an Olympiad being the four-year stretch between one great religio-athletic festival and the next at Olympia. When citing a date the name of the victor in the foot-race – the earliest of the various events in the games – was frequently mentioned too, and the first recorded name, Koroibos, was held to mark the First Olympiad, in the year 776 B.C., as the standard Hellenic era. Competitors in the race wore a very brief loin-cloth, until at the fifteenth festival in 720 B.C. a certain athlete, Orsippos, discarded it, ran completely naked, and won the event. From that moment his practice was universally followed, first in the games for Zeus at Olympia, then at other athletic festivals, and so in gymnasia and in many public places, outdoors and in, all over ancient Greece. In Sparta, and possibly in some other states, where athletics for girls and young married women were encouraged by the State, the same custom was presently adopted by them.[1]

It is natural for men and women to experience an emotion known as 'modesty', though of course they have to feel that they have something to be modest about. Frequently it takes the form of a shrinking from exposing certain parts of the body, but, if circumstances should cause that special and particular inhibition to disappear, men and women must value another kind of 'modesty' instead, and such is bound to be a modesty of mind and spirit – that which the Greeks called *aidōs*, which connotes 'respect, sense of honour, moderation, regard for others'. Such 'modesty' entailed the lavishing of no more thought upon any one portion of the human body than upon another portion, its opposite being 'pudency', which implies an overwhelming and embarrassing awareness of certain parts of the body. It was, indeed, revolutionary that from about the seventh century B.C. onward modesty should become of the mind and *not* of the body; that it should be

[1] See Seltman in *Cornhill Magazine*, 1950, pp. 296 ff.

in moderation and *not* pudency; that it should show a suscepti-
bility to self-respect but *not* to ashamedness; that it should be preoccupied with honour but *not* with bawdy. But, as a word of
warning, one may add this: that there must have been some
Greeks who exceeded, who coddled the body, who felt prudish
and ashamed, and who dwelt mentally in a slough of wantonness.
Yet the uninhibited framework of their society discouraged re-
pressed persons so naturally that they seem to have been remark-
ably few in number.

When the great Hero of the *Odyssey* was shipwrecked on the
shore of Phæacia he was eager to conceal his naked manhood, just
as any other Greek would have done in the Homeric age. Nevertheless, in order to understand how the Greeks could so quickly
change in a matter of Custom and Conduct – all because one
Olympic runner ran without his loin-cloth – one must realise that
overdressing, dressing, skimping, and nakedness are simply
matters of fluid convention.

Yet once the convention of athletic nakedness had been adopted,
the Greeks maintained it for close on a thousand years, because it
seemed to them to be consistent with their principles of liberty,
moderation, and good breeding. It seems that a free and aristo-
cratic-minded people, of Northern stock like the Greeks, happen-
ing to have acquired a convention of nakedness, is not easily
turned from it. Neither the Catholic Church nor the English
migrants into Ireland could overthrow the healthy habits of the
ancient nobility of Ulster, where, in Queen Elizabeth's reign, the
great O'Cane himself, who spoke fluent Latin as well as his own
tongue, welcomed a Bohemian nobleman to the hall of his Great
House in which The O'Cane and all his sixteen ladies sat down
naked, inviting the embarrassed and unwilling foreigner to
undress and be comfortable.[1]

It has been necessary to put some emphasis on the ancient
Hellenic convention of convenient and natural nakedness, because
it had a powerful, even a profound, effect on the Greeks' religious
outlook and on their conception of Zeus and of other deities.

[1] Fynes Moryson, *An Itinerary, Containing his Ten Yeares Travell*, London, 1617,
pp. 180 ff.

God created man in his own image,
In the image of God created he him:
Male and female created he them.[1]

A similar idea in the Greeks' mind caused them to make their
gods in the likeness of perfect men and women. In either case, and
whichever way you have it, a compliment is implied, a *rapproche-
ment* is on the way, and a wish is there to love God and be loved of
God. Indeed, the Greeks were *never* idolaters in the sense of wor-
shipping actual images which they had made. Rather was an
ancient statue a statement of praise about a god, no more and no
less than a hymn was a song of praise about a god, but human
language was requisite for the song, and human likeness for the
statue.

That Greek art operated in the service of anthropomorphic
religion is obvious, but it was an exceptionally high standard of
anthropomorphism, because athletics in the service of religion
had given the Greeks so high a standard of human physical perfection. They felt convinced that the man who came closest to human
perfection was the athlete; and therefore to express the divine perfection of Zeus you must depict him too as a divine athlete. That is
the explanation of a glorious bronze statue of the naked Zeus.

In April 1926, some fishermen, plying their trade near Cape
Artemision off the north-east coast of Euboea, drew up in one of
their stronger nets the bronze arm and hand of a figure over life-
size. With that instinctive sense for the antique which so many
Greek peasants and islanders possess, they seemed to know that
this was important, and they persuaded a professional sponge-
diver to go down and look for more. His observation of a bearded
head and a torso satisfied them that the time had come to report
their discovery. Accordingly, by the autumn of 1928 the requisite
steps had been taken and the splendid statue, which proved to be
complete, was raised to the surface and transferred to the National
Museum in Athens. There I had the good fortune to be one of the
first Englishmen to set eyes upon the figure as it lay in a huge tank
of distilled water, which was absorbing impurities from the

[1] *Genesis*, I, 27.

bronze. Later this great masterpiece, seven feet high and dating from about 460 B.C., was set up as one of the chief glories of Greece. The place of its discovery in the company of some other broken bronzes suggests the possibility that it formed part of ship-wrecked loot being conveyed from Greece to Constantinople in the fourth century of our era, or possibly to Rome at a somewhat earlier date.

All other considerations apart, this Zeus is the most perfect bronze athlete statue that has survived from antiquity. Balance, rhythm, proportion, tension, and restraint – all are blended. In looking at the picture (Plate II facing page 17) one must allow for the fact that the right shank and the left foot are somewhat out of shape because of injuries sustained in the shipwreck; but having made this allowance, one observes that the nearest approach to perfection for a fully developed, but not over-developed, mature male athlete has here been achieved. As a conception of Zeus it holds one thing left over from the past, a thunderbolt – now miss-ing from the right hand – about to be hurled to earth by the god. Zeus was the thunderer; Zeus is the prototype of mankind, sane and healthy, created in his own image; Zeus shall be the one primary Being, who has begotten, and again absorbs into himself, all things and all gods – and such a conception was on the way.

III. *Zeus the Eternal God*. This third stage in Greek religious thought about Zeus was already implicit in the ideas which Phei-dias expressed when – about thirty years after the bronze Zeus was made – he created a statue, the most famous, not only of any in ancient Greece, but in the history of mankind – the colossal gold-and-ivory god in his temple at Olympia. The upper part of the figure was naked, but a corner of the ample cloak which was round the thighs fell over the left shoulder. Classed as one of the 'Seven Wonders of the World' until it perished in A.D. 462, it received more praise from the ancients themselves than any other work of art.[1] Quintilian wrote about A.D. 95:

The beauty of the Olympian Zeus is thought actually to have added something to the received religion: so far did the majesty of the work go towards equality with godhead.

[1] Cook, *Zeus*, III, pp. 960 ff.

It was told of a certain Neo-Pythagorean sage named Apollonios of Tyana, who flourished in the first century of our era, that when he first set eyes upon the statue enthroned at Olympia he prayed aloud with the words:

Hail, All-good Zeus, for good Thou art in this, even that Thou givest Thyself unto men.

However, among ancient authors one man, Dion, gained most of his fame because of a discourse, a kind of combined lecture and sermon, which he gave in the summer of A.D. 97 before the Greeks assembled at Olympia; since the main part of it concerned the gold-and-ivory statue of Zeus. Dion, a distinguished and well-born citizen of Prusa, was nicknamed 'mouth-of-gold' for his fine voice and rounded phrases. He called Pheidias 'this wise, inspired maker of a creation at once solemn and supremely fine'. 'Of men', he continued:

whosoever is utterly weary in soul, having drained many sufferings and sorrows in his life without the solace of sweet sleep, even he, methinks, if he stood over against this statue, would forget all the terrors and hardships of humanity. Aforetime in lack of clear knowledge we dreamed our several dreams and fashioned our individual fancies, or at most combined the unconvincing likenesses produced by previous craftsmen. But you, Pheidias, through the potency of your art, have conquered and combined Hellas first and then the rest of the world by means of this marvel, a work so amazing and brilliant that no man who had once set eyes on it could afterwards find it easy to form another conception of god.

Finally, Dion puts into the mouth of Pheidias the following words:

Ours is a god of peace and universal mildness, overseer of a Hellas free from faction and at harmony with itself. By the help of my art, and the counsel of Elis, a State both wise and good, I have established him, gentle and solemn with untroubled mien, the giver of livelihood and life and all good things, the common Father and Saviour and Keeper of mankind, imitating so far as mortal thought can imitate the nature that is divine and beyond our ken.

Although these writers were of a later age, it had nevertheless come about that already in the fifth century B.C. there were Greeks who thought of Zeus as a god to be loved. Yet he must be loved not by way of unthinking dumb obedience, but by the way of reflection and reason; not by the way of pretence bolstered up by foolish tales of the pointlessly miraculous, but by the way of visible reality contemplated in tranquillity.

This was in agreement with the trend of Plato's ideas, for it is possible to regard the Platonic System as the projection of a mental process into an imaginary world of absolute values. The Pheidian Zeus was the result of a mental process expressed in matter by a mighty artist. Did he achieve expression by projecting his mind into an imaginary world?

On the emotional side the thinkers and poets tended to drive more and definitely into a monotheistic theology which was completely developed by the time that the Stoic philosopher Cleanthes wrote – about the middle of the third century B.C. – his celebrated Hymn to Zeus, containing verses such as:

> Oh, Father, cleanse our soul, grant us to find
> Wisdom wherewith Thou governest all aright,
> That honoured thus we too may honour Thee,
> Hymning Thy deeds for ever.

Lines such as these, and others from the hymn, would slip appropriately into any modern devotional manual. Not so, however, the extraordinary myth of Zeus – violent in its contrast with the high thoughts of philosophic men.

In the whole history of mankind no obedient believer has allowed himself to be disturbed consciously by glaring inconsistencies in his myths and gospels. But since man is often a reasoning being, these inconsistencies trouble his 'deep-down' mind badly; and the firmer his conscious obedience to faith, the more troublesome are his inward doubts, which he may label 'Furies', or 'the Tempter', or 'the Subconscious'. Some of those who are thus troubled become philosophers, some saints; but such are deviators from the norm, for the former drag forth their doubts to examine them, while the latter drive them down to remoter depths, covering them with the dusty veils of muted mysticism. And mysticism can easily become the religion not of hope, but of despair.

It has just been remarked that man is often a reasoning being; but often he is not. When he is not he is capable of reckless credulity, all too ready to confide in those who, he thinks, 'know better', because they are the people who have assured him that they do know better. He questions neither their knowledge nor their motives. There were, of course, plenty of credulous men in ancient Greece who were prepared to accept without question what Hesiod had said as though he were some pontiff or apostle of the gods. It was only his supposed nearness in time to Homer that brought him this measure of attention. Now Hesiod, so it happened, had been a farmer-man living in the eighth century B.C., and having a gift for poetry; and his poem *Works and Days* was admirable stuff. His *Theogony*, or 'Birth of the Gods', was not, for he was as unsuited to compose a *Theogony* as Robert Burns would have been to write *Paradise Lost*. Accordingly, it is not surprising to discover that of all ancient god-myths the Zeus-myth, having regard to the unique nature of Zeus, is the most wildly absurd. But it is probable that not many of the Greeks permitted their subconscious minds to be severely troubled by the kind of tale that follows, since none of it was ever *de fide*.

The first of the gods had been Ouranos, who mated with Ge – the Earth – and begat the Titans and the Giants, and last of all, the youngest, Kronos, who married his sister Rhea. By the advice of his mother, Ge, Kronos castrated his father and ruled in his stead. As already recounted in the Myth of Hera, Kronos swallowed all his children by Rhea save the youngest, Zeus, for whom a stone was substituted. The infant was now hidden in a cave in Crete and nourished by animals while armed spirits, called Kuretes, danced around it. Then Zeus, growing up quickly, forced Kronos to disgorge his brothers and sisters, and dethroned him. The Titans, elder brothers of Kronos, having come to his help, there ensued somewhere in Asia Minor the 'battle of the Gods and Giants', and the latter were beaten by the Olympian Gods and imprisoned. Zeus, secure on Olympus, began – apart from other activities – to visit many goddesses and mortals. From the indices of a famous modern work[1] one may compile a list of the goddesses, nymphs,

[1] Cook, *Zeus*, I, II and III.

and mortal girls with whom Zeus was reputed to have consorted, and these collected stories are evidence for the irresponsibility of ancient myth-mongers. The tales are mainly Hesiodic, but certain 'learned' contributions were also made by others.

Five separate strands of story-telling have got themselves plaited together to make this extraordinary rope of a myth:

(I) There is the bloody and dismal part now known to be Hittite and Hurrian, with some Babylonian affinities, already discussed.[1] This is now regarded as the concoction of Anatolians about 1600-1200 B.C., handed on to Phoenicians, and passed by the latter to Greeks like Hesiod. It is independent of the other strands.

(II) The pre-Hellenic beliefs concerning a great Mother-goddess have also got into the myth. The emphasis on Ge, Rhea, and lastly Hera, and on the parts they played, arise from these beliefs, as do many of the love-affairs attributed to Zeus, who succeeded to the chain of lovers of the Great Goddess.

(III) There is a strand deriving from ancient Minoan legend. Not only is the infant Zeus hidden in a Cretan cave and brought up in the island, but there was shown in one place the holy sepulchre where Zeus had been buried. A dead Zeus rising to live again was certainly a reflection of the tale about the annual god-boy-lover of the Great Goddess of Minoan days.

(IV) A very strong strand was the one supplied by the pedigree-makers, for no family was royal unless it was god-descended. You might trace your line from Poseidon, Apollo, or Hermes, but to be Zeus-born was the most distinguished of all. The palace bard who could not sing of some lovely queen or princess whom Zeus, beholding her from high Olympus, visited, would soon lose his job. Desperate opponents of the old religion, like the unhappy Clement, made great play with these imaginary scandals, and a careful catalogue of the god's love-affairs can supply him with one wife, one ex-wife, and – over a vast span of centuries – fifty-three mistresses. Yet in the heyday of a single lifetime King Solomon in all his glory was able, so it is alleged, to acquire a far more splendid company.[2]

[1] pp. 33 f.   [2] *I Kings*, XI, 1 and 3.

(v) Last comes a strand, slender perhaps, but enduring, which accounts for the long life of the stories of the god's affairs. The myth had an appeal to the unsophisticated in many Greek lands. Every male simpleton secretly longed to become a great lover such as Zeus; and every simple girl secretly hoped to be loved by him.

Now that the Hurrian–Hittite monster-tales can be totally discarded, one tendency has become clear. There is a thread that runs through from the simple Greek farm-girl's prayer to be loved of a god, through from an early notion of a god who died and rose again, through from the love-poem in Homer's *Iliad*, and through from the athlete dedicating to God his body trained to perfection, through to the mallet and chisel in the hands of Pheidias, and so to the poem written soon after 300 B.C. by Aratos of Soloi:

From Zeus let us begin: Him do we mortals never leave unnamed. Full of Zeus are all the streets and all the market-places of man; full is the sea and the heavens thereof. Always we have need of Zeus; for we also are His offspring.

The thread is a kind of love of God with an affection for mankind, and it is humanism.

It is for humanism that Zeus ultimately stands.

IV. ATHENE

THE last two chapters dealt with the most exalted of the Olympians; this and the next are to tell about much more personal deities. If a philosophic Greek had told you that they are but aspects of the central 'Idea' of a godhead – which is God – you would perhaps remark that they were both exceptionally attractive aspects.

Athene cannot fail to be interesting. Her origins from two different sources can be traced in a satisfactory manner. The sources merge to make the Homeric Athene, who is conceived of in terms of the *Iliad* and *Odyssey* in many Greek cities down to 600 B.C. Then in her chief city, Athens, one can watch her altering into another kind of goddess.

The brilliant civilisation of Minoan Crete began from about 1900 B.C. to grow up in and around a few luxurious palaces wherein civil and sanitary engineers vied with one another in the creation of many-storeyed buildings, functional bathrooms, and water-closets. The kings and princes who owned these palaces appear to have given special devotion to a 'Palace Goddess', who was one aspect of the all-pervading Mediterranean mother-goddess discussed in Chapter II. However, in her role of Palace Goddess emphasis was not upon motherhood, but upon that kind of feminine wisdom, intuition – call it what you will – which is comforting to the male; even as masculine stability and resourcefulness comfort the female. The attributes of the Palace Goddess were a shield, a snake, a tree, and a bird. When presently the Greek-speaking peoples moved down into Greece and came, about 1700 B.C., under cultural influences from Crete, their kings and princes took over this young goddess, adapting her for their own Achæan and Mycenæan Palace Shrines, identifying her, at the same time, with their own young warrior-goddess, daughter of Zeus, known simply as 'the Maid' and called by various titles: *Korē, Parthenos, Pallas*, meaning 'girl, virgin, maiden'. Thus her usual double appellative was 'Pallas Athene', the latter name being pre-Hellenic in origin.

Because she was the Palace Goddess, she was from the women's point of view skilled in all household arts and crafts; yet from the man's point of view she was the Wise One, the strategist – even the tactician – leader in warfare. In classical times one will always find that where her worship is, there an ancient palace had been. Thus she became the goddess not only of the palace, but also of the fortress and of the fortified city. That is why she was worshipped at Sparta and Corinth, at Argos and Thebes, as well as in many lesser city-states.

Some scholars think that she gave her name to – others that she derived it from – her greatest city. However, whichever way it was, her cult, her dominion over men's minds, and their deep affection for her were far stronger in her own Athens than in any other Greek state. There was, of course, the right attitude to Zeus and Apollo, to Poseidon and Hephaistos, as well as to other gods within Athens and Attica. Yet Athene, daughter of Zeus, had an absolute supremacy in the thoughts and hearts of the people of Athens, and it appears that this was due primarily to one man, for the title 'Apostle of Athene' is one that could well be applied to the famous Peisistratus. This brilliant and popular politician of an ancient and horsey family secured for himself the position of autocrat of Athens about 566 B.C.,[1] resting his powers on the approval of the merchants and the goodwill of the workers, and gradually overcoming the ill-will of many – but not all – of his fellow-nobles. The first recorded fact concerning his administration is his founding of the Greater Panathenaia – that is, of the athletic, poetical, musical, and race-course contests held every fourth year. in Athens in honour of Athene. Since the foundation, more than two centuries earlier, of the quadrennial Olympic festival[2] other athletic games had been started in other centres, and now Athens took her place as a city to be visited by competitors from all over Greece. The prizes for the winners were large vases, with a painted figure of Athene on one side, containing oil from an olive-grove sacred to the goddess. An integral part of the festival was the great Panathenaic Procession, which followed a long route up to the Acropolis, where special rites in the goddess's honour took place.

[1] Seltman, NC, 1946, p. 101.   [2] See p. 45 above.

At the same date the autocrat introduced a new kind of coinage for the state, having, upon the obverse, a head of Athene – an owl, her bird, upon the other side – and because of this head the coins began to be spoken of as *korai*, or 'girls'. Moreover, at this very time the Athenian painted-pottery industry was already booming, and it is possible to see from pictures on vases painted in Athens the general attitude to and thoughts about the goddess herself, while from the contemporary monuments in stone and marble upon the Acropolis of Athens more may be deduced.

Thoughts about Deity tend to correspond to human interest and emotions, ambitions and loves. And so the pictorial presentations of an important anthropomorphic deity like Athene may help one to understand some of the personal interests and emotions which, at a given time, prompted men to think of her in that presented way. If they were representing her frequently as a child-goddess or a young girl-goddess, clumsy though some such pictures might be, it means that many influential Athenians were, at that given time, rather devoted to their own youthful daughters. Now from 566 B.C. onward for a long time young unmarried girls of good family were, more than wives, very important in the eyes of their relatives, partly because they might get appointed as basket-bearers and temporary attendants on the goddess or on other deities, thereby winning congratulations for their parents, partly because it is natural for a father to be proud of a comely marriageable daughter. It is evident that Athene, at least as an art type, became an interesting sublimation of this idea and, until about 440 B.C., she was frequently represented as a girlish divinity, while the great bulk of the statues dedicated to her were statues of girls. A favourite theme with the vase-painters was the Birth of Athene,[1] shown as a baby-figure emerging from the brain of Zeus, or a child standing upon his knees. The Greeks liked stories about 'new-born babe' divinities; and even a later poet like Callimachus was to write of this quaint legend:

> No mother bare that goddess, but the head of Zeus.
> The head of Zeus bows not in falsehood, nor
> In falsehood hath his Daughter any part.

[1] Cook, *Zeus*, III, figs. 474 ff., and Plates L to LVI.

By about 460 B.C. some sculptors began to represent Athene as a girl of about twelve, the most famous of them being Myron, whose bronze group of the young Athene with Marsyas, the satyr, must have given much delight. A small bronze in New York (Plate IV facing p. 33) shows a rather similar girl-goddess letting fly her owl from her right hand. A helmet of the shape called Corinthian is on her head, and she wears a plain Doric *chiton* fastened with a pin on each shoulder and girt up at the waist. Gods like Zeus, Poseidon, Apollo, Hermes, and others might be, and constantly were, represented as naked; but not goddesses, unless they granted permission to be thus revealed, and only Aphrodite came to permit this often. Indeed, to catch unawares a goddess bathing could have terrible consequences. Handsome hunters in Greece were well advised to be careful how they approached mountain tarns and woodland bathing-pools. The youth who from shelter of rock or thicket had observed some lovely creature shedding her simple *chiton* in order to bathe was incurring no great risk if the vision were mortal girl or mountain nymph, but if she were a goddess disaster was certain. They said of Actæon that he surprised Artemis herself bathing in the silvery pool of a mountain stream and that he was instantly changed into a young stag and torn to pieces by his own hounds.

Callimachus – the poet already cited – wrote early in the third century B.C. a hymn known as 'The Bath of Pallas' in honour of Athene, and worked into this an older legend which he had learnt as a youth in Athens.

The story is not mine, but told by others. Girls! there was one nymph of old in Thebes whom Athene loved much, more than all her companions, the mother she was of Teiresias, and she was never apart from her.

This nymph, Chariklo, was, like all her kind, ageless; for enduring youthfulness was the fortune of nymphs, even though they might be the mothers of mortal men.

Yet even her did many tears await in the days that followed, albeit she was a friend so pleasing to the heart of Athene. One day those two undid the buckles of their robes beside the fair-flowing Fountain of the

Horse on Helicon and bathed; and noontide quiet held all the hill. Those two were bathing and it was the noontide hour and a great quiet held that hill. Only Teiresias, on whose cheek the down was just darkening, still ranged with his hounds the holy place. And, athirst beyond telling, he came unto the flowing fountain, wretched man! and unwillingly saw that which is not lawful to be seen. And Athene was angered, yet said to him: 'What god, O son of Everes, led you on this grievous way? hence you shall never more take back your eyes!'

She spoke and night seized the eyes of the youth and he stood speechless; for pain glued his knees and helplessness stayed his voice. But the nymph cried: 'What have you done to my boy, Lady? Is such the friendship of you goddesses? You have taken away the eyes of my son. Foolish child! You have seen the breasts and thighs of Athene, but the sun you shall not see again.'

And the goddess Athene pitied her friend and spoke to her and said, 'Noble Lady, take back all the words that you have spoken in anger. It is not I that made your child blind. For no sweet thing is it for Athene to snatch away the eyes of children. But the laws of Kronos order thus: Whosoever shall behold any of the immortals, when the god himself chooses not, he shall behold at a heavy price.'

Then Athene went on to tell of the terrible fate of Actæon when he saw Artemis bathing, and to declare that by comparison blind Teiresias was fortunate, and Athene gave to him in compensation many honours, making him 'a seer to be sung of men hereafter, more excellent by far than any other, both in this world and in the after-life'. Wisdom indeed was in the gift of Athene.

There is no clearer proof of the love which the Athenians felt for their goddess than the temple which they built for her. The Parthenon, made, all of it, of solid Pentelic marble, was not the largest Greek temple, but it was incomparably the finest. Yet its very splendour was the symptom of a change in feelings about Athene. The pleasing concept of Pallas Athene as a young goddess, fresh-emerged from childhood, was not to endure, even as the youthful vigour of Athens, crowned by her courage and daring against the Medes at Marathon, was not to last. Athens developed into an imperialist power; Athene, under the very inspiration of Pericles and Pheidias, into a symbol of empire. In both

gable-groups of the Parthenon she was depicted as one grown to
the full estate of goddess-womanhood: the statue of her inside the
temple made her a giantess of gold and ivory.[1] It has been destroyed; but we know small copies of this, the second in fame of
the works of Pheidias. Two question must be posed. If we could
see that figure could we admire it except as a *tour de force* of engin-
eering and a brilliant piece of craftsmanship? Could it have possessed any of the deep religious and numinous qualities which we
must believe that Zeus – Pheidias' other work in gold and ivory –
possessed? Perhaps a reluctant 'No' is the answer to both questions.
Be that as it may, Athene had changed to another kind of goddess,
emblem of the state, symbol of empire, from which symbol there
were to be copied as time marched on other very similar female
symbols named 'Roma', 'Britannia', and 'Columbia'.

Yet when Pheidias had completed his statue of her these sym-
bolical derivatives were still far off, and she was venerated by the
Athenians and by other Greeks for another eight hundred years.
More than that, Alexander himself, the World Conqueror,
adopted her, placing her head upon the gold coinage of his empire. His successors followed suit, and she figured upon the money
not only of the Kings of Macedon, Thrace, Pergamum, Cappa-
docia, Syria, Egypt, and Syracuse, but even on the coins of a series
of Greek kings who ruled in North-west India. At last, when the
closing of all pagan temples was ordained, the Parthenon became
a Christian church, and the cultus of the virgin goddess of Athens
was replaced by that of the Virgin Mary. A string of titles and
epithets for god or goddess in ancient Greece was frequently
rather favoured; thus, among a variety of such tags, the goddess of
Athens had been addressed as *Pallas Athene Parthenos Gorgo Epēkoos*, meaning 'Girl Athene, Virgin, Terrible, Hearkening-to-
prayer'. When the Virgin Mary replaced Athene she, in her turn,
became *Mater Theou Parthenos Athenaia Gorgo Epēkoos* – that is,
'Mother of God, Virgin Athenian One, Terrible, Hearkening-to-
prayer'. It is those last two epithets which especially emphasise
the smooth transmutation.[2]

The sculptures of the Parthenon set forth two important myths

[1] A. W. Lawrence, *Classical Sculpture*, pp. 195 ff.   [2] Cook, *Zeus*, III, p. 588.

about the goddess. Without the co-operation of any god, hero, or mortal, Hera had parthenogenetically borne a son – Hephaistos, the divine craftsman. The implication of feminine self-sufficiency in this deed was both disturbing and displeasing to Zeus. It gave him a headache. The headache got worse; it became insupportable. He summoned the ancient spirits called Eileithyiai, who preside over birth, and their diagnosis was that Zeus was with child in his brain. So the headache was the answer to Zeus' worry about Hera. Hephaistos, her son, was next summoned and commanded to open the skull of Zeus with a stroke of his axe. Having complied, he took rapid evasive action, even as he saw the tiny child Athene spring from the brain of Zeus. Some witnesses declared she came forth fully armed and quickly grew to god-like majesty; but there are tales about her childhood and youth. Skilled in many arts and crafts, she one day invented the double-flutes, and was delighted with the music she could make, until of a sudden she looked into a clear pool of water as she played them, and was horrified at the ugliness of her puffed-out cheeks. As she threw them away in disgust a satyr named Marsyas was passing and carried them off, to his own undoing. Elated with pride as he taught himself to play them, the wretched creature dared to call himself a better musician than Apollo, and to challenge the god to a contest. What happened to him will be described in another myth in the chapter about Apollo.

Athene's girlhood friendship with the nymph Chariklo and the fate that came to Teiresias, who saw them bathing, has already been told. But now another strange story must be mentioned concerning an attempt to get Hephaistos as a husband for Athene. The proposition of a marriage between his wife's parthenogenetic son and his own 'phrenetictic' daughter seemed to Zeus a sensible way of stabilising the family; therefore, when Hephaistos asked the 'Father of gods and men' for the hand of his daughter, Zeus gave a ready consent. Yet the plan miscarried either because of the reluctance of Athene or because of the clumsiness of Hephaistos. She had been given leave by her father to 'repulse his attentions'. They struggled together, and his seed fell on the earth, which thus became fertile and in due season produced a boy.

Athene took charge of the infant, hid him in a chest guarded by serpents and gave it to the daughters of Kekrops, King of Athens, to keep, with instructions not to open it. They disobeyed, and at the sight of the serpents they were so terrified that they leapt off the Acropolis and so perished. The child was called Erichthonios and remained a favourite of Athene.[1]

Another episode in the myth concerns the Judgment of Paris, when Athene was a competitor against Hera[2] and Aphrodite for the prize of beauty. Her failure to win it was held in some measure responsible for her hostility to Trojans and her partiality for Greek heroes in the Trojan War. At any rate, of all the Greek kings and princes of that day, Odysseus was evidently her favourite. The tendency among gods to oppose one another was not displeasing to mortals, who were flattered by the belief that a god could think of a mortal man as having some importance. Thus the final story, the contest of Athene and Poseidon, proved to be a myth which could gratify the inhabitants of Athens. The deities strove for the ownership of the land, performing miracles with the ancient Heroes of Attica present as judges. Poseidon, striking the Acropolis rock with his trident, created a salt spring of water, whence there sprang a horse. Athene smote the rock with her spear and created the olive-tree, which was adjudged the more valuable gift.

The first episode in the myth of Athene – her birth from the brain of Zeus in the presence of a brave company of gods – filled the whole gable at the east end of the Athenian Parthenon. The last episode – the contest, in the presence of the Heroes of the land, between Athene and Poseidon for the ownership of Attica – filled the whole gable at the west end. The great frieze of the Parthenon depicted that famous quadrennial event founded in the goddess's honour, the Panathenaic Procession; and in the centre of the east end of the frieze on the temple there were carved the Twelve Olympian Gods, so arranged that the central places of honour were given to two pairs of gods: on the one hand Zeus and Hera, and on the other hand their children, Athene and Hephaistos. All this may be seen in the British Museum when a visit is paid to the Elgin Marbles.

[1] H. J. Rose in *OCD*, p. 114.   [2] See p. 35 above.

On the whole these are satisfactory myths, for not only do they hold a gay tale full of symbolism and psychology, but they also contain the three essentials of mythological form.

(1) There is more than one strand of symbolism in the story. Firstly, that Athene came forth from the mind of Zeus does make her the divine embodiment of God's Wisdom. Her real successor in Christian mythology is not the 'Virgin Mother of God, Terrible, Hearkening-to-prayer', who succeeded to her temple on the Acropolis; but Saint Sophia, or *Hagia Sophia*, or 'the Holy Wisdom' of God. Indeed, it is a remarkable fact that the two most sublime, most perfect creations that man as an architect has ever made are the Parthenon upon the Athenian rock and the Church of Saint Sophia beside the Golden Horn of Constantinople. And both are consecrated to the Holy Wisdom of God.

But *sophia*, the Greek word, is a word which calls for further examination. What precisely did it mean?

Until about 400 B.C. *sophia* meant adroitness of hand and brain; therefore 'skill'. The person who possesses *sophia* is *sophos*, and is accordingly an expert. It means 'knowingness' before it begins to mean 'wisdom'. After 400 B.C. it begins to apply especially to the expert in thinking – the philosopher, the 'liker of thinking'. And from then on *sophia* tends to become specialised as 'wisdom'. But the sense of 'knowingness' is never quite absent from the word. 'What a knowing fellow you are!' has more than one meaning.

So Athene sprung from the brain of Zeus is the symbol and the patroness of *sophia*, which means 'skill-plus-wisdom', and therefore is the protectress of every man and woman who is definitely keen on and good at his or her job. That means the potter and the spinner, the goldsmith and the weaver, the cobbler and the sempstress, the mason and the miller, the carpenter and the cook; but also the soldier, the strategist, the statesman, the schoolmaster, and finally the philosopher. In fact, for Man the city-dweller, Man the member of the prosperous proletariat, Man whom Aristotle called 'a political animal', Athene is the perfect divine patroness. Therefore she attained her fullest development in the best organised of all Greek city-states – Athens. There she had, besides the other titles already set down, the epithets *ergane* and *promachos* – that is,

'Athene the Worker' and 'Front-line Athene' – the former un-armed, the latter in the panoply of battle.

(II) The psychology behind the myth of the goddess is pleas-antly expressed, illustrating as it does several subtleties of human response or reaction to a number of situations. There is Zeus, mightily jealous and upset because his queen has produced a child really and truly all by herself. There is Athene, growing up and aware of herself mirrored in the unruffled pool, aware of her good looks and of the fearful mistake of playing the flutes. Then again there is the problem story of her and Hephaistos: two people united by a common interest, united by their work and their pride in exquisite craftsmanship, utterly suited to one another but for a fortuitous and unfortunate sexual incompatibility. That is what one would be saying if they were mortals instead of gods; and one would have deplored the boorish clumsiness of the artisan 'god of the smithy'. But as the myth stands, since Athene and Hephaistos still remained partners in Athens, you are left guessing whether they were just work-mates or more closely linked. Lastly, there is the well-understood psychology of the woman of independence with a job of her own, who nevertheless intensely desires to have a child – but without trouble! And there are to be nurses! Pallas Athene achieved this in the most satisfactory manner by the adop-tion of Erichthonios, who, in the given circumstances, might be considered her child.

(III) Like the Zeus myth, this one also contains the three essen-tials of mythological form, which are birth, mating, and death; but they are all presented in strange and unusual fashion, the death part being supplied by the suicide of the daughters of Kekrops – the nurses of the infant Erichthonios.

If the story of Athene is, like several other myths, in its sim-plicity rather earthy, bluff, and odd, one must remember that it had scarcely any relation to the dignified cult of the goddess, or to the emotional love which men could give to her divinity.

'THE non-criminal classes have always been apt', as *The Times* once declared,[1] 'to take a rather romantic view of the malefactors who prey upon them.' Robin Hood and Dick Turpin are not quite 'saints', but they surely are heroes. Today in Greece it is a fine breadth of a letter that distinguishes between *kleptēs*, the thief or pickpocket, and *klephtēs*, the brigand or guerrilla, and this still encourages among non-criminal urban classes an almost tolerant attitude towards the romantic mountain 'Kleft'. But what is too easily overlooked is that both the pickpocket and the brigand sometimes say their prayers and often feel the need of supernatural aid in their enterprises against people whom they regard as anti-social plutocrats.

It would, indeed, be unwise to regard divine patronage of thieving as something peculiar to the ancient Greek world, because there is adequate evidence of a similar phenomenon in much later times. A legend was told in Winchester concerning a certain thief who was about to be hanged for his crimes; but, owing to his great devotion to the Blessed Virgin Mary, she appeared and held him up by his feet so that he escaped hanging. In the Lady Chapel at the east end of Winchester Cathedral there was painted between 1486 and 1498 a series of pictures showing miracles of the Virgin, and this episode of the thief, her devoted worshipper, is among them.

Whosoever retains a memory of some lesson learnt in school about ancient Greek beliefs is apt to recall the fact that there was a 'god of thieves' called Hermes and to reflect in consequence upon the 'immoral' nature of Greek religion. A readiness to aid thieves and brigands was unquestionably one of that god's functions; but it was only one of many, and it promptly raises the point that he was once a god of an earlier, conquered, and suppressed body of people who felt every justification in taking what they could – like Taffy the Welshman – from their oppressors. Nevertheless, in the classical age Hermes is discovered to be a full Olympian, a son of

[1] May 21, 1951, p. 5.

HERMES, herald, guide of souls and of the lonely traveller. This bronze, about 10 inches high, shows him carrying a ram. Made about 500 B.C., perhaps in Sparta.

Silver coin of Aenus with head of Hermes, struck about 470 B.C.

Silver coin of Sybrita with head of Hermes, struck about 360 B.C.

PLATE V

APOLLO, the god and guardian of law and right. This gigantic marble figure from the centre of the western gable of the Temple of Zeus at Olympia was made about 460 B.C.

(LEFT) *Silver coin* of Leontini, Sicily, with head of Apollo, struck about 370 B.C.

Silver coin of Clazomenæ with head of Apollo, struck about 370 B.C.

PLATE VI

Zeus, and a younger brother of Apollo. His great variety of functions and his double origin make him a most genial and fascinating deity.

It is now becoming apparent that, just as in Christian theology there are always two distinct influences, one Jewish, the other Greek, so in Pagan theology – that is to say, the lore about Pagan gods – there are for all the most important Olympian deities two distinct influences, one pre-Hellenic, the other Hellenic. This is certainly true of Hermes, whose name is Greek, but whose nature and functions are mainly derived from the beliefs of earlier folk. He appears to emerge as a pastoral god and a guide to travellers for the reason that in remote antiquity he is the spirit immanent in stone-heaps – such a spirit of the cairn as is still an occasional feature of Northern European belief. The stone-heaps are put up gradually by shepherds as landmarks, and in unexplored country are of the greatest help to wayfarers. Mountain country may abound in wild animals, which such a spirit may be able to control. When the Greek-speaking peoples came down into the peninsula and observed these friendly heaps, they referred to each one as *herma*, meaning 'stone-heap' in their language, or as *hermaios lophos*, meaning 'stone-heap mound'. They did not know the name which the pre-Hellenic inhabitants gave to their god; and the name – as often in similar cases elsewhere – was doubtless withheld from them, therefore they could only refer to the god as 'Hermes', or, in the Laconian dialect which some of them spoke, as 'Hermanos', which being translated must mean 'He of the stone-heap', or familiarly, 'Old Heapy'.[1] A large grey stone embedded in a stone-heap was discovered on a hill-side in Laconia, and it bears in letters of the sixth century B.C. the god's name 'Hermanos'.[2]

As an alternative name the Greeks constantly referred to the god simply as *Diaktoros*, which means 'the Guide', and coupled with this another epithet *Argeiphontes*, or 'Argos-killer'. Now Argos is a name constantly given to dogs; and, since Hermes also

[1] Jacqueline Chittenden in *Hesperia*, 1947, pp. 89 ff., and in *AJA*, 1948, pp. 24 ff. The form Hermanos is genitive.

[2] Chittenden, *loc. cit.*, Plate XV. See also Guthrie, *The Greeks and their Gods*, p. 90.

bears as variants similar epithets meaning 'dog-throttler', this points to his function as a spirit protecting the lonely wayfarer from the savage dogs which are still a bane to travellers in Greece today. But he who can protect a man from dogs can also save him from more terrible animals: wild boar, wolves, and lions. Now the incoming Greeks also encountered another somewhat different god who was worshipped in Minoan Crete and who was also associated with stone-heaps, and especially with domination over wild creatures. This 'Master of Animals' was in some way associated – either as lover, son, brother, or all three – with the Great Goddess whose worship prevailed in Asia and in Crete, and one of her most important aspects was that of 'Mistress of Wild Beasts', concerning whom more must later be told. The Greeks appear to have made a synthesis of this Minoan 'Master of Animals' with the mainland pastoral god, the guide to travellers whom they named Hermes. Presently other interesting traits purely Greek in origin began to accumulate, adding to the subtlety and variety of a most friendly divine personality.

Hermes in the *Iliad* is a divine guide to the living; by the time the end of the *Odyssey* is reached he has begun to conduct souls on their last journey, and that function of guide to the dead became, in classical times, a most important one. Again, he never appears as a messenger in the *Iliad*, because it was Iris who, as servant of Zeus, filled that role. But in the *Odyssey* the change takes place, and he is presently a messenger frequently despatched by Zeus to men. From this notion there grew the concept of Hermes as the divine herald, and he is represented in art as carrying the herald's staff, the *caduceus*, made of a rod with forked twigs that are twisted into a shape like a figure '8' left open at the top. Himself, as the divine herald, becomes the god of heralds, and therefore of those who set a pause to war, bringing armistice and then peace. Peace revives or leads to trade, restoring prosperity to the market-place, and he is now chief deity of the market and of business. Yet it is in this very market – where not only customers but also commercial rivals soon start to impute to certain traders thievish proclivities – that thievishly inclined persons (alternatively described as 'really live business men') need a god to pray to and to give them protection. Hermes is the only answer; especially because, long before urban life developed, he had already been the god of the older race of peasantry in Arcadia and adjoining places, where the down-trodden 'natives' sought his help in such raids as they could make on the cattle and chattels of their oppressors. After all, it depends in these cases entirely upon which side we are taking whether we call a man a thief or a social benefactor. This makes a long catalogue of Hermes' functions and of matters for his divine concern, and it is surely appropriate that as god of business he should be the busiest of deities. But there is more to come.

Nowadays one of the first things which a good man of business contemplates is insurance, that is to say an effort to give to family life some sort of security and to the home itself some kind of protection. Anything like 'policies' financially arranged was far away indeed, for the civilised Greek world really held a more slender sense of security than does ours, and there was nothing for it but to put your faith in some god – the kindlier the better – and hope for his benevolence. But the civilised world was much less inhibited, and therefore much more courageous, than ours of today. The importance of fertility for crops and herds and for humanity was something which must so obviously be emphasised with complete frankness that no Greek could think of it as a matter for unseemly sniggers. When we come to examine, in a later chapter, the history of the incoming worship of Dionysos, youngest of the Twelve Olympians, we shall find that his most serious impact made itself felt upon the larger urban communities of the Greeks early in the sixth century B.C. That powerful and alarming god, imported from more simple Northern neighbours of the Greeks, being essentially a god of fertility, was sometimes represented as a squared wooden stump with a mask on top for a face and a phallus attached half-way down it. In Athens and in a number of other cities this crude but honest image appears to have been taken over from Dionysos by the more sophisticated Hermes. One may venture a guess that, while the conspicuous symbol of human fertility was highly respected, men inclined to associate it with a god who, in their view, possessed far greater stability, reliability, and familiarity with the economics of town life than did the

wild new god from beyond the Hellenic regions. Be that as it
may, we find that a custom dating from before the mid-sixth
century soon spread, and that at the entrance to each public building and beside the front-door of each private house there was set
up a stone pilaster, square in section with rough stumps for arms,
a phallus in the centre, and a formal bearded head, meant to present Hermes, on top of it, and that this object was called a 'Herm'.
Symbolically it meant the best of good luck. Hermes, who in the
countryside could give increase of flocks and herds, could assuredly enhance the fertility of the household. As god of thieves, was
he not the best of all deities to keep the thieves away – provided,
of course, you wooed him with prayers and gifts? As god of the
market-place and trade, his benevolence to your household was
much to be desired, and his image stood almost as a token of insurance against all harm that threatened your family and your
residence. Meanwhile, out on your country estate, large or small,
to which you all moved in the hot weather, other Herms of the
very same type were there as tokens of a god's goodwill. And it is
to be observed that when a death occurred in the family it was
this same Hermes on whom you relied to conduct the loved soul
on an untroubled journey. He is constantly shown on Athenian
painted funeral vases as the soul's guide to the other world.

Two more activities became his concern during the classical
age. Hermes was thought of as the god of orators and the general
patron of men of letters, this being perhaps a natural development
from the herald, to whom the fine voice and persuasive tongue
were assets, as, of course, they also were to the successful trader
and man of affairs. Lastly, Hermes became a patron of athletic
games and exercises. The line of thought here was perhaps as follows: the god of fertility is a deity of good luck, which is needed
by athletes who compete against one another; and, as these are
the young men whose training is an essential part of Greek education, Hermes, too, is commonly represented from the mid-fifth
century onward as a young athletic type. But for more than a
century before this it was customary to represent him as somewhat older and bearded, as he appears on a superb bronze statuette (Plate V, facing page 64) from Peloponnesus made about

500 B.C. and now in Boston. Hermes the Guide is dressed as a traveller; his long hair protects the back of his neck, and he wears a hat of felt and a short garment buttoned on the shoulders and belted at the waist, while his high, buttoned shoes have wings attached to show him as the divine messenger. Tucked under the left arm of the god of flocks and herds is a contented ram, whose fore-legs are held in his left hand. In his right, now empty, he held the *caduceus* – the herald's staff.

Recent research[1] has provided us today with a clearer perception of what the Greeks at different times thought and felt about Hermes, and we know more about him than about several other deities. Yet the multiplicity of his titles and functions must not be allowed to disguise the fact that Hermes is one of the very earliest and most primitive of all the gods of Greece.

In the official myth Hermes is the son of Zeus and Maia, but that was just her title and no more than a mode of address. Indeed, the word *maia* has almost a slangy quality, meaning 'mother' as used for 'Old Mother Hubbard', and in Greek it is applied to elderly nurses and domestics. Yet in some older stage of the Greek language it must have denoted 'mother' in the true maternal sense, even as the title was used to denote Hermes' mother, Maia, the mountain-nymph of Mount Kyllene in Northern Peloponnesus. Her real name – the one that was given to her by the initiates among the pre-Hellenic people – has vanished, just as the original name of her son vanished long ago. Of course, she was an aspect of the Great Goddess[2] of many names who passed something of herself to almost every goddess and many a nymph. Here the simplicity of the title seems like a token of something ancient and more than half-forgotten. But among mortal men the god whom she bore was one of the best-loved of gods.

There was preserved in Greek literature a series of hymns to various gods, varying greatly both in quality and in length, and composed between about 700 and 450 B.C. One of the longest, most important, most enchanting and humorous is the Hymn to Hermes, which has been assigned to a date close to 600 B.C. It tells the story of the early adventures of the infant god following

[1] Especially by Chittenden, *loc. cit.*   [2] See pp. 31 f.

immediately on the day when he was born in the cave on Mount Kyllene.

Sing of Hermes, the son of Zeus and Maia,
Lord of Kyllene and Arcadia, rich in flocks,
The luck-bringing messenger of the immortals whom Maia bare,
The long-haired nymph, when she was joined in love with Zeus,
A shy goddess, avoiding the company of the blessed gods,
She lived within a deep cave. There the son of Kronos
Would lie with the long-haired nymph, unseen by deathless gods
    and mortal men,
At dead of night, when sweet sleep held white-armed Hera fast.
And when the purpose of great Zeus was fulfilled,
And the tenth moon with her was fixed in heaven,
She was delivered and a notable thing was come to pass.
For then she bare a son, of many shifts, blandly cunning,
A robber, a cattle-driver, a bringer of dreams,
A watcher by night, a thief at the gates who was soon to show
Wonderful deeds among the deathless gods.
Born with the dawning, at midday he played on the lyre,
And at eve he stole the cattle of far-shooting Apollo,
On the fourth day of the month;
On that day our Lady Maia bare him.
So soon as he had leaped from his mother's heavenly womb,
He lay not long waiting in his holy cradle,
But he sprang up and sought the oxen of Apollo.
As he stepped over the threshold of the high-roofed cave,
He found a tortoise there and gained endless delight.
For it was Hermes who first made the tortoise a singer.
The creature fell in his way at the courtyard gate,
Where it was feeding on rich grass before the dwelling,
Waddling along. And when he saw it, the luck-bringing son of Zeus
    laughed
And said:
'An omen of great luck for me so soon! I do not slight it.
Hail, comrade of the feast, lovely in shape, sounding at the dance!
With joy I meet you! Where got you that rich gaud for covering,
That spangled shell – a tortoise living in the mountains?
But I will take and carry you within; you shall help me
And I will do you no disgrace, though first of all you must profit me.

It is better to be at home: harm may come out of doors.
Living you shall be a spell against mischievous witchcraft;
But if you die, then you shall make sweetest song.'

The infant proceeded to convert the shell of the tortoise into the
first seven-stringed lyre that had ever been made; and after tuning
it, began to sing.

He sang of Zeus, the son of Kronos, and dainty-sandalled Maia,
Of the converse which was theirs in the comradeship of love,
Telling all the glorious tales of his own begetting . . .
But while he was singing of this, his heart was bent on other matters.
And he took the hollow lyre and laid it on his sacred cradle,
And sprang from the sweet-smelling hall to a watch-place,
Pondering sheer trickery in his heart – deeds such as knavish folk
Pursue in the dark night-time; for he longed to taste flesh.
The Sun was going down beneath the earth towards the Ocean
When Hermes came hurrying to the dark mountains of Pieria,
Where the divine cattle of the blessed gods had their steads,
And grazed the pleasant unmown meadows.
Of these the son of Maia, the sharp-eyed Argos-killer,
Cut off from the herd fifty loud-lowing kine,
And drove them straggling-wise across a sandy place,
Turning their hoof-prints aside. Also, he bethought him
Of a crafty ruse and reversed the marks of their hoofs,
Making the front behind and the hind before,
While he himself walked the other way.

There follows a long tale of how Hermes drove the cattle all the
way from Pieria near Mount Olympus to the River Alpheus in
Peloponnesus and killed and flayed two of them, making a burnt
offering and sacrifice to the gods. When he had duly finished he
quenched the embers and covered the ashes with sand.

Then the god went back again at dawn to the bright crests of Kyllene,
And no one met him on the long journey either of the blessed gods or
    mortal men,
Nor did any dog bark. And luck-bringing Hermes, son of Zeus,
Passed edgeways through the key-hole of the hall like the autumn
    breeze,

Even as mist: straight through the cave he went,
And came to the inner chamber, walking softly,
And making no noise as one might upon the floor.
Then glorious Hermes went hurriedly to his cradle,
Wrapping his swaddling clothes about him as though he were a feeble
    babe,
And he lay playing with the covering about his knees;
But at his left hand he kept close his sweet lyre.

It was not long before the great Apollo, son of Zeus and Leto, discovered how serious a raid had been made upon his herd, and seeking information on this side and on that – one of the earliest detective-stories here – he finally concluded that in some way this magical new-born child must be responsible. Therefore,

... the lord Apollo, the Son of Zeus, hastened
And came to the forest-clad mountains of Kyllene,
And the deep-shadowed cave in the rock where the divine nymph
Brought forth the child of Zeus who is son of Kronos.
A sweet odour spread over the lovely hill
And many thin-shanked sheep were grazing on the grass.
Then far-shooting Apollo himself stepped down
In haste over the stone threshold into the dusky cave.
Now when the Son of Zeus and Maia saw Apollo
In a rage about his cattle, he snuggled down
In his fragrant swaddling-clothes; and as wood-ash covers
Over the deep embers of tree-stumps, so Hermes
Cuddled himself up when he saw the Far-shooter's anger.
He squeezed head and hands and feet together in a small space,
Like a new-born child seeking sweet sleep,
Though in truth he was wide awake, and he kept his lyre under his
    armpit.
... Then when the Son of Leto had searched the recesses of the great
    house,
He turned and spoke to glorious Hermes:
'Child, lying in the cradle, make haste and tell me
Of my cattle, or we two soon will fall out angrily.
For I will take you and cast you into dusky Tartarus
And awful hopeless darkness; and neither your mother
Nor your father shall free you or bring you up again to the light,

But you will wander under the earth and be the leader amongst little
 folk.'
Then Hermes answered him with shrewd and crafty words:
'Son of Leto, what harsh words are these you have spoken?
And is it cattle of the field you are come here to seek?
I have not seen them: I have not heard of them: no one has told me.
I cannot give news of them, nor win the reward for news.
Am I like a cattle-lifter? Am I a stalwart person?
This is no task for me: rather I care for other things:
I care for sleep, and milk of my mother's breast,
And for wrappings round my shoulders,
And for warm baths. Let no one hear the cause of this dispute,
For this were a great marvel indeed among the deathless gods
That a child newly born should pass through the forepart of the house
With cattle of the field: herein you speak extravagantly.
I was born yesterday, my feet are soft and the ground is rough;
Nonetheless, if you will have it so, I will swear a great oath
By my father's head and vow that neither am I
Guilty myself, nor have I seen any other who stole your cows –
Whatever cows may be: for I know them only by hearsay.'

Then Apollo took up the child and began to carry him.

But now the strong Argos-killer had his plan
And while Apollo held him in his hands, sent forth an omen,
A hard-worked belly-serf, a rude messenger, and sneezed thereafter.
And when Apollo heard it, he dropped glorious Hermes
Out of his hands on the ground: and sitting down before him,
Though eager to go on his way,
Spoke mockingly to Hermes:
'Fear not, little swaddling baby, son of Zeus and Maia,
I shall find the strong cattle presently by these omens,
And you shall lead the way.'
... Now though Hermes had many wiles, he found that the other
Had also many a shift, and he began to cross the sand,
Himself in front, while the Son of Zeus and Leto came behind.
Soon they came, these lovely children of Zeus,
To the top of fragrant Olympus, to their father, the Son of Kronos;
For there were the scales of judgment set for them both.
There was an assembly on snowy Olympus,

And the immortals who perish not were gathering
After the hour of gold-enthroned Dawn.
Then Hermes and Apollo of the Silver Bow stood at the knees of Zeus;
And Zeus who thunders on high spoke to his glorious son and asked
    him:
'Phoebus, whence come you driving this great spoil,
A child new born that has the look of a herald?
A weighty matter this, to come before the council of the gods!'

Apollo made his lengthy accusation, which the infant Hermes
proceeded to rebut, all to the delight of Zeus, who sent him off to
show his elder brother where he had hidden the cattle and to return them. This done, Hermes produced his tortoiseshell lyre and
began to play upon it for his brother's enchantment.

But Apollo was seized by a longing not to be allayed,
And he opened his mouth and spoke winged words to Hermes:
'Slayer of oxen, trickster, busy one, comrade of the feast,
This song of yours is worth fifty cows, and I believe
That presently we shall settle our quarrel most peacefully.
But come now, tell me this, resourceful son of Maia:
Has this marvellous thing been with you from your birth,
Or did some god or mortal man give it to you – a noble gift –
And teach you heavenly song? For wonderful
Is this new-uttered sound I hear,
The like of which I vow that no man nor god dwelling on Olympus
Ever yet has known but you, O thievish son of Maia!
What skill is this? What song for desperate cares?
What way of song? For verily here are three things to hand,
All at once from which to choose – mirth, and love, and sweet sleep.
And though I am follower of the Olympian Muses
Who love dances and the bright path of song – the full-toned chant
And ravishing thrill of flutes – yet never I cared
For any of these feats of skill at young men's revels
As now I care for this: I am filled with wonder, O son of Zeus,
At your sweet playing.'
. . . Then Hermes answered him with artful words:
'You question me carefully, O Far-worker; yet am I not jealous
That you should enter upon my art: this day you shall know it.
For I seek to be friendly with you both in thought and word.
Now you well know all things in your heart since you sit

Foremost among the deathless gods, O son of Zeus,
And are goodly and strong. . . .
But since, as it seems, your heart is strongly set on playing the lyre,
Chant and play upon it, and give yourself to merriment,
Taking this as a gift from me, and do you, my friend, bestow glory
   on me.
Sing well with this clear-voiced companion in your hands;
For you are skilled in good, well-ordered utterance.'

That was how the lyre which Hermes had made became the
property of Apollo; and father Zeus looked down from Olympus
happy in his children and

. . . himself gave confirmation to their words,
And commanded that glorious Hermes should be lord over all birds of
   omen
And grim-eyed lions, and boars with gleaming tusks,
And over dogs and all flocks that the wide earth nourishes,
And over all sheep; also that he only should be the appointed
Messenger to Hades, who though he takes no gift,
Shall give him no mean prize.
Thus the lord Apollo showed his kindness for the Son of Maia,
And Zeus gave him grace.
He consorts with all mortals and immortals:
A little he profits but continually through the dark night
He cozens the tribes of mortal men.

The long Hymn to Hermes,[1] running to nearly six hundred
lines, was written for recital at a feast or holy day of the god,
probably held on his birthday on the fourth day of the month.
The words have the freshness, the metre, the rapidity of the great
epics, *Iliad* and *Odyssey*, but there is less of seriousness and nothing
of terror. Here is a story of 'gods, who being exempt from death
and pain live a life that men would like to live but may not'. So it
is 'full of humour and joy'.[2]

When he had grown to full godhead Hermes was set a hard
task by Zeus. It happened as follows: Zeus, like a great Lord

[1] My version of the passages selected is adapted from the late H. G. Evelyn-
White's translation in the Loeb volume.
[2] C. M. Bowra, *Ancient Greek Literature*, 1933, p. 46.

enamoured of one of his Lady's waiting-maids, fell in love with
the beautiful Io, a young priestess of Hera, and to conceal her
from his ever-jealous spouse he changed the girl for a while into a
young heifer. The Lady Hera, aware of what had happened, asked
her husband in seeming innocence for the pretty little cow as a
gift, which Zeus could hardly refuse. Having thus gained a point,
Hera set the savage Argos to guard the heifer. Some said he had
eyes in the back of his head, or eyes all over him, or a hundred
eyes, but these were later elaborations of a tale in which originally
he was probably an extra-large and savage dog.[1] Zeus, thwarted
of his love, remembered that he had given the son of Maia power
over wild animals and dogs and so sent Hermes off to kill Argos.
This accomplished, the god won the title of Argos-killer by which
he was so constantly described.

Hermes remained a bachelor-god, and, for a son of Zeus, he
seems to have had a modest number of love-affairs; or else with
his gift of cunning kept some of them secret. There were old families in Attica, where his worship was of such importance, who
traced descent from him, and it was claimed that not only had he
loved one of the daughters of Kekrops, King of Athens – Herse by
name – and begotten the hunter Kephalos, but also that he loved
one of her sisters – Aglauros or Pandrosos – and was the father of
Keryx, founder of an Eleusinian clan. Another son of his was the
hero Eleusis, whose mother was called Daeira – the 'knowing one'.
This was a title given to Persephone, bride of Hades; and when
Pausanias avers that she was an Ocean nymph this may represent
an Attic or Eleusinian priestly version meant to cover an earlier
tale of divine intrigue.

But the most important love-tale about Hermes is set in Arcadia. There was a girl named Ameirake,[2] who as a child was cast
into the sea but rescued by a wild duck (in Greek *penelops*) and
was thenceforth named Penelope – or 'Ducky'. Yet in another
version her name was Dryope, or 'Woodpecker' (the Greek is
dryops), not a very duck-like bird. At any rate, bird-like she was,
and Hermes loved her; and in the second book of his history
Herodotus said that she – Penelope he calls her – was mother by

[1] Chittenden in *AJA*, 1948, p. 27.   [2] Cook, *Zeus*, II, p. 691.

Hermes of the fantastic Arcadian god Pan, who was born at Mantinea, where his mother's tomb was shown. All this was imagined as having occurred before ever Penelope became wife of the great Odysseus of Ithaca, himself Hermes' great-grandson. There is a Homeric Hymn to Pan which begins:

> Sing to me, Muse, that dearest son of Hermes,
> Goat-footed and two-horned, who takes delight
> In loud noise, and about the tree-girt lawns
> Roams with the dancing Nymphs, who range the tops
> Of cliff-scarped mountains, calling upon Pan,
> The bright-haired unkempt deity of flocks.[1]

Another son of Hermes was Autolykos, master-thief, cattle-rustler, faker, and trickster; but who his mother was it is hard to know, for some said her name was Chione, others Philonis, and yet others Telauge. One might hazard a guess that there was rivalry among the daughters of chieftains to claim motherhood of so fine a brigand by so great a god. An ancient story was told in Rhodes about a girl named Apemosyne, grand-daughter of Minos, King of Crete, who repulsed all Hermes' offers and always ran from him, until one day the trickster spread in her path some slippery raw hides, on which she fell, and so possessed her. Apart from this last episode, he showed great politeness to goddesses and nymphs. In the twenty-first book of the *Iliad*, when numerous gods, having lost their sense of proportion on account of partisanship either for Greeks or for Trojans, began to line up ready to attack one another, Hermes found himself facing the great Leto, mother of Apollo and Artemis. With true tact Hermes the Guide, the Argos-killer, called across to her and said:

> Do not be afraid, Leto, that *I* am going to fight you. People who come to blows with Consorts of the Cloud-compeller Zeus seem to have uphill work. No; you can boast to your heart's content and tell the gods that you got the better of me by brute strength.[2]

Although Hermes had so rich a mythology, and although he was a god much loved and of great importance in many places,

[1] R. C. Trevelyan, *Translations from Greek Poetry*. [2] Translation by E. V. Rieu.

there seems to have been only one great and prosperous Greek city – Ainos on the Thracian coast – in which he was the chief and dominant deity.[1] But there were shrines and statues and 'Herms' of him all over the civilised world for many centuries, and it is diverting to recall the story that the great oratorical gifts of the Apostle Paul caused him on one occasion[2] to be paid the highest compliment in a Greek city of Asia Minor when he was taken for the god Hermes. His violent rebuttal of the intended compliment raised some trouble, and the Apostle came near to becoming himself submerged in a stone-heap.

In the Western world the god had a great vogue under his mercantile name of Mercury, being especially popular in Gaul, where he was the most important god of all. The same applies to those small parts of Germany which came under Roman influence, for in them Hermes–Mercury was identified with the great Teutonic god *Wodanaz* (Norse, *Odinn*; Old English, *Wōden*), and his name-day is therefore Wednesday. At the eastern end of the Roman Empire another transformation occurred. Because earlier Greeks had once equated the Egyptian god of letters, Thoth, with Hermes, certain Gnostic writers of the third century A.D. with a mystical devotion to Thoth invented for him the title of 'Thrice-great Hermes', which had, however, no true association whatsoever with the humorous, kindly Greek deity, messenger of Olympian Zeus, herald, guide of souls and of the lonely traveller, guardian of the home – perhaps the most loved of them all.

---

[1] In Arcadian Pheneus he was also the dominant god, but it was not a very large city.   [2] *Acts*, xiv, 12 ff.

IN the introductory chapter reference was made to the effort required by modern men and women to adjust themselves to the Greek point of view in order to sense the reality of ancient Greek belief in personal deities. For many of us, at certain periods of our lives, when we find or have found our whole being obsessed, to the exclusion of all else, with passionate and unfulfilled desire for the bodily presence of another, it has seemed as though some external daimonic force held us in thrall. It is then that we hesitate to ascribe the erotic enslavement of our minds to an Almighty and All-merciful God, perhaps because we still sense within us some of the happier Paganism of our own remote ancestors. Therefore we may resort to symbolic allusions concerning the bow of Cupid or the arrows of Eros, or – employing her Latin name – to the unconquerable power of his mother, Venus. In fact, many of us, for at least some periods of our lives, still believe in Aphrodite, though hardly with that intensity known to the ancient Greeks.

There will be something to say a little later about her origin, but for the moment it is important to set on record the dual meaning of her name, which can conveniently be expressed by the manner of spelling it either with a capital or with a small initial. A Greek got the meaning from the context: but for us it is useful to write 'Aphrodite' when the goddess is intended, and *aphrodite* when we mean sexual desire and union, the word having been employed in both senses by the Greeks.

Of all the Twelve Olympians she is the most alarming and the most alluring, so much so that many writers have tended to edge away from a discussion of her. It is not that people write against Aphrodite, but rather that they avoid her as a topic, as though there were fear in their hearts of offending. But in this present time, when Western civilisation is witnessing great changes in the conventional attitude to the relations of the sexes, when the Registrar-General's *Statistical Review* showed as long ago as 1939 that one bride in every six was pregnant on her wedding-day – in such a time as this present age it is far easier to write naturally about *aphrodite* and to achieve some understanding of the ancient Greeks' attitude to the powerful goddess. Today we are free to recognise the reality which informs all that she stands for, free to recall that, while most men can remember acts of folly and of careless hurt performed in her service, most men and women have likewise been made aware of mystical experiences in the deeds of love. Some there are who have learnt that the deepest pleasures are those which are both subjective and objective at the same moment. This moment is then timeless and appertains to eternity. The only true rewards are imagination merged in reality and, simultaneously, reality merged in imagination. These are the mystical things of the body – as well as of the soul – which Aphrodite has to offer. Indeed, the view is tenable that only one who has in youth and maturity known temperate experience of *aphrodite* and who has always looked on pleasure as something to be given to another is qualified to write of the mystical splendour of love, even as in his old age Pindar, the greatest lyric poet of his day, once wrote when celebrating the gentle votaries of the goddess in ancient Corinth.[1] By the fifth century B.C. some such attitude to *aphrodite* had been adopted by many Greeks. But it is not to be forgotten that their concern with sex was moderate and occasional, and that since it was not mixed up in their minds with ideas of sin, they were less preoccupied therewith than were people in subsequent ages. For Greeks in this context self-denial was as much of a perversion as self-indulgence, since both are evidence of excess.

Leaving the fifth century, we may now move back to contemplate a remoter past and to consider what is known about the origins of Aphrodite.

Long before the Olympians were established in the affections of the Greeks, an older religion, based on a society of a very different kind, had centred on the worship of a Great Goddess[2] whose cult existed in Iran, Babylonia, Anatolia, Syria, and Cyprus as well as in Greek lands. Her name took various forms such as Ishtar, Ashtoreth, Astarte, and her spouse was addressed as Bel or Baal, meaning 'Lord'. A feminine form of that title was Baalath, Bilit, or

[1] See pp. 83f.   [2] See pp. 31f.

Silver coin of Cnidus with head of Aphrodite, struck about 470 B.C.

APHRODITE, the most alarming and the most alluring of the Twelve Olympians. Bronze statuette, about $18\frac{1}{2}$ inches high, made about 330 B.C.

Silver coin of Lycia with head of Aphrodite, struck about 470 B.C.

PLATE VII

DEMETER, 'Mater Dolorosa', mourning for Persephone. Marble, over life-size, made about 330 B.C. by Leochares. Found at Cnidus.

Silver coin of Metapontum, South Italy, with head of youthful Demeter crowned with corn. Struck about 340 B.C.

Silver coin of Delphi with head of Demeter, struck in 335 B.C.

PLATE VIII

Milit, meaning 'Lady', which came into Greek as 'Mylitta', about
whom the historian Herodotus had much to say. In Babylon it
was a social rule that every girl once in her life must go to the
temple of the goddess and whatever her status must sit down with
the other women.

And there are always many women there; for some come, as others
go. And thoroughfares marked with the line extend in every direction
among the women, along which the strangers pass and make their
choice. And whensoever a woman sitteth down there, she departeth
not home before a stranger cast money in her lap and lie with her inside
the temple. And as he casteth in the money, needs must he say this
much: I adjure thee by the goddess Mylitta. And the money is of any
amount; for a woman will never reject it (for that is not allowed her
for the money is sacred); but she followeth him that first casteth money
in her lap, despising no man. But when he hath lain with her, she hath
performed her duty to the goddess, and departeth home; and thereafter
thou canst not give her anything so great as will entice her.[1]

What is, from the Greek point of view, important here is that
Herodotus goes on with the remark: 'Now there is a custom very
like this in some parts of Cyprus also.'

Aphrodite was 'the Cyprian'; she was 'the Paphian', named
after the famous city of Paphos, where she – the foam-born goddess – first landed from the sea. Primitive images there showed her
naked like the images in Babylon of Ishtar, and in Syria of
Astarte, and the girls of Cyprus performed the same duty in her
honour. The dove – most amorous of creatures – was her sacred
bird. From the flourishing, part-Semitic, part-Greek, island of
Cyprus her worship was transferred, certainly by Phœnicians, to
Cythera, an island off Southern Peloponnesus. In the *Iliad* Aphrodite is called 'Cypris'; in the *Odyssey* a little later 'Cytherea'; and
at last her cult was established in one of the greatest and most
flourishing of Greek states, Corinth, perhaps as late as the eighth
century B.C. Long before, in the Bronze Age, the early Greeks had
some knowledge of a goddess similar in type and like Astarte, for
in a shaft-grave at Mycenæ a little gold *repoussé* image made
about 1500 B.C. was found, representing a naked goddess with

[1] Herodotus, Book I, 199.

doves.[1] But the introduction to a Dorian Greek city-state like Corinth of a specialised – though modified – kind of fertility religion was something unique and probably rather sudden; and though the precise circumstances of the introduction are not known, there can be little doubt that the peculiar religious practice came from a partly Phœnician place like Cyprus. It involved a dedicating of *aphrodite* in honour of Aphrodite, goddess of procreation, supreme deity in the state of Corinth. This special form of devotion and duty done to the goddess *once* by *every* girl in Babylon and in Paphos was something which could not be fitted into the Greek social pattern, rooted in the family and patriarchal in type. Nevertheless, the character of the goddess – and men would never dare to thwart her primæval nature – required feminine dedication and self-abnegation. Aphrodite needed her 'religious', her servants who 'professed' their devotion; and a girl might find her happiness as a mystical handmaid of the goddess. For what happened was that the Corinthian State handed over the cult-duty to 'professionals' who lived for long years in the precinct of Aphrodite, high up on the splendid summit of Acrocorinthus, not down in the city itself. If their profession automatically involved unchastity, they none the less practised 'poverty', since what they earned went into the coffers of their 'Order'. For that reason the girls of Corinthian Aphrodite were not despised among the ancient Greeks, who were prone to the same heartless and flippant attitude towards ordinary prostitutes which has been the mark of ancient Roman, mediæval, and modern men.

The large number of girls who lived on Acrocorinthus were not slaves, for slavery, it seems, was frowned on anyhow, since Periander, despot of Corinth about 600 B.C., passed a law against it. Some were of the free-citizen class, like certain girls mentioned by Athenæus,[2] others, who had been purchased by donors, were automatically freed by being given to the goddess, whose ministers they became. Those who found a protector might leave the

[1] H. Bossert, *AAC*, 194e.

[2] His great work should perhaps be called *The Gourmets*, but is commonly named *The Sages at Dinner*, XIII, 572, a, b.

'Order', exchanging security for adventure. Nowadays women, even more than men, quest after both security and happiness. Yet these states of mind cannot co-exist, save for a very brief period. Security soon entails boredom, a major form of unhappiness; happiness calls for excitement and adventure – things incompatible with security. But one thing the girls of Aphrodite did receive, and that was honour, being hymned by very great poets. Whenever in a grave crisis the city of Corinth ordered a national day of prayer to the goddess the Government would invite as many of these girls as possible to join in with their petitions, adding their supplications and being present at the sacrifices. Accordingly, when the great invasion of the Persians occurred, threatening to enslave all Greece, the Corinthian girls entered the temple of Aphrodite and prayed for the salvation of the Greeks. Hence, when the Corinthians dedicated in honour of the goddess a bronze tablet on Acrocorinthus, they inscribed upon it the name of every girl who had made supplication upon that day, and the great Simonides wrote them an epigram:

> For the Greeks and for their hard-fighting armies
> These girls stood forth to pray to the Lady Cypris.
> And Aphrodite willed that none should betray
> To Persian archers this Citadel of Hellas.

Not long after this an even more famous poet, Pindar, wrote an ode[1] for a number of Corinthian girls, when in 464 B.C. a rich citizen named Xenophon won two events at the Olympic Games after having promised his city-goddess a present of twenty-five girls should he be successful. It is an enchanting little poem, deep in its knowledge of love's fragility, light in its gentle mockery of his solemn self in unaccustomed role, and in the conceit of five and twenty girls as a hundred limbs for *aphrodite*.

> Young hospitable girls, beguiling creatures in wealthy Corinth,
> You who burn the amber tears of fresh frankincense
> Full often soaring upward in your souls to Aphrodite,
> Heavenly Mother of loves;

[1] *Enkomia*, 122.

To you, girls, she has granted
Blamelessly upon lovely beds
To cull the blossom of delicate bloom;
For under love's necessity all things are fine.

Yet I wonder whatever the lords of Corinth will be saying
Of me –!
Devising as I am a prelude to sweet song
All for the pleasure of anybody's girls!
But we've tested their gold with a pure touchstone.

O Lady of Cyprus! Hither to your sanctuary
Xenophon has brought fillies –
A hundred limbs of girls –
Glad for the fulfilment of his vows.

Within the orbit of Hellenic influence there was another sanctuary which seems to have had much in common with that of Acrocorinthus. It was on a mountain named Eryx in Western Sicily. From Lechaion, seaport of Corinth, to Aphrodite's sanctuary on the summit, 1,886 feet above sea-level, is nearly two and a half hours' walk; and from the ancient Sicilian port of Drepanon to the top of Mount Eryx, 2,465 feet over sea-level, the ascent takes a good three hours. A temple on the summit and a great sanctuary peopled by professional girls completed the parallel, though the goddess was variously named according to the race of people in control of Western Sicily. At first, when Carthaginians held it, she was called Astarte; in the fifth century B.C., when a Greek coinage was minted there and Greeks possessed Eryx, she was named Aphrodite; lastly, when Sicily became a Roman Province she was known as Venus Erycina, whom the Romans, despite their strong taint of puritanism, greatly respected.

In other Greek states the worship of Aphrodite does not appear to have taken on the special character of the cults at Paphos, Corinth, and Eryx, but to have been more akin to the cults of goddesses like Hera and Athene, so that she might figure as a powerful protectress of cities. Even in Cyprus one statue of her held a spear; in Thebes, Sparta, and Smyrna she was armed, and in Argos dubbed 'bringer of victory'. Her favourite title in Athens was

Aphrodite *Pandemos*, whereby she was raised to the level of Zeus *Pandemos* with an honourable epithet meaning 'of the whole people', and it represented the highest political idea to which the goddess attained. Plato, in the *Symposium*,[1] put a philosophical interpretation upon this title, treating it as representing common love, which he wanted to contrast with another title of Aphrodite's, *Ourania*, that was to symbolise intellectual love. Plato, who knew the facts as well as his listeners did, never intended this to be more than a *jeu d'esprit*; but when later readers took it in all seriousness some confusion ensued. The real origin of her name *Ourania* will emerge when the myths about the goddess are related.

In art Aphrodite appears in early times as a naked goddess standing; or else draped, seated, and holding a dove; while in the fifth century sculptors amused themselves by representing her in thin transparent clothing. But in the fourth century B.C. a new and apparently sensational type was created by the famous sculptor Praxiteles, who showed the goddess naked, dropping her garment over a vase before taking her bath. This statue was the inspiration of many others in which the motif varied, and among them is a lovely bronze (Plate VII, facing page 80) now in the city of Providence. But the original by Praxiteles elicited the highest praise of all from that industrious Roman polymath, the Elder Pliny.

The Aphrodite, to see which many have sailed to Knidos, is the finest statue not only by Praxiteles, but in the whole world. He had made and was offering for sale two figures of Aphrodite, one whose form was draped, and which was therefore preferred by the people of Kos – to whom the choice of either figure was offered at the same price – as the more chaste and severe, while the other which they rejected was bought by the Knidians, and became immeasurably more celebrated. King Nikomedes wished to buy it from the Knidians, and offered to discharge the whole debt of the city, which was enormous: but they preferred to undergo the worst, and justly so, for by that statue Praxiteles made Knidos famous. The shrine which contains it is quite open, so that the image, made, as is believed, under the direct inspiration of the goddess, can be seen from all sides: and from all sides it is equally admired.[2]

[1] 180D–181.　[2] *Natural History*, xxxvi, 20 ff.

In the sculpture galleries of the Vatican a later but ancient copy of this celebrated figure is preserved, its nether limbs swathed in modern, metal, whitewashed drapes.

The myths about Aphrodite are complicated by the fact that there is more than one story of her divine parentage. Some account has already been given in the chapter on Hera[1] of a collection of grisly tales now known to derive from an ancient Hurrian and Hittite civilisation in Syria and Asia Minor and to have been composed about 1500 B.C. Some of these tales got into Greek myth, and a dynasty of Hittite gods named Anu, Kumarbi, and Teshub was equated with the Greek Ouranos, Kronos, and Zeus. Kumarbi attacked his father Anu and deprived him of his manhood, which, falling upon the goddess Earth, made her pregnant, and one of the children was a girl.[2] In the Greek variant the seed of Ouranos fell into the sea, causing foam – Greek *aphros* – from which Aphrodite was born, and she stepped on to land at Paphos in Cyprus. Thus, because she was sprung from Ouranos, who is the heavens, she was called *Ourania* or 'Heavenly' Aphrodite. This myth arose in Cyprus, an island part Phœnician, part Greek, and the Phœnicians had certainly derived much of their theology from their Hittite neighbours. From Cyprus it passed into Greek lore and was accepted by the poet Hesiod, who was better as a farmer than as an exponent of exalted notions of godhead.

Now Homer, who came from a social group superior to that of Hesiod, would have none of this crude mythology, and so invented another parentage for the goddess, making her the daughter of Zeus and Diōne; which was rather inconsistent, for those two were the most Hellenic of gods and she an undoubted alien. In addition to this, Homer called her the wife of Hephaistos and made Ares her paramour. It is only in later periods that Eros, the boy god of love, and Hermaphroditos were alleged to be her children. Within the Homeric corpus she already became what she remained till the end – the goddess of rapture. Her portion of honour among the gods, as among men, is – so Hesiod declared – 'girlish babble, and tricks; sweet rapture, embraces and caresses'. This same divine rapture, by which those who are separated find

[1] See pp. 33f.   [2] H. G. Güterbock in *AJA*, 1948, pp. 124 ff.

their unity in love, became later – after all odd Anatolian myths
had dropped away – a great cohesive force in the philosophic view
of the cosmos. She, goddess of the eternal miracle of love, alone
has power to assure the peace of the world. In the early phase of
mythology there is a tale of how she gave herself to a mortal
man and became the mother of a Hero. It is set down in one of
the most exquisite of the Homeric Hymns, which was probably
composed early in the seventh century B.C.

The poet begins by telling us that golden Aphrodite sends love's
sweet desire upon the gods in heaven, upon mortals, and upon
birds, beasts, and creatures of the sea. Yet there are three whom
she cannot touch, Pallas Athene, Huntress Artemis, and Hestia of
the hearth.

These three, then, Aphrodite has never the power to move,
These three the sweet cheat snares not. Else from the might of Love
Nothing escapes – not mortal men, not Gods above.
Yea, Zeus, the Lord of Thunder, Allmightiest, Prince of Praise,
She has beguiled his wisdom and led him wandering ways,
Oft as she would, and laid him by many a mortal's side
Forgetting the love of Hera, his sister and his bride . . .

So, in return, Zeus wounded the Cyprian's own white breast
With sweet desire for a mortal's love. Once she had lain,
She, too, at last in a mortal's arms, then never again
Should she vaunt in the halls of Heaven with sweet, disdainful smile,
The laughter-loving Cypris, how oft she could beguile
High Gods to seek the kisses of the daughters of the earth,
And from their seed immortal bring mortal sons to birth,
Or daze the daughters of Heaven with love for mortal men.

Therefore Zeus awakened in Aphrodite a longing for the handsome young Anchises, cousin of Priam, King of Troy, who had
his farm on Mount Ida of the many springs of water.

Over the hill, to the neatherd's byre she passed; and as she came,
The grey wolves followed, fawning, and lions with eyes on flame,
And bears, and lightfoot leopards, devourers of the deer.
The Goddess smiled to see them; and on all, both far and near,
She cast her lure of longing – back to their forest-dens,

Pair by pair, they vanished, down the darkness of the glens.
But herself to the herdsmen's huts she came, built well and fair,
And alone she found Anchises. . . .
Then Zeus-born Aphrodite stepped forward and drew near,
Changed to the form and stature of a young unwedded maid,
Lest his eyes discern her godhead and the hero grow afraid.
Then Anchises saw and wondered – so beautiful she seemed,
So tall she towered before him, so gay her garments gleamed.
For the robe that rippled round her shone like a fire ablaze,
Richly her twisted armlets, her ear-rings flashed their rays,
Round her soft throat fair chains of gold glanced fitfully,
Light from her soft breasts shimmered, like moonlight, strange to see.
Then passion gripped Anchises. Swift was his greeting given –
'Hail to Thee, Queen, whoe'er Thou art among the Blessed in
    Heaven!. . .'

   Yet Aphrodite, dissembling, answered him:

'Why liken *me* to a Goddess? Mine is no Heavenly birth.
I am but a mortal woman, that of earthly mother came,
Daughter of famous Otreus – if ever you heard his name –
Lord of the well-walled cities of all the Phrygian land.
Yet the tongue of the Trojans also, like mine, I understand. . . .'

   She was dancing with other girls around Artemis, she said,
when suddenly Hermes the Argos-killer caught her away unseen:

'The Argus-slayer seized me, God of the Golden Wand –
O'er many a tilth and ploughland he bore me, and beyond
Many a waste and wilderness, untilled of men,
Where beasts devouring wander, deep in the shadowy glen –
I thought that never again should I feel the kindly ground.
For the bride-bed of Anchises the God said I was bound,
To be the wife you wedded and bear strong sons to you;
He said it, and pointed towards you, then swiftly away he flew,
The mighty Argus-slayer, back to the Heavenly Gate –
And to you I came – for upon me hard lay the hand of Fate.
But now, by Zeus and the noble hearts that gave you birth,
I beg you (for, sure, no dastards bred such a son of worth),
Take me a maid as I am, that nothing know of love,
Home to your noble mother, home to your sire, to prove;
And to your brothers show me, bred of the selfsame race –

Let them judge if this bride before you will bring your blood
    disgrace. . . .'
So in his heart she made the sweet love-longing stir,
And passion gripped Anchises, and swift he answered her:
'If you are a mortal maid indeed, of woman bred,
And the great Otreus is your sire, as you have said;
If Hermes, the Herald of Heaven, truly has brought you here,
To be my wife for always, unto my latest year,
Then there is no man living, there lives no hand divine,
Shall have the power to hold me before I have made you mine,
Now! – no, not even Apollo, though from his silver bow
The Archer-king should slay me with the arrows of his woe.
Face fair as the Immortals, once let me share your bed,
And then the House of Hades may close above my head!'
Hard by the hand he gripped her. With eyes cast down for shame
Upon the earth, and bending her face away, she came,
The laughter-loving Cypris, to the bed of the prince spread fair,
With many a fleecy mantle, and furs of the forest bear
Above them, and hides of deep-mouthed lions, that his own hand
Had stricken to death aforetime, high in that mountain-land.
But when they two together in that fair bed were laid,
He drew the gems aglitter from the body of the maid,
Brooches and twisted armlets, ear-rings and chains of gold;
And loosed the girdle round her, and drew off fold by fold
Her garments in their glory, and laid them, soft and still,
On a seat with silver studded. Then, by the high God's will,
Mortal beside the Undying he lay – and knew it not.

But at the hour's returning when the herdsman seeks his cot
With his fat sheep and his cattle, home from the flowery field,
Then the eyes of Anchises deep in sweet sleep she sealed.
Once more she clad her body, a Goddess glorified,
In the beauty of her raiment, and stood at his bedside.

She awakened him, and, as he shrank in terror because he had
lain with a goddess, consoled him:

'Fear not too much – from me thou hast no ill to fear,
Nor from the other Immortals. For Heaven holds thee dear.
And now a loved son shall be born thee. He shall reign as the Trojan's
    king,

And children of thy children, years without end, shall spring.
His name shall be called Æneas, for deep and bitterly,
When I sank to the bed of a mortal, the heart was shamed in me.
But indeed, of all earth's peoples, the children of thy race
Have ever stood next the Immortals in comeliness and grace. . . .

And now beneath my girdle I bear, I too, a child.
But him, when he sees the sunlight, the Nymphs of the mountain-wild
Shall take to their deep bosoms. This high and holy peak
Is theirs, and no haunts of mortals, no haunts of the Gods they seek. . . .

These, then, shall be the nurses to watch and tend my son.
And when to lovely childhood he grows, as the seasons run,
The Nymphs shall lead him hither, for thine own eyes to see:
And again in his fifth summer will I bring him back to thee,
And thou shalt learn my purpose. At sight of that young face
In the first flower of its springtide, fair as the Gods in grace,
Thy heart shall leap rejoicing. Then shalt thou take the boy
And bring him down beside thee to the windy walls of Troy.
But as for thy dear son's mother, if thou art asked of men,
'Who bore him under her girdle?' – beware, Anchises, then!
This be thine answer (remember!) – 'They say he was the child
Of a flower-faced Nymph of Ida, where wave the woodlands wild.'
But if, with the mind of a madman, thou boast vaingloriously
That the fair-crowned Cytherea once gave herself to thee,
Then Zeus shall loose in his anger his reeking bolt on thy head.
Therefore take heed what I tell thee. My latest word is said.
Mind well thy mouth, nor name me. Of the wrath of the Gods beware.'
She ceased, and vanished, soaring, through the windy wastes of air.[1]

In all literature there are few poems to equal this Hymn, radi-
antly alive with its vision of unspoilt youth. 'Greece', as Mr Lucas
has said, 'looked in many different ways upon the Paphian; but
hardly ever with that sense of inherent guilt, sin, and shame which
was to warp the European mind for many centuries to come.' If
any parallel to the Greek attitude exists in our own day it is perhaps to be found in Samoa, where, according to a modern anthro-
pologist, sex is an experience 'which will not be sufficiently en-
grossing to threaten the social order. The Samoans condone light
love-affairs, but repudiate acts of passionate choice. . . . Pre-marital

[1] The lines are quoted from the fine translation by F. L. Lucas, *Aphrodite*, 1948.

affairs and extra-marital affairs are conducted with enough lightness not to threaten the reliable sex-relationships between married couples.'[1] But not every Greek had such an attitude to *aphrodite*, and even to Plato the Hymn from which we have quoted would have seemed one of those impious immoralities of the poets; to the Fathers of the Church it was devil-worship; to the Middle Ages something to lure souls into the ante-room of Hell.

Before such sad times and thoughts befell Europe the myth concerning the love of Aphrodite and Anchises had exercised a mighty influence in the history of the world. Their son was the famous Trojan Hero, Æneas, who fled from burning Troy with his small son Ascanius, whose other name was Iulus. After much wandering Æneas came at last to Central Italy and there founded Lavinium, so the later writers from the fifth century onward began to tell. His son, Iulus, founded on the Alban Mount Alba Longa, whence came Romulus and Remus, founders of Rome. Moreover, that most illustrious of all patrician families, the Julii, were originally from Alba Longa and claimed descent from Iulus himself. Long before Julius Cæsar accepted the supreme power in the Roman Empire, other famous rulers had been claiming divine ancestry. Alexander asserted his descent from Zeus, and Ptolemy did likewise; Seleucus claimed Apollo for his ancestor; Demetrius claimed Poseidon. The world had grown accustomed to such notions of divinity in kingship, and when Julius Cæsar set, time and time again, the head of Venus upon his coinage, when he built her a temple on the Palatine beside his own house, there were millions who believed not only that the great Dictator was directly descended from Iulus of Alba Longa, but also that Iulus had been grandson of the goddess Aphrodite.

Meanwhile in her favourite island, Cyprus, she still lives on, at least in name. In more than one Cypriot village church the Paphian has been merged in the Virgin Mary, who is supplicated there under the title of *Panaghia Aphroditessa*.[2]

---

[1] Margaret Mead, *Male and Female*, 1949, p. 114.
[2] Guthrie, *The Greeks and their Gods*, p. 30; Sir James Frazer, *Adonis, Attis, Osiris*, I, p. 36.

Aɴʏ study of the origins and of the cult of the Olympians reveals the fact that most goddesses and gods show traces of a dual personality. There are conflicting stories and incompatible views – they can hardly be called 'beliefs' – which point to diverse derivations. For Hephaistos, however, this is not the case, and his growth as a divine concept may be observed as a clear phenomenon, since he was gradually transformed from an indefinite spirit into a definite artisan-god; next into a noble craftsman-god and mighty Olympian artist. Yet when his own worshippers fell in public estimation, when – starting with the fourth century B.C. – potters, bronze-workers, and sculptors began gradually to sink in the social scale, Hephaistos, too, seemed to lose much of the respect due to him, and to appear in the guise of a decayed nobleman rather than as a powerful god. His subsequent identification with Vulcan, an Italian volcano-god whose full name was Volcanus Mulciber, 'Incendiary' and 'Fire-extinguisher', did not greatly improve his status.

The early development and transformation proceeded in the following manner. In the distant age of bronze the inhabitants of Greece and the islands held the skilled worker in metal in very high regard. His art was both a mystery and a delight, and he was thought to owe his gifts to supernatural beings, around whom many legends grew. There were creatures called Dactyls, smelters of bronze; Curetes and Corybantes, armourers; Cabeiroi, who were skilful smiths; Telchines, gifted workers in gold, silver, and bronze, who made weapons for gods and the earliest statues; and lastly, the mighty Cyclopes forging the bolts of Zeus. All these are vague giants, goblins, and godlings – patron saints of the workshop and the forge whom you might do well to appease and some of whose names just meant 'Fingers', 'Hammer', 'Tongs', 'Anvil', and 'Fire'. Then, by the time that the Homeric epic began to take form, one of these beings seems to have grown in stature until he attained Olympian rank. Men said he was a lame god because Zeus had once hurled him to the earth, but this is just a story to explain the fact that smiths constantly at work at the anvil tend to have powerful arms and weak legs. In the Homeric world blind men would become minstrels and lame men smiths. An artist's god must resemble the artist. The Olympian smith was named Hephaistos, a name of great antiquity belonging to some language spoken before ever the Greek-speakers came to Greece.[1] Perhaps his name simply means 'Fire'.

The artist, dreaming his dreams of what wonders he would like to make, attributed to his god the power to create just such things of surpassing fineness, and the minstrel set them in epic form. And so, in the eighteenth book of the *Iliad*, Homer told of the wonderful shield of Achilles made by the famous god.[2] Here once again we may note the closeness of Olympian gods to Homeric heroes who claim to be god-descended. Indeed, 'the Quality' – Lords and Ladies in the Palace – are proud to be artists and skilful with their hands like their god Hephaistos. The Lady Penelope in the *Odyssey* wove the great web upon her own loom; her Lord, Odysseus, himself once built, fashioned, and inlaid their marriage-bed. When at last he returned from his long wanderings, weather-beaten and no longer young, his wife, fearing that some stranger might be impersonating him, looked for some proof that this man was really her husband. Then came the enchanting recognition scene in the twenty-third book, when Odysseus began to describe to her his handiwork.

'A great secret went into the making of that complicated bed; and it was my work and mine alone. Inside the court there was a long-leaved olive tree, which had grown to full height with a stem as thick as a pillar. Round this I built my room of close-set stone-work, and when it was finished, I roofed it over thoroughly, and put in a solid, neatly fitted, double door. Next I lopped all the twigs off the olive, trimmed the stem from the root up, rounded it smoothly and carefully with my adze and trued it to the line, to make my bedpost. This I drilled through where necessary, and used as a basis for the bed itself, which I worked away at till that too was done, when I finished it off with an inlay of gold, silver, and ivory, and fixed a set of purple straps across the frame.

[1] W. R. Halliday in *CAH*, II, p. 616.   [2] Seltman, *AGA*, pp. 12 ff.

'There is our secret, and I have shown you that I know it. What I don't know, madam, is whether my bedstead stands where it did, or whether someone has cut the tree-trunk through and shifted it elsewhere.'

Her knees began to tremble as she realised the complete fidelity of his description. All at once her heart melted. Bursting into tears she ran up to Odysseus, threw her arms round his neck and kissed his head. 'Odysseus,' she cried, 'do not be cross with me, you who were always the most reasonable of men. All our unhappiness is due to the gods, who couldn't bear to see us share the joys of youth and reach the threshold of old age together. But don't be angry with me now, or hurt because the moment when I first saw you I did not kiss you as I kiss you now. For I had always had the cold fear in my heart that somebody might come here and bewitch me with his talk. . . . But now all's well. You have faithfully described our token, the secret of our bed, which no one ever saw but you and I and one maid, Actoris, who was my father's gift when first I came to you, and sat as sentry at our bedroom door. You have convinced your unbelieving wife.'[1]

When it is realised that one of the finest things in the life of so heroic a fighter, so intrepid a sailor, as Odysseus was his subtle skill with his hands, then one understands why Hephaistos was a god loved and venerated by a people who for centuries produced and enjoyed so many of the best works of art that mankind has made. There is one respect in which Greece of the Classical Age and Italy of the Renaissance era differ from other historic periods; for in those two epochs a greater number of persons had a ripe judgment and a critical appreciation of works of art – large and small – produced by their contemporaries than European mankind had in any other age. Classical Greece and Renaissance Italy were both humanist, but the latter was also, effectively though not openly, rationalist. Not so the Greeks, for which reason they had great need, in order to help to explain many phenomena, of a god of arts and crafts. In those states where such a need was felt – and most of all in Athens – Hephaistos was precisely the symbolic aspect of godhead which was urgently required. Indeed, at the time when Athens attained the summit of artistic and intellectual

[1] Translation by E. V. Rieu.

domination over the civilised world, Hephaistos rose to a status of near-equality with Zeus himself, for in the central portion of the Parthenon frieze he and Athene are grouped together to form the natural counterpoise to Zeus and Hera. But this high rank was not to endure.

The pre-Hellenic origin of this classically Hellenic god is not hard to trace. If Hestia was 'fire' in one sense – the natural home-kindled wood-fire on the hearth – Hephaistos was 'Fire' of quite another kind, for he was in origin Gas; he was Mineral Oil; he was Petroleum. Besides the great and famous Macedonian Mount Olympus, home of the gods, there were at least seventeen other Mounts Olympus,[1] and we must now consider one of their number situated in Lycia in the south-west corner of Asia Minor.

The country known as Lycia is a mountain *massif* almost square in plan, which thrusts southward from the western end of Asia Minor. On the east coast of this country but well to the south was a mountain called Olympus, about 3,350 feet in height, which was famed in ancient times for a peculiar phenomenon. Early in the fourth century of our era a well-known Christian bishop named Methodios wrote an account of a fire which he had seen with his own eyes burning on the top of the mountain and springing from a vent in the earth, but which was harmless to the vegetation growing around. He compares it to the episode recorded in the Old Testament of Moses and the Burning Bush, and this very mountain is nowadays named *Musa Dagh*, meaning 'the Mountain of Moses'. This impressive fire on the summit was observed by a traveller as late as 1811. Not far away, due north of the Lycian Mount Olympus, there is a similar phenomenon still to be seen at the present day – a strong jet of flaming gas which leaps up like a fountain from crevices in the rock. In antiquity several such fiery jets were known, and the site was called either *Hephaisteion* or *Hephaistia*, or 'the Mountains of Hephaistos'.[2]

There is reason to believe that at some period before 1000 B.C.

[1] Cook, *Zeus*, I, p. 100.
[2] Cook, *Zeus*, II, p. 972; Sir Boverton Redwood, *Petroleum* (1922), p. 187. See also Freya Stark's reference to the fire, *The Times*, March 13, 1953. It is still burning.

some inhabitants of Lycia and neighbouring regions emigrated to numerous Greek islands in the Ægean Sea, where they became known as Pelasgians, or 'Peoples of the Sea'. One of the islands occupied seems to have been Lemnos, and those Lycians, or Pelasgians, who went to Lemnos were fortunate to discover on a mountain in that island a gaseous phenomenon exactly like the one they had left behind at Mount Olympus in their homeland. The flame issuing from the summit of Mount Mosychlos on the island was referred to by various ancient writers, to whom it was an inexplicable wonder. Here, just as in Lycia, they were perfectly aware that it was not in the least volcanic in origin, and they worshipped the mystery as God, just as for many centuries certain Parsees have worshipped as God the columns of fire among the great oil-fields of Baku, and just as, in classical times, the Persians revered 'Fire' above their other gods, since in places – now known as oil-fields – mysterious fire issued from the earth. Both in Lycia and in Lemnos the flame was the sanctuary and the very image of the godhead called Hephaistos – a belief which was naturally adopted by the Greeks.

In the Near and Middle East one may observe on the map a roughly parallel series of oil-wells running from north to south with a slight swerve towards the east. The most famous of these is the long line which runs down between Mesopotamia and Persia. It appears that there was a lesser line running approximately parallel to this, but much farther west. At its northern end there is today the great complex of oil-wells in Rumania, and at its southern end the oil-wells of the Sinai peninsula and Eastern Egypt. Between these two groups and on the appropriate slightly swerving line there lie Lemnos and the Lycian Olympus region. The Rumanian fields produce some paraffin crude oil; and it is fair to assume that the oil which produced the Hephaistos-flames in Lemnos and in Lycia was asphaltic crude oil. This oil gives what is known as a 'low-pressure field', which generally results in a seepage of subterranean gas given off by the oil, which makes its way up through fissures in the rock and, when it appears at the surface, can become ignited. Since it has a low flash-point, it is found to burn with a comparatively cool flame, and vegetation

fairly close to it is not scorched.[1] Thus we have the very phenomenon observed by the most reverend bishop, Methodios.

The cult of Hephaistos may be traced from Lycia to Lemnos;
and there can be little doubt that it passed from Lemnos to Athens
at some period before Homer wrote about the god, whom he
already looked upon as one of the Twelve Olympians, and as the
magical smith and the creator of fine art. There were legends of a
'Pelasgian' settlement in Attica, and it is difficult to dissociate these
particular 'Peoples of the Sea' from Lemnians, since by no other
means can the advent of Hephaistos be explained. In Athens he
remained, though there was no miraculous Fire with which to
associate him; in Athens he grew in importance and distinction;
and in Athens there still stands, upon an eminence dominating the
region where craftsmen and artists worked, the most perfectly
preserved of all extant Greek temples, which is wrongly named
the 'Theseum', for it is in reality the 'Hephaisteion', or temple of
Hephaistos, built between 450 and 440 B.C. But to the north on
the slope of the hill there once existed the temple of his first wife,
Aphrodite Ourania or Heavenly Aphrodite. Within the Hephaisteion there stood two statues: the one of Hephaistos himself, and
the other of his second 'wife', Athene Hephaistia.

The hymn in his honour is brief, but to the point, and may have
been written about the time when the temple was built.

Sing, clear-voiced Muse, of Hephaistos famed for inventions.
With bright-eyed Athene he taught men glorious crafts throughout
    the world –
Men who before used to dwell in caves in the mountains like wild
    beasts,
But now that they have learned crafts through Hephaistos the famed
    worker,

---

[1] See *Our Industry* (Anglo-Iranian Oil Co. Ltd.), 1947, plate following p. 16.
Much later, towards the end of the second century B.C., Roman observers re-
ported a similar seepage and flame in the neighbourhood of a Greek colony in
Illyria close to the same north-south line as the bitumen seepage at Zante
(*Herodotus*, Book IV, 195) and as the gas-jet seen by Pausanias (second century
A.D.) at Bathos beside Karytæna in Arcadia.

Easily they live a peaceful life in their own homes the whole year round.
Be gracious, Hephaistos,
And grant me success and prosperity![1]

Apart from Lemnos and Athens, the cult of the god was quite
insignificant in other states of old Greece, for such seepages as
might be observed in Greece in post-Homeric times were not
associated with him; and when his worship did pass to the Western Greeks of Sicily and South Italy it underwent a complete
change. The Italian peninsula, rich in so much, is almost without
any mineral oil, for there is only one small unimportant oil-field
in the very north – never discovered until recent times. But there
were other manifestations of nature less gentle than the friendly
gas-jets which enlivened the heights of Lemnian Mosychlos and
Lycian Olympus. There were great and active volcanoes like Etna
and Stromboli as well as lesser, though sinister, volcanic terrors,
all thought by the inhabitants to be produced by a local subterranean deity whom they named Volkanus or Vulcanus.

Volcanic activity being full of terror, the cult of a volcano-god
is marked by nervous fear and anxiety to appease. The Romans
kept on assuring him that he was in reality a 'gentle monster',
gave him the *sobriquets* of 'Soother', 'Quiet One' – *Mulciber*,
Quietus – and married him to a goddess called 'Steady Mother',
Mater Stata. Moreover, it occurred to them that when he did get
rough there was one part of creation beyond his reach – the world
of fish. Therefore they would on occasion prepare a sacrifice of
appeasement, lighting a fire by the river-side and flinging in it for
his delectation live fish. This is 'nursery stuff' such as fear of a
volcano seems to induce even today. It is not long since the inhabitants of Cremano under Vesuvius became angry with their patron
saint, San Giorgio, when they were aware of a stream of lava
rolling towards their township. Accordingly, they took his silver-
plated image from its shrine and planted it in front of the advancing molten mass, as though to say, 'Save us, San Giorgio, or burn
yourself!' The lava stopped; and he is now a highly respected
godling.

[1] Translation by H. G. Evelyn-White.

All this is very remote from Greek conceptions and emotions concerning Hephaistos. But when Greeks settled in Sicily they began to use the name of their Fire-god for the local volcano-god, and so it came about that the actual Forge where the Great Artificer worked with the help of the Cyclopes was alleged to be situated underneath Mount Etna in Sicily.

The myths about Hephaistos are mainly concerned with three things: his birth, his lameness (a deformity which made him seem almost ugly to the other Olympians), and his absolute genius as a creator of works of art and craftsmanship. He had no father, and this is most appropriate for a god who is a flame of fire rising from a hole in Mother Earth. Hera, who inherited so much from the primitively imagined Earth-goddess, was his mother. 'Hera', as Hesiod tells in his *Birth of the Gods*, 'without union with Zeus – for she was very angry and quarrelled with her mate – bare famous Hephaistos, who is skilled in crafts more than all the descendants of Ouranos.'[1] Later, when he was fully grown, another quarrel was under way, and Hephaistos presumed to interfere on his mother's behalf and suffered hard punishment. At the end of the first book of the *Iliad* Hephaistos tells of his misfortune:

Zeus seized me by the foot and hurled me from the threshold of Heaven. I flew all day, and as the sun sank I fell half-dead in Lemnos, where I was picked up and looked after by the Sintians.

Milton, always in two minds about the ancient world – abhorrent to the puritan, adorable to the poet – was fascinated by this episode. Vulcan he knew, and found his Latin title *Mulciber* fitting for a fallen angel turned devil, and so tacked on to his satanic creature the tale of Hephaistos' fall.

> From Morn
> To Noon he fell, from Noon to dewy Eve,
> A Summer's day; and with the setting Sun
> Dropt from the Zenith like a falling star,
> On Lemnos, th'Ægæan Ile.

It was after this that he was said to have been married to

[1] See p. 60.

Aphrodite – the ugliest god to the loveliest goddess – a kind of 'Beauty and the Beast' myth, which has an allegorical twist to it.

All the trouble had started for poor Hephaistos because he had tried to help his mother. Yet, when after long convalescence he returned, a limping god with a crooked foot, she hated him; and in the eighteenth book of the *Iliad* we find him complaining: 'After my great fall my wicked mother tried to do away with me because I was a cripple!' Homer's gods have the faults and foibles of a spoilt aristocracy, and his choleric Zeus bears as slender a relationship to the Zeus of Cleanthes[1] as does Baal to the Yahweh of the great Hebrew prophets.[2]

The genius of the divine smith for making works of art is a constant and popular theme. Weapons for Athene, a sceptre for King Agamemnon, a necklace for Harmonia – he can make them all; but his delight was in pleasing Thetis, who had been kind to him, by making the splendid and famous armour for her son, Achilles – armour the description of which is the main theme of the eighteenth book of the *Iliad*. It is here too that we can read the description of his own delectable residence.

Thetis of the Silver Feet made her way to the palace of Hephaistos, which the god of the Crooked Foot had built, with his own hands, of imperishable bronze. It shines like a star and stands out among the houses of the gods. She found Hephaistos hard at work and sweating as he bustled about at the bellows in his forge. He was making a set of twenty three-legged tables to stand round the walls of his well-built hall. He had fitted golden wheels to all their legs, so that they could run by themselves to a meeting of the gods and amaze the company by running home again. . . .

Hephaistos raised his monstrous bulk from the anvil. He limped, but he was nimble enough on his slender legs. He removed the bellows from the fire, collected all the tools he used, and put them in a silver chest. Then he sponged his face and hands, his sturdy neck and hairy breast, put on his tunic, picked up a thick staff and came limping from the forge. Golden maidservants hastened to help their Master. They looked like real girls and could not only speak and use their limbs but

[1] See p. 50.
[2] H. St J. Hart, *A Foreword to the Old Testament*, 1951, pp. 39 ff., 173 ff.

were endowed with intelligence and trained in handwork by the immortal gods. Supported by his toiling escort, the Lord Hephaistos made
his clumsy approach to the spot where Thetis was seated, and himself
sat down on a polished chair, took her hand in his and greeted her.[1]

Here is poetic imagination to perfection. And is there prophecy
(whatever prophecy may be)? His 'robots' are no cube-headed
monsters, radio-activated, but golden girls that look real and use
their limbs. What of his three-wheeled run-about tables? It may
divert us to toy with the notion that here is the forerunner of the
motor-car made by that very god who – we have seen – was himself the actual divine gas, the essence, the petrol which activates
the internal-combustion engine.

[1] Translation by E. V. Rieu.

THERE is no deity in the whole august company of immortal gods, evolved and worshipped by anxious humanity, who is more deserving of our commiseration than is Ares. This was the most unloved of all the divine aspects and concepts invented by mankind, which too often approaches godhead in ignominious fear, but rarely with such veiled hostility and suspicion as were the lot of Ares. The poets delighted to present him in unpleasant situations. It will be well to illustrate this by two stories from the Ares-myth, especially as they both belong likewise to the Hephaistos-myth with which we ended the last chapter.

The divine smith of the crooked foot was deeply hurt at his mother's unkindness and planned a punishment, so he fashioned exquisitely a chair for her, and sent it as a gift to high Olympus. But he had put a magic spell upon it so that once the Queen of Heaven had seated her royal person she could not rise again. And he, Hephaistos, alone of all gods and mortal men, knew the spell that could release her. Ares, her favourite son, attempting to lift her off by force, only made things worse; so he armed himself, and entering the divine smithy threatened the lame god – all to no purpose, for of what use is the finest of rapiers when your opponent advances on you with a great bar of white-hot iron?

The Lady Hera would have been sitting upon the beautiful magic throne even to this day had not another god – the youngest of the Olympians – thought of something better than military compulsion. Dionysos and a rout of his jovial *Seilenoi*, well equipped with skins of wine, visited the forge upon a hot day; nor was it long before they brought Hephaistos to so genial a frame of mind that he was ready to forgive and to forget. Mounted upon a magnificent donkey, he was conducted by his new friends up to Olympus, where he pronounced the liberating spell, and Hera was able to rise from the chair.

The story is old, for it was already familiar in Athens by about 550 B.C., when the painter Kleitias set the scene in black-figure upon a big Athenian mixing-bowl made of glazed pottery (Plate

IX, facing p. 112). The tale is clearly told, for all the divine actors are named. On the left is Ares in full armour, crouching upon a block of stone, his whole attitude confessing his inadequacy. Athene looks back at him, but her right forefinger points to the approaching visitors. Hera, seated rigidly upon the throne, seems about to clap her hands with pleasure at the hope of rescue. Dionysos – not shown in our picture – leads the big donkey, on the back of which rides Hephaistos astride, his near foot pointing forward and his farther foot, bent feebly backwards, appearing under the animal's belly. While he smiles engagingly he points back with two fingers at one of several following horse-legged *Seilenoi*, who carries a full skin of wine, and he seems to say, 'These people brought me here!' Perhaps the strangest thing about this stylised painting is the artist's success in making us feel sorry for the soldier-god who is so ashamed of his failure. So few early Greek pictures exist of either Hephaistos or Ares that this vase-painting is a precious document that enlightens us on the attitude of Athenians to both these gods.

The other story in which Ares gets the worst of it in a situation of great embarrassment is an heroic tale known as 'The Lay of the Minstrel Demodokos', which is incorporated in the eighth book of the *Odyssey*.

Then to his harp uplifting his beautiful voice did the minstrel
Sing of the passion of Ares for fair-crowned Queen Aphrodite,
How they as lovers at first held tryst at the house of Hephaistos
Secretly meeting; and how by his gifts he prevailed, and dishonour
Brought on the bed of her lord. But as messenger hastened to tell him
Helios, he who had noted them meeting in tender embracement.
Then did Hephaistos, as soon as the grievous tidings had reached him,
Go to his forge, devising revenge in the depths of his bosom.
Here on the stithy he set the enormous ánvil and forged him
Fetters not to be broken or loosed, to entrap and to hold them.
Now when at last he had fashioned the toils, in his anger at Ares,
Into the chamber he entered wherein, as of old, was his bedstead.
Here to the posts of the bed, all round it, he fastened the netting;
Much of it also he fastened above it, attached to a rafter,
Fine as the web of a spider, that none could ever perceive it
E'en of the blessed immortals: so cunningly fine was it fashioned.

So, when at last he had fastened the toils all over the bedstead,
Then he pretended to go to the well-built city of Lemnos,
Land that was dear to his heart – far dearer than every other.
Neither was blind as a watcher the god, gold-glittering Ares.
Seeing Hephaistos, the worker renowned, set forth on a journey,
Speedily unto the house of the far-famed god he betook him
Filled with the longing of love for the fair-crowned queen Cytherea.
Newly arrived from the home of her father, Zeus the almighty,
Resting she quietly sat; and he entering into the mansion
Tenderly clung to her hand; then he opened his lips and addressed her:
'Come, let us go, my beloved, and lie on the bed and enjoy us!
Nowhere nigh is Hephaistos, but started already for Lemnos,
Gone to the Sintian folk, that people of barbarous language.'
Thus did he speak, and a thing right pleasant it seemed to the goddess.
So they ascended the bed and reclined them; but the netting
Cunningly wrought by the crafty Hephaistos descended upon them:
Suddenly gone was the power of lifting a limb, or of moving.
Then at the last they perceived it when all too late to escape it;
Ay, and already at hand was the famed deft-handed Hephaistos,
Back from his journey returned ere reaching the island of Lemnos.
Helios, still on the watch, had remained and had brought him the
    tidings.
Homeward straight he returned with a heart sore troubled within him;
Up to the portal he strode, and he stood; fierce anger possessed him;
Then with a terrible cry to the gods of Olympus he shouted:
'Father Zeus and ye other immortals eternally blessed,
Come and behold! 'Tis a matter to laugh at, but not to be suffer'd.
Lo now, me that am lame this daughter of Zeus, Aphrodite,
Ever dishonours and loveth instead man-murdering Ares,
Since he is fair to the sight and in limb he is straight; but a body
Weakly was mine from my birth – nor verily blame I another,
Only my parents. I would they had never begotten and borne me!
Come! ye shall see these twain now lying in loving embracement;
Here on my bed they are mounted – behold! At the sight I am
    maddened!
Scarce for a moment more, do I think, they are longing to lie here,
E'en though hotly in love – nor quickly again will be longing
Thus to be bedded together. But here they are trapped and imprisoned
Till that her father repay, to the last one, every bride-gift,
All that I left in his hands as the price of the impudent baggage –

Ay, for his daughter is fair, but she knows not to bridle her passions.'
Thus did he speak, and the gods to his brass-floor'd mansion collected:
Hither Poseidon himself, Earth-shaker, hastened and Hermes,
Bringer of fortune, and hither the prince, far-shooting Apollo,
While that at home with womanly shame stay'd every goddess.
Soon at the porch were standing the deities, bringers of blessings.
Then an unquenchable laughter rose mid the blessed immortals
While they beheld the device that was wrought by the cunning
  Hephaistos,
Looking whereon thus whispered the one to the other beside him:
'Ill deed prospereth never; the slow oft catcheth the nimble:
Even as now by the tardy Hephaistos o'ertaken is Ares,
Ares, the swiftest of all of the gods that inhabit Olympus,
Caught in the toils of the Limper – and compensation he oweth.'
Thus conversing together, they whispered the one to the other;
Then spake lordly Apollo, the son of great Zeus, to Hermes:
'Zeus-born Hermes, herald of heaven and bringer of blessings,
Say now, feel you a longing in such strong fetters imprisoned
Lying beside her in bed to embrace Aphrodite the golden?'
Him thus answered the herald of heaven, the Slayer of Argos:
'Had I but only the luck, O lord, far-darting Apollo!
E'en though triple in number the toils – yea endless – that held me;
E'en though all of you gods stood gazing, and every goddess,
Give me to lie by her side and embrace Aphrodite the golden!'

And now Poseidon, senior god of Olympus, brought his tact to
bear in order to end the scandal, for he persuaded Hephaistos to
loosen the magical net and release the lovers.

Then did the twain, set free from the grievous constraint of the netting,
Spring straight upward and vanish. To Thracia Ares departed,
She to the Cyprian isle, Aphrodite, lover of laughter –
Even to Paphos – for here is her shrine and her altar of incense.
Here did the Graces receive her and bathe and anoint her with unguent
Not of the earth; but it lieth as bloom on the limbs of immortals.
Then did they clothe her in beautiful raiment, a wonder to gaze at.[1]

Here is a strange tale to tell about gods, for though Ares is disliked, Hephaistos is truly admired, and Aphrodite adored. Yet it is
certain that Homer is neither a cynic nor is he detached and

[1] After H. B. Cotterill's translation.

sophisticated. The best comment has been made by the most recent translator of the epics:[1]

He does believe in his gods, and that very vividly, but whereas the Christian conception of godhead is based on our creation by God in his image and likeness, with imperfections introduced by Satan, Homer regards his gods, though immortal, as made in the image and likeness of man. Mixed with deep respect for their almost unlimited powers and his æsthetic appreciation of their beauty, he betrays a very tolerant understanding of their motives and frailties. This leads quite often, as in the famous Lay of Demodokos, to a treatment that we can only regard as humorous. But it was neither flippant nor irreverent. These powerful beings, who were so intimately connected with men's passions and desires, were there to administer, not necessarily to obey, man's moral code. Christian apologists of a later age made a mistake when they suggested that the pagans had invented the gods and their iniquities as an excuse for themselves. Homer never censures a god nor lets a mortal use a god's misdeeds as a pretext for his own.

Ares, the undesirable alien, was a god of Thracian origin, and his worship extended thence, through Macedonia, into the northern portion of Greece, down to Thebes, in which city he was held to be the husband of Aphrodite rather than her paramour. In Athens, too, since Hephaistos had virtually become the mate of Athene, Ares and Aphrodite were associated. There were temples for him in several cities of Peloponnesus, especially, of course, in Sparta. But even the Spartans, most warlike of all Greeks – Greeks who were then, and still are, the best fighters of the Mediterranean peoples – even the Spartans treated Area roughly and with suspicion. Near his temple there was a statue of the god in fetters, for it was the notion of the Spartans that if they kept him in chains he could never run away from them. No one even felt confidence that he would support a fighter who showed courage, and in the sixth century B.C. the poet Anacreon wrote a brief epitaph for a friend who fell in battle:

> Timokritos fought well. This is his grave.
> For Ares spares the coward; not the brave.

It was in the war-god's character to be a great pursuer of

[1] E. V. Rieu. *Odyssey*, p. XIII.

women, though in this respect he did not differ from the other Olympians. His sons, however, grew up as violent and outrageous men, murderers, brigands, impious raiders, and ferocious fighters. They were generally unpopular.

When Greeks and Romans came into frequent contact with one another Ares was naturally identified with the Roman Mavors, or Mars, a deity of far greater importance and one held in high esteem, for in Rome Mars was second in importance only to Jupiter himself. But, like the half-civilised Thracians from whom Ares was derived, the Romans were generally partial to war, wherein, owing to the superior organisation of their military machine, they were almost uniformly successful. There were no purely Roman tales of the amorous deeds of Mars, until such time as his identification with Ares was established, whereupon the whole mythology of Ares was taken over and given to Mars as well.

One may well ask how it came about that a people with such views as the ancient Greeks held – a people who had as great a fundamental hatred of war as the English have – should have persisted in the cult of an unpopular god. The answer, perhaps, is that there are sometimes historical and vital crises in the lives of nations when ultimate values must be assessed and ultimate decisions taken and when a whole nation knows – as we in our time have twice known – that the choice lies between Ares and 'slavery'. Yet, except for Satan, there never was, and surely never can be, a 'god of servitude'. Add to this the emotional factors of the deadly tedium of security and the exhilaration of danger; and sometimes – though happily not too often – even the best may be driven, like Rupert Brooke in 1914, to welcome Ares:

> Blow, bugles, blow! They brought us, for our dearth,
> Holiness, lacked so long, and Love, and Pain.
> Honour has come back, as a king, to earth,
> And paid his subjects with a royal wage;
> And Nobleness walks in our ways again;
> And we have come into our heritage.

Seven Olympians have so far been passed in review: Hera, Zeus, Athene, Hermes, Aphrodite, and her two mates Hephaistos and Ares. Before proceeding to tell about five more yet to come, we may pause and attempt an assessment as to which deities – among the seven described – held the highest place in the minds and hearts of the Greeks. First one must put Zeus. Before the end of the fifth century B.C. a thoughtful Greek's view of Zeus would be much like a thoughtful modern believer's view of his God. Many a Greek would hold that poetry, music, temples, statues, and all other works were things offered by creative man to the glory of Zeus; for the relation of Zeus to the world was both that of Creator Artist and of Father and Ruler of mankind. The poet Epimenides wrote already by about 500 B.C. the famous words, 'In Him we live and move and have our being'.

Second one must put Aphrodite. The view that one of the other highest concepts of godhead appears embodied in the Paphian is, I am aware, much more difficult of acceptance in our time. That is because men have for so long clothed and cloaked and muffled themselves in the wrappings of sin-belief; and have held sex to be at worst the most sinful of all phenomena, and at best something to be deplored in whispers. As the result the modern world has too frequently offered Aphrodite its insults and now pictures her through the symbols of celluloid dolls and molls with meaningless Hollywooden faces. This is an impious attitude to a Power whom even the Immortals feared, and whom mortals adored because they had no tendency to regard what was pleasant and pleasurable as suspect and sinful. Total abstinence seemed as hateful as total indulgence, for of all things the Greeks despised the violence of excess. Moderation and self-knowledge were of as great value in the service of Aphrodite as they were in that of the god next to be described – one who stood as high as Zeus and Aphrodite in the thoughts of men – Apollo.

IN historical times Apollo became a great Panhellenic god second only to Zeus himself. The other Olympians who were held to be the sons of Zeus – Hermes, Ares, Dionysos – seemed, as it were, younger sons who were never regarded with quite so much awe and reverence as the Greeks gave to Apollo. Indeed, he is the embodiment of the Hellenic spirit, because almost everything which distinguished the Greek outlook on life from that of other peoples around them – sensitivity in art, music, and poetry, a deep interest in the health and gaiety of youth, respect for law, love of moderation – all these things are symbolised by Apollo. Nevertheless, he may not have been in origin a Greek god, even if one of the divine concepts which contributed to the Apollo-godhead came from a Dorian source. Opinions about him among modern students of Greek religion are more sharply divided than are opinions about any other deity, and the authorities are found to be ranged in two camps which favour, the one a Northern, the other an Eastern origin of the god. If controversy has not raged with the uttermost force of an *odium theologicum*, it has nevertheless raged.

More than twenty-five years ago Professor Gilbert Murray suggested that a compromise night be found in the view that Apollo might derive from *both* regions,[1] and there is more recent evidence to support such a view. About 1100 B.C. Dorians, the last wave of Greek-speaking people to come down from the North, entered Greece, and a number of them got as far south as Crete, which thenceforward became a predominantly Dorian island. These people had the custom of holding an Assembly of all adult male voters – rather like an Anglo-Saxon Shire-moot – which was named the *apella*. In the Dorian-Greek dialect Apollo was always called *Apellon*, and it is almost certain that the two words are closely connected, which means that *Apellon* is in origin a Dorian tribal deity, and Nordic.

Yet in Central Asia Minor, in that Hittite region from which –

[1] Gilbert Murray, *Five Stages of Greek Religion*, pp. 71 ff. Guthrie, in *The Greeks and their Gods*, gives approval.

as we have already seen – strange tales were derived and incorporated in the myths of Kronos, Zeus, and Aphrodite, an Apollo-like god also once existed. From Lycia, one of the strongest centres of his cult in the south-west corner of Asia Minor, came his surname *Lykios*, by which the Greeks constantly called him; and farther east on the high plateau has been found a Hittite dedication to a god probably called *Apulunas*. Here is the most powerful of a cumulative mass of reasons for saying that the god is Eastern, or Anatolian.[1] It was always one of the agreeable characteristics of the Greeks to welcome the god or gods of a stranger and to say to him, 'But of course! Your gods *x*, *y*, and *z* are obviously the very same as my gods *a*, *b*, and *c*!' Therefore, if Ionian Greeks, living in the Islands and on the coast of Asia Minor, became familiar with a god of Hittite origin named *Apulunas* they would be ready to point out to Dorian Greeks, of other Islands and the Greek mainland, that this was unmistakably the same god as *Apellon*, and the Dorians would readily concur. Thus the coincidence of like-sounding names would hasten the process of merging two separate divine concepts into one undivided godhead.

Apollo's twofold origin is stressed by the fact that there were two distinct and separate primary holy places devoted to him – his Ionian sanctuary of Delos and his Dorian shrine at Delphi. To the former he owed such appellatives as *Phoibus*, or *Shining* (which seems to make him akin to a sungod), *Delian* and *Lycian*; to the latter names like *Delphinian*, *Pythian*, *Ambiguous*, and *Founder*. One might, indeed, compare the two centres of his cult with the Roman Vatican and the Byzantine Phanar, though Delphi and Delos never enjoyed thundering at one another retaliatory excommunications, and no Delian Photius caught out a Delphic Leo subscribing to heresy.[2] In times of war the two places might find themselves backing the politics of rival states, but beliefs remained entirely unaffected.

One particular point of difference between the two holy places deserves notice. Apollo had a twin-sister, Artemis, who among the Ionians and in Delos was of greater importance than she was

[1] The whole question is concisely set out by Guthrie, *loc. cit.*, pp. 74 ff.
[2] See Steven Runciman, *Byzantine Civilisation*, p. 122.

among Dorians and at Delphi. It will therefore be convenient to consider Delian Apollo in the next chapter, in company with Artemis, but to devote the present chapter to the story of Delphic, or Pythian, Apollo. What the god meant to the ancient Greeks can still be perceived to some extent today, for it is open to anyone who can travel to Greece to visit Delphi, to linger there, to drink in the air of that extraordinary place, and to learn a little of the feelings men have had about the god.

There is a shelf of land, stony and sloping, on which Dorians from Crete built the god's Sanctuary of Delphi beside the Castalian Spring. Looking from the shelf to the south-west, one may see the distant Gulf of Corinth and some of the mountains of North Arcadia beyond. Below the shelf is a drop of near 2,000 feet into the deep and narrow gorge of the River Pleistos. A traveller may descend with difficulty, ford the river, and climb more easily the south side of the gorge in order to get from the south, looking north, the best view of the ancient sanctuary and the modern village of Kastri beside it. Then one sees the cliffs towering behind Delphi to the height of another 2,000 feet. Later, the ascent of those same cliffs having been made by a rock-track called 'the Bad Stair', the traveller comes on to a high undulating plain at about 4,000 feet above sea-level. There are patches of forest, small tarns, meadows covered with the perfect wild-flowers of a Greek spring and early summer; and beyond and over all this, to the east, there rises the great snow-capped dome of Parnassus, yet another 4,000 feet above the plain on which it stands.

That very condensed description of the situation within Greece of the Holiest Place of the Greeks is needed, because the position and the atmosphere of awe created for them a sense of the numinous combined with authority such as gave the place much power in historical Greece. Delphi, always one of the very little Greek towns, exercised an influence on the rest of Greece which now appears – and in the ancient world often appeared – most disproportionate to its small size; and this influence was derived very largely from a curious procedure: the employment of the Spirit of Divination in the service of Politics. It is of considerable interest to study the mechanism of prophecy and the results achieved by its careful application to the lives and actions of individuals and states.

Apollo, god of the place in historical times, had replaced earlier female divinities who were thought to have prophesied. The legend told that he had slain a great she-serpent, whose putrid remains gave rise to the name Putho, or Pytho, whence the god received the title of Pythian Apollo, for which reason his priestess was known as the Pythia. In later times such a title could be given to lesser women, like the young slave-girl who followed Paul and his companions at Philippi, causing them much trouble, and who was described as possessing a 'Python' spirit.[1] But only the inspired official priestess at Delphi was really entitled to such a name. Successive Pythian priestesses were thought of as mystical brides of Apollo and were in earlier times virgins; but, after a young Pythia had been raped by a rough laird from the mountains of Thessaly, a change was introduced, and the prophetess was always elderly – over fifty – though dressed symbolically in the garb of a young girl. In the days when Greek states and neighbouring kingdoms and empires flourished there were usually two or three Pythias available to take turns of duty in the *adyton* – the oracular vault situated below floor-level in the basement of the temple.

Nowadays if one stands beside the theatre of Dionysos and looks down on to the huge platform of Apollo's temple – several Doric columns of which stand up at the east end – one may see, nearer to the west end, a deep, dark cavity which was approached by a steep stair. Later one may scramble down into it and wonder at its small size.[2] But in ancient days this *adyton* was the Holy of Holies to which few but a Pythia and her priest-interpreter might have access. He started to burn, over an oil-flame, barley-grains, hemp, and chopped bay-leaves, the fumes of which filled the little vault with clouds of smoke; and at that moment she began to chew the leaves of a bay-sprig in her hand. Cyanide of potassium is the name we give now to the essence she got from those leaves – a small quantity, of course, or she would die, but insidious, ex-

[1] *Acts*, XVI, 16 ff.
[2] This account of the oracle is founded mainly on A. B. Cook, *Zeus*, II, pp. 169–210. Views divergent from some of Professor Cook's have recently been expressed by Pierre Amandry, *La Mantique Apollinienne à Delphes*, Paris, 1950.

ARES, shame-faced, finds all his brute force unavailing while (below)
HEPHAISTOS is brought to the rescue by Dionysos and his *Seilenoi* (see p. 102).
Both from a large mixing bowl painted in Athens by Kleitias about 560 B.C.

(LEFT) *Copper coin* of Lipara,
off Sicily, with head of Hephaistos, struck about 350 B.C.

Silver coin of Calymna, near
Rhodes, with head of hel-
meted Ares, struck about
540 B.C.

PLATE IX

APHRODITE leaning on a rock and holding the young Eros, who learns how to use bow and arrow. Bronze mirror cover made about 350 B.C.

Silver coin of Syracuse with the head of Artemis Arethusa, struck about 408 B.C. and signed by the engraver, Kimon.

PLATE X

citing, and intoxicating. The *adyton* filled up with smoke, a small grating in the ceiling allowed some fumes to escape, otherwise the celebrants would have suffocated, but the escaping fumes exercised their dizzy influence on the postulants anxiously awaiting above the answer of the Prophetess. According to another view, however, there was room for one postulant within the *adyton*. Now we may imagine that the Pythia has attained 'ecstasy' and has gone under – under the 'influence'. She talks, talks, and talks – incoherently, but not entirely so. She has heard the question that was put and, since she has a 'spirit of divination' in which she herself completely believes, since she is possessed of 'second sight', since she has got that 'something' which we have all at some time met in some otherwise-foolish fortune-teller – 'something' we have failed to explain – since she has all this, the Pythia is saying things often well above the nonsense-level. The priest-interpreter memorises or takes down her words as quickly as may be; then there is a pause, for the words require editing and interpreting by another, the *prophētēs*, or 'speaker' for the god, who may give them out either in verse or in prose. Lastly, there awaits the postulant an *exēgētēs Pythochrēstos* – another member of the staff, doubtless appointed for natural good manners and adroitness – whose job it is to explain the obscure and difficult bits to the satisfaction, if possible, of the serious enquirer, for these obscurities caused Apollo to be referred to frequently as 'Loxias', *the Ambiguous*.

Such was the mechanism of prophecy in the holiest and most celebrated of all oracles in ancient times. Its application to the active world, gay or grim, outside Delphi was worthy of note, both through its successes and through its failures.

Why did the outer world fall for the snare with such ease? Firstly, perhaps because divination, carrying the message of the god himself in that magnificent situation, with crag and crevice, gorge and rushing water, eagles wheeling among towering cliffs, skies of the bluest, but often black with deafening thunder, and ever the deep, dark olive groves and distant sea – divination in that setting must more impress the imagination than any prophetic words given in less majestic, god-touched landscape.

Secondly, because the Pythia was quite frequently right; and those who subconsciously wish to be persuaded of something remember all the times when the answer was right, forgetting most of the times when it was wrong. The Pythia had what the gipsy-woman has: an unexplained ability to skip Space – and sometimes Time – where the little affairs of individuals are concerned. She could tell a man that his maternal aunt would die within the month, she could know about King Crœsus and his silly cookery test (of which more below), because trivialities could pass into a trivial mind emptied of its own trifling preoccupation. But where major issues were concerned, conflicts or policies, statesmen in conspiracy, kingdoms plotting the overthrow of kingdoms, she cannot really have functioned, unless by pure chance.

And here one must recognise the third reason for which Greek and barbarian alike could be impressed by prophecy from Delphi: the place must certainly have had an exceptionally efficient international and political Intelligence Service. The adroit priestly attaché, the *exēgētēs Pythochrēstos* – call him the exegete – who explained obscurities in the answer a man had received, was a member of this Service, which must have possessed a valuable and important collection of archives, together with dossiers on all important persons. In all Greece the Delphic priesthood was the only one that came near to being what we mean by the term today – a whole-time priestly caste differentiated from other men. But even in Delphi they were not really whole-time men and must have had other jobs as well; nor were they all Delphic-born. That famous and brilliant polymath, Plutarch of Chaeronea, who flourished between about A.D. 46 and 125, was an honorary 'life-priest' of Delphi.

In the process of time the Delphic college must have collected and filed a great deal of useful information about the shores of the Mediterranean Sea, because every visitor from afar had plenty to tell. Constant correspondence with the kingdom of Lydia and with some lesser barbarian – that is, foreign – principalities kept Apollo's Foreign Office well informed; but the farther a land was removed from the sea the less they knew about it. At one time it was fashionable to draw a comparison between the influence of Delphi and that of the mediæval Papacy, but this will not hold except in a few minor details. Pythian Apollo possessed no authoritative control over the whole of Greek religion; he might give advice about it, but his moral instruction went little further than what was implied by the famous maxims of the Seven Sages inscribed in the entrance of his temple: 'Know thyself', 'Don't exceed', 'The Mean is best'; and Apollo's representatives could not exercise anything comparable to the powers of interdict and excommunication. Only the wide knowledge which the Papacy possessed of kingdoms and of men was matched by a parallel store of knowledge possessed by Delphi. It was this which first made a great reputation for the place because of the wise and helpful advice Apollo was enabled to give to prospective colonists, especially in the seventh century B.C. – the great age of Greek colonisation.

Postulants might be roughly classified as follows: colonial pioneers, Oriental potentates, Spartans, other Greeks; and they all derived some benefit, and some hurt, from the Pythian prophetic machine.

The help given to Founding Fathers of Greek colonies has been mentioned, and the successful colony ever afterwards kept up its links with Delphi. Greek religion, it has been observed, was quite free of the proselytising urge, for the Greeks never thought themselves possessed of the sole faith, and were therefore more interested in learning the beliefs of others than in propagating their own. It was only in this one matter of colonisation that a touch of the missionary seemed to appear, for every new Greek colony was commanded to worship in the new settlement not only the gods of the motherland whence it derived, but also very specially 'Founder Apollo', and to build him a temple in the new land. He was to accompany – certainly not to displace – any other gods. And for the Pythian Sanctuary there was great benefit, since it would be a graceless colony indeed which did not send to Delphi a regular supply of gifts.

Oriental potentates – and especially the multi-millionaire kings of Lydia from Gyges to Crœsus – not only helped greatly to augment the reputation of Delphi, but also conferred upon it gifts of such immense wealth as to raise oracle, temple, sanctuary, and town to the height of prosperity. Gyges, who usurped the Lydian throne about 685 B.C., agreed with his opponents to abide by Apollo's decision as to whether or no he should rule, and when the Pythia duly pronounced in his favour he began to shower gifts on Delphi. The last of his line was the celebrated Croesus, who, meditating a preventive war against the dangerously growing power of Persia under Cyrus after 550 B.C., decided to put all the well-known oracles of the day to the test. Accordingly, he sent trusted Lydian envoys to try them out. The story of this episode as recounted by Herodotus in the first book of his *History* is entertaining:

Now his purpose in sending hither and thither was to learn if the oracles had any wisdom; so that, if they were found to know the truth, he might send a second time and ask them whether he should make war against Persia. And when he sent the Lydians to test the oracles, he charged them thus, that from the day they set forth from Sardis they should keep count of the days and on the hundredth enquire of the oracles and ask what Croesus the son of Alyattes, King of the Lydians, was doing; and whatsoever each of the oracles should prophesy they should write down and bring back to him. Now what the other oracles prophesied is told by none; but at Delphi, as soon as the Lydians entered into the hall to enquire of the god, before they asked the question they were charged with, the Pythia spake thus in hexameter measure:

I know the number of the sands and the measures of the sea;
I comprehend the dumb, and hear him that speaketh not.
A smell is come about my senses of a stout-hided tortoise,
Seethed in a vessel of brass with the meat of a lamb;
Brass is spread beneath it, and with brass it is clad.

These things, when the Pythia prophesied them, the Lydians wrote down; and they departed and returned unto Sardis. And when the others that had been sent out were also come bringing their answers, then Croesus unfolded the writings one by one and looked thereon. And none of them liked him, until he read that which came from Delphi, which straightway he did accept and worshipped, deeming that the only oracle was that at Delphi because it had found out what he did. For after he had sent the messengers to the several oracles, he waited for the appointed day, and devised a thing impossible to guess: he cut in pieces a tortoise and a lamb, and himself seethed them together in a cauldron of brass, which he covered with a brazen lid.

This episode, which in all probability actually occurred, may have been evidence for the Pythia's 'second sight' and veridical vision under drugs; it was assuredly no token of her political judgment. But the King of Lydia – unable to distinguish between the trivially Inexplicable and the cosmically Ineffable – was so deeply impressed by the answer given that he put unquestioning faith in Delphi. Gifts to astound were bestowed on the sanctuary, and every townsman of Delphi received a generous money-prize. Then came the next question – the important question for which all this elaborate plan had been made – 'Crœsus, the King of the Lydians and of other nations, now asketh you whether he shall make war against the Persians'. And the answer of 'Loxias' came back, 'that if he made war against the Persians he should humble a great empire'. This was no Pythia talking, but the 'interpretation' of a cautious exegete, uncertain about the balance of power and strength of armies east of the Lydian kingdom. In the event Crœsus was defeated and became the prisoner of Cyrus, who permitted him to transmit to Delphi a long message of protest and reproach. The written answer he received was simple:

Touching the prophecy that was given him, Crœsus doth ill to find fault; for Apollo foretold him that if he warred against the Persians he should humble a great empire; and he thereupon, if he would have been well counselled, ought to have sent and enquired whether he spake of his own empire or of the empire of Cyrus. But because he comprehended not the saying, neither enquired again, let him declare himself the guilty one.

The Spartans as a whole were quite a trial to Delphic patience, for the Faithful who display an excess of fidelity are always a liability to any well-organised religious machine. During the sixth century B.C. those intrepid fighters were not happy in a fast-expanding world of art and commerce. They were simple soldier-men, only too conscious of a sense of inadequacy – except, of course, in battle – who needed direction, so they were ready to surrender personal initiative and to seek on every trivial matter advice from the god through his Pythia. From the Delphic point of view they were a burden, being poor and frugal folk who could not bring rich presents like Eastern kings or even like great Athenian landowners. Sometimes the Spartan State would consult the oracle in clumsy fashion, as when they plotted to invade and annex neighbouring Arcadia, but advertised their whole plan by enquiring publicly at Delphi whether they should attack. This at least afforded the god opportunity to administer a sharp rebuke through the Pythia, who said: 'Dost thou ask of me Arcadia? It is a big thing thou askest: I'll not give. There are many acorn-eating men in Arcadia, and they will stop thee!'

But it was the private, almost unremunerative Spartan who was always getting into the queue of postulants. The Pythia prophesied only on certain days of the month, and the priests determined the order in which questions were taken. The Lydian king and his nobles had automatic and lifelong right of precedence over all other strangers. Next came those who arrived with the best sacrifices and richest gifts, and penurious but persistent persons were put last. From this system there arose a scandal which shook the oracle badly.

While the great despot Peisistratus and his son Hippias ruled in Athens, the Alcmæonids – the most powerful Athenian family opposing the despots – had to live in exile. They settled in Delphi and proceeded to work for the downfall of the tyranny in Athens. It was apparent that nothing less than the armed intervention of Sparta could bring about this end. Accordingly, they bribed the Pythian priestess to give a uniform monotonous answer to every Spartan who asked any question on any matter personal or official. Whatever question was put she answered with depressing irrelevancy, 'Athens must be freed'. After a while Spartan nerves gave way under this treatment; they sent an army to Athens and expelled the tyrant, enabling the Alcmæonid family to return. Then, when it was all over and the end achieved, the scandal came out. The Spartans were greatly distressed, for they had a firm belief in the virtues of playing the game according to the rules – the Spartan rules, of course – and were shocked when the bribery was exposed. They were not bemused by discovering that Apollo had allowed it, nor angry at the Pythia for accepting money, since they themselves fell easily for the lure of gold. But they were exceedingly angry at the misbehaviour of the Athenian Alcmæonids.

Nevertheless, in the opinion of the Greek world as a whole, Delphi suffered greatly in prestige, for a venal Pythia in the sixth century B.C. could hurt the reputation of the Tripod as easily as a fifteenth-century libertine Pope could hurt that of the Chair. Yet Delphi continued to prosper, though to a lesser degree than in the days of Crœsus; and the same Alcmaeonids who had bribed the Pythia built for Pythian Apollo a new and splendid temple. But the priesthood was perhaps more conscious than men in certain other states of the grave threats which were slowly building up in the East against the liberties of Greece. At last the vast expedition of Xerxes started to lumber on its way, and for every questioner Apollo had only words of doom. Housman, in *The Oracles*, pictures the Pythia's deathly despair as she cries the warning:

The King with half the East at heel is marched from lands of morning;
Their fighters drink the rivers up, their shafts benight the air.
And he that stands will die for nought, and home there's no returning.
The Spartans on the sea-wet rock sat down and combed their hair.

The Spartans did – before Thermopylæ, where those bravest fighters in all history died with Leonidas.

At this point the great bureau of international information gave up hope. Herodotus has a rather confused account of what ensued, because later on the priesthood managed to muddle him – and others – and to cover their tracks when events turned out contrary to expectations, Probably their archives were stuffed with accounts of the vastness and power of Persia – accounts sometimes exaggerated. They had seen the mighty Crœsus fall before Cyrus; what hope for the little states of Greece before the far mightier Xerxes? The priests, and perhaps the Pythia, stayed at their posts. Collaboration or extinction seemed to face them; they chose for themselves – and counselled for others – the former. After Thermopylæ a Persian force left the main army to cross the pass, to occupy Delphi, and to take over the Sanctuary with its stores of wealth. One of the Delphic priests, Akeratos by name, casting about for a visible token of their surrender that might be understood by a foreigner, took down a suit of dedicated armour and laid it in front of the temple even as the Persians came into sight.

Yet the Persians never got there. The priests with their staff and attendants, some sixty souls, were ready to bow before the inevitable. But the citizens of Delphi would not have it thus. They had sent their women and children across the gulf into Peloponnesus, and the men ascended the crags of Parnassus by 'the Bad Stair', carrying their valuables up to the Corycian cave, sacred to Pan and the Nymphs, which became the headquarters of the Resistance. That fund of courage, daring, and resource with which modern Hellenes astonished the world in 1941 has always distinguished the Greeks; and the Delphians showed it in 480 B.C. So far the invaders' triumph had been complete; the dead still lay unburied at Thermopylæ; Salamis was yet to be fought, and no Pythian citizen or farmer could have foreseen that surprising victory and the annihilated Persian fleet. Many of the Delphians were shepherds – the coins of Delphi all bore the heads of rams and goats – and any herdsman in search of pasture for his flocks on the rugged flanks of Parnassus knew every rock and ledge above the shelf of land and the Castalian gorge. Up on the crag called Hyampia – above the angle where the road from Arachova bends sharply round the towering rocks and where Delphi comes suddenly into view – the shepherds seem to have been able to dislodge a great mass of rock, the perilous instability of which may have been already known to them. The timing was perfect. A thunderstorm – constant phenomenon in that region – helped with the stage effects. 'From Parnassus', says Herodotus, 'two mountaintops were broken off and rolled down upon them with a great crashing and overthrew exceeding many of them. Dismay fell upon the barbarians. And when the Delphians perceived that they fled, they descended and pursued after them and slew no small number of them.' Akeratos, the priest who had grounded the armour in front of the temple, and his despondent colleagues, recovering from their surprise, may have been startled into belief in divine intervention. They promptly issued an official version, which was that the sacred armour had moved out miraculously, and that there were seen two warriors of greater than human stature – ancient heroes of the place – pursuing and slaying Persians. Not a very convincing tale!

After the relentless attacks on the barbarians and after their expulsion from Greece thanks were offered up to the gods, and not least to Pythian Apollo. If the citizens and shepherds, rather than the priests, had saved the Holy Place, it was still Apollo acting through his people. Victorious states dedicated splendid offerings at Delphi, partly because anything set up there was bound to be seen by other Greeks. Yet amid all the celebrations men sometimes remembered that a Pythia had within living memory been bribed, and that a priesthood had counselled collaboration. For most Greeks such happenings were no reflection on Apollo, nor even on his Pythia; but the wisdom, reliability, and impartiality of the priestly body fell under suspicion, and things were never quite the same for many years to come. The glory and the authority of sixth-century Delphi were departed.

From this time on, the oracle seems to have been rather less frequently consulted than in former days, partly for the reason just given, partly because among very many of the Greeks a respect for human reason was overshadowing superstitious practices. But, since Apollo was himself the greatest promoter of law and reason, there were still postulants, there were spectators and competitors for the quadrennial games, there were pilgrims and sightseers. Because of this the Delphians, like the population of any famous place of pilgrimage anywhere, presently became little better than profiteers in the faith of simpletons and parasites on God.

Nevertheless, for the Greeks the first and most important aspect of Apollo was certainly his championship of law and order, an aspect which his famous temple maxims 'Know thyself', 'Don't exceed', 'The Mean is best', really emphasised. And what has been called his 'legal activity' embraced criminal, civil and constitutional codes, for which reason his help was precious to every newly founded Greek colony in the Mediterranean lands. Politically the small town was assured of the protection of a union of

surrounding states called the Amphictionic League, and when in
346 B.C. Philip of Macedon obtained membership of that League
the oracle naturally became pro-Macedonian. After Alexander it
maintained good relations with all the Successor Kingdoms and
later with the neighbouring confederacy of the Ætolians, who
appear to have saved the place from robbery and destruction at the
hands of a vast horde of Gauls who invaded Greece in 279 B.C.
The generals of the Roman Republic treated Delphi well until the
ruthless Sulla stripped it of all its remaining wealth to pay his
soldiery. A hard period of poverty followed until the reign of
Nero, who patronised the oracle and gave it much money, though
he offset this by robbing the Sacred Precinct of five hundred
bronze statues destined to decorate his 'Golden House' in Rome.
Yet imperial patronage, which reached its climax in the reign of
the magnanimous Hadrian, provided for Delphi an Indian summer of elegant tranquillity before the corrosive action of Gnosti-
cism, Mithraism, and other half-Eastern proletarian beliefs began
in the third century of our era to undermine Apolline faith. Early
in that century Clement of Alexandria pretended that the oracle
was moribund, but for most Christian apologists the oracular
powers of the place were never in doubt, and only the emphasis
was changed: Pythia and priests were Satanic; Apollo a devil in
disguise. The last of all oracular responses is said to have been
given in A.D. 363 to the Emperor Julian, philosopher, soldier and
apostate, but a man inadequate to champion or to heal the
ancient faith of Hellas:

> Say ye to Cæsar: 'Fallen our fair-built columns lie.
> Phœbus hath left his temple, his laurel of prophecy,
> His speaking spring – yea, even the spring that spake is dry.'

Balance and toleration finally disappeared before A.D. 400, for
the Emperor Theodosius was able to close the sanctuary, and the
Emperor Arcadius to demolish it; but the actions of those blunder-
ing men could not for ever stifle humanism sprung from the
worship of Apollo.

The myths about the god belong to his two main centres of
worship, and one can generally tell which are suitable to the

Delphian and which to the Delian canon. Naturally, both groups were equally acceptable in both places, since the god had become a Unity as much as Pallas Athene. Here we may note some of his myths that have a Delphic frame, leaving a consideration of the island and Eastern myths until later. Two Homeric Hymns were written: one at the behest of the Delphic priesthood, the other in praise of the holy island where the god was born. The former tells firstly how Apollo came to Delphi, took it for his own, and then got him Dorians from Crete to be the Keepers of his temple. Down from Olympus he came and travelled south through the plains of Thessaly to Iolkos and crossed to Euboea; thence he struck west over the narrows, into Boeotia, and on into the mountains.

And thence he went speeding swiftly to the mountain ridge,
And came to Crisa beneath snowy Parnassus,
A foot-hill turned towards the west: a cliff hangs
Over it from above, and a hollow rugged glade runs under.
There the lord Phoebus Apollo resolved to make his lovely temple.

It was then that he met the she-dragon, Python, and killed her, taking over the ancient oracle of Earth.

Then Phoebus Apollo pondered in his heart
What men he should bring in to be his ministers
In sacrifice and to serve him in rocky Pytho.
And while he considered, he became aware of a swift ship on the wine-like sea,
In which were many men and goodly Cretans from Cnossos,
The city of Minos, they who do sacrifice
To the prince and announce his decrees, whatsoever Phoebus Apollo,
Bearer of the golden blade, speaks in answer
From his laurel below the dells of Parnassus.
These men were sailing in their black ship for gain and profit to sandy Pylos,
And to the men of Pylos. But Phoebus Apollo met them:
In the open sea he sprang upon their swift ship, like a dolphin in shape,
And lay there, a great and awesome monster, and none of them gave heed so as to understand
But they sought to cast the dolphin overboard. But he kept shaking
The black ship every way and making the timbers quiver.

Then in the end he brought them to the port of Delphi in the Corinthian Gulf, and led them up to the shelf of rock upon the mountain-side so that they and their descendants might be his servants from generation to generation.

Another favourite Delphic story is about the Hyperboreans, or the 'Folk-beyond-the-north-wind'. or the 'Over-the-mountains-people'. Every year for at least three of the winter months Apollo left his younger brother Dionysos in charge of Delphi while he himself flew north in his swan-drawn chariot to the 'never-never' land of those fabulous folk who know neither disease nor old age, toil nor war, but they dance and make music, sing and feast, and betimes they sacrifice hecatombs of wild asses to Apollo, 'who laugheth as he looketh on the brute beasts in their rampant lewdness'. All this is mainly fairy-tale of a familiar type, which, however, holds some small foundation of fact concerning some fortunate folk living, possibly, in a rich Danubian plain among corn and orchards, who worshipped a god of Apolline semblance.

Many girls were loved by the god, but several of them rebuffed or cheated him – to their own undoing, like Daphne, who was changed into a bay-tree, and Cassandra, who, though he gave her the gift of prophecy, refused him her favours, wherefore (since he could not take back his gift) he added another: that no one should ever believe her. Coronis – whom he dearly loved – was, while pregnant, unfaithful to him, and Artemis slew her and her lover. But Apollo snatched from her dead body the infant, his son Asklepios, at first a hero and later a god of Healing. Enamoured of the girl Marpessa, he took her from her bridegroom, Idas, who, being the strongest of mortals, drew his bow against the god. Zeus made peace, giving Marpessa the choice between them, and she preferred Idas. Apollo was more fortunate with Akakallis, a Cretan girl, who bore him twins; and most of all with a huntress-nymph called Cyrene, whom he found one day in Thessaly as she was strangling a young lion with her bare hands. The happy god carried her off to that part of North Africa which was presently named after her, and of which she became in time the patron goddess, and she bore him Aristaios, a hero and protector of cattle and fruit-trees.

Among painters and sculptors Apollo was through long centuries one of the favourite subjects of all in Greek art, from his primitive, pillar-like image in Laconia to the latest Græco-Roman polished marble representing him as an effeminate youth. By far the finest statue of Apollo – many would say the finest surviving marble statue of any god – is the giant figure from the centre of the west gable of the temple of Zeus at Olympia (Plate VI, facing page 65).

The master who carved this figure showed the god in the semblance of a perfectly developed – but not overdeveloped – man of about forty years still in perfect training. Around him is the fight of civilised Lapiths against savage centaurs, and the god trails an idle bow because he can overcome lawlessness with weapons of the spirit. Because *he* is present – the god of law and right – to help those who know him, we can understand that goodness and fineness of spirit will prevail. And now, when we reflect on his worshippers in the ancient world, we are made aware that those who followed the way of Apollo had need of fine qualities: lucidity, moderation, courage and tact, as well as wisdom born of self-knowledge and an experienced acceptance of the physical world wherein man is not all inner conflict but a unitary whole.

X. ARTEMIS

Midway between Delphi and Ephesus – between the holiest oracle of Apollo and the holiest shrine of Artemis – lay Delos, where, according to the commoner legend, their mother Leto gave birth to the younger twin – Apollo. This story and the hymns to Delian Apollo and to Artemis will be discussed later; Delos, however, was something of a half-way house for both gods. Artemis, like her brother, had a dual aspect, seeming a purely Greek concept of young godhead when she is Huntress Artemis, but also carrying some powers of the age-old nature goddess of Asia Minor when she is Artemis Ephesia. Despite the fact that in the Homeric poems she is a partisan of the Trojans, she is pictured as a purely European type of goddess, for she is a huntress roaming the woods and mountains, delighting, like her brother Apollo, in music and the dance; in fact, leading the life of many an unmarried daughter among the gay and brilliant feudal families pictured by Homer.

This concept had come down from an earlier, more primitive society when she – or her like – was first worshipped by wandering tribes whose livelihood came mainly from hunting and fishing. As they were not agricultural, and probably not yet patriarchal, they gave their women great freedom, perhaps because some of the actual burdens of food-finding fell upon them as well as upon the men. Artemis was first the goddess of such energetic women as these, who held that the wild beasts belonged to her, and especially their cubs, so she became known as 'Mistress of Animals', a title which helped her gradual merging with the Asiatic Artemis. Hare and stag, wolf and boar, bear and lion, all were hers, yet her favourites were the wild deer. Since fish are valued food, they too came under her care, and in the uplands of Arcadia – her special country – there was an image of her fish-shaped from the waist down; but she was not of the sea, rather a fresh-water mermaid. Lakes, marshes, streams, and rivers were her care, and all the wild-growing trees of grove and forest. Here was the fleet young Huntress whose followers so much resembled

her. No better type of the goddess can be found than the famous
Atalanta, who would hunt and wrestle with the men and get the
better of them, though she was unwilling to wed any of them.[1]

Perhaps the ancient Greeks and Romans of the late Hellenistic
period thought of Artemis-Diana as a 'chaste huntress' who preserved her virginity. Romantic Europe certainly adopted that belief. But it was not the earlier Greek view, according to which,
although she practised celibacy, she was no rigid upholder of
chastity, which, indeed, no sunburnt, free-living, huntress girl of
the heroic age would have held as either needful or pertinent. The
Greek word *parthenos*, normally translated as 'maid' or 'virgin',
has not really got such a meaning. In the *Iliad*[2] and in Pindar[3] it is
used of unmarried girls who are not virgins, while in Sparta the
children of concubines were called *partheniai*, implying that the
mother remains a *parthenos* in name. The word, indeed, has a wide
range, and can denote maid, girl, young woman, mistress, but not
wedded wife who is a mother. Possibly the simplest English word
to carry a like meaning is 'wench'. A usage similarly indeterminate
has been observed in Hebrew, for it is interesting to note that
parthenos is used in the Jewish–Greek version of the Old Testament, known as the Septuagint, to translate the Hebrew *almah* in
the famous and controversial verse of *Isaiah*, vii, 14: 'Behold a
virgin shall conceive and bear a son'.[4] Yet 'the word *almah* means
a girl or young woman above the age of childhood and sexual
immaturity . . . it asserts neither virginity nor the lack of it'.[5]

It has been necessary to stress the fact that, although Artemis
later figured as the 'chaste huntress', she was originally no special-
ist in virginity, and was therefore the protectress of all human
femininity. Childhood, girlhood, womanhood in every stage was
her concern; she was invoked by all women in childbirth, and
other birth-goddesses are in a sense only variants of her. When the
end came she was said to make death easy for them. With the
actual marriage rite she had no association at all, for she had come
down from an earlier stratum when hunters and nomads attached

---

[1] For a recent account of Atalanta see Seltman in *Cornhill Magazine*, 1950,
pp. 296 ff. [2] Book II, 514. [3] *Pythian Ode*, III, 34. [4] Quoted in *Matthew*, I, 23.
[5] G. B. Gray, *International Critical Commentary*, *Isaiah*, Vol. I (1912), p. 126.

little value to such a rite; and unlike Hera, who contracted the
Holy Marriage with Zeus, she retained her happy independence
of males. Her earlier forerunners, Britomartis and Dictynna,
whom the Minoan Cretans worshipped as huntresses, appear to
have made a contribution to the early Greek concept of Artemis,
since they sprang from a familiar social order. One may observe
a parallelism between the growth of the classical Hermes[1] and of
the classical Artemis, both with origins part Minoan and part
mainland Greek.

In general, she had less importance as a city goddess than Hera,
Athene, or Aphrodite, though women in the towns prayed to her
as fervently as did peasants. But there were three important exceptions to this, for she was the chief divinity in three great cities:
Ephesus, Marseilles and Syracuse.

Tradition said that somewhere about 900 B.C. certain Ionians
from Greece, escaping from invading Dorians, founded, under
the leadership of an Athenian prince, the Greek city of Ephesus.
There had been a Carian township and a temple there before it was
annexed, and many of the Ionians took Carian wives and with
them certain customs that entailed considerable freedom for
women. The same applied in other famous Ionian cities, like
Miletus and Clazomenæ, and this accounts for the swift urbanisa-
tion of the divinity whom the Greek colonists of Ephesus brought
with them, Artemis. All this occurred before Apollo's oracle at
Delphi had taken to itself any political influence in the matter of
colonisation, for no important Apolline cult went to Ephesus,
though such a cult became very important in many other Ionian
states.

The worship of Artemis at Ephesus centred on the huge, impressive, and fabulously wealthy temple, which later became
known as one of the Seven Wonders of the World. We can note
several stages in the development both of the temple and of the
principal image within it. At some distant date – possibly as far
back as 2000 B.C. – the inhabitants possessed a small sacred stone
believed to have fallen from Zeus in heaven and known as a
diopetes in Greek. This *diopet* was probably no meteorite, but some

[1] See pp. 65f.

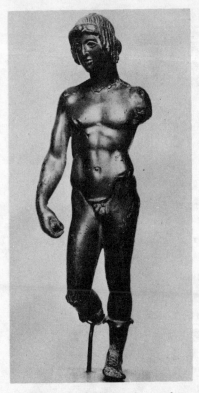

DIONYSOS: his cult seemed a terrifying incursion when first it came to Greece. 9 ins. high, made about 470 B.C.

POSEIDON the Earth-Shaker, tamer of horses and saviour of ships. Bronze, about 4 ins. high, made about 300 B.C.

(LEFT) *Silver coin* of King Antigonus of Macedonia with head of Poseidon, struck about 258 B.C.

Silver coin of Naxos, Sicily, with head of Dionysos, struck about 460 B.C.

PLATE XI

HERAKLES introduced by Athene to Zeus. Athenian black-figure cup, *c.* 550 B.C.

DIONYSOS at sea, in a ship with a vine growing up the mast. Painting on the inside of an Athenian cup, made about 540 B.C.

PLATE XII

neolithic implement – an axe or, more likely, a pounder – and was held in the greatest veneration. Later, when Christians reproached pagans for revering images made by the hands of Man, the Ephesians, at least, could reply 'that which *we* most revere was not made with hands but fell to earth from God Himself'. For that small sacred *diopet* endured to the end of the ancient religion, when it was hidden away.[1]

The second stage is not yet historical, and involves a story about Amazons. Now Amazons – as is well known – had a tremendous attraction for the Greeks, to whom the idea of a tribe of man-ruling, battle-fit huntresses was a matter of perpetual interest which provided a theme popular in Greek art for many centuries. Critics until recently have inclined to the view that all the Amazon legends were merely expansions of travellers' tales about barbarous nomads living on the remote outer fringes of the ancient civilised world. But we, who some while ago heard much about the actual battalions of women soldiers on the Eastern Front and in China, are bound to be less sceptical, and it is possible that among Phrygians and Carians such people did exist. Anyhow, it was alleged that Amazons founded the first shrine at Ephesus, possibly before the Greeks got there, and had a very primitive image of a goddess, later identified with Artemis. It is likely that this idol was made of a palm-trunk, for that tree continued to be associated with the real Artemis whom the Greeks brought over with them. Moreover, Theophrastus, the founder of scientific botany, described palmwood as both tough and easy to carve, and therefore popular for making images.[2] About 650 B.C. barbarous Cimmerians destroyed the shrine of Artemis, which lay outside the walls of Ephesus, and almost certainly the image with it.

Though an attempt at restoration was then begun, it was not until the reign of the famous Crœsus, 564–546 B.C., that anything on a big scale was started; and this brings us to our third stage. The munificent gifts of Crœsus to Apollo have already been mentioned,[3] and it seems that the King was almost as generous to Artemis of Ephesus as to her brother of Delphi. Fragments,

[1] An object in the Liverpool City Museum is probably this very *diopet*.
[2] *History of Plants*, v, 3, 6.   [3] See p. 115.

inscribed with his name, of columns which he gave for the temple are preserved in the British Museum, and the 'Crœsus-temple' was famous in its day as the biggest of all Greek fanes.

At this time a new and delightful statue of the goddess was carved in hardwood by a celebrated sculptor of the day named Endoios. It resembled other standing figures of *parthenoi* made in the sixth century – long-haired, upright, feet together, elbows to sides, forearms held out, the garment clinging. One may compare a superb bronze figure about $9\frac{1}{2}$ inches tall[1] said to have been found near Olympia, depicting Artemis holding a young doe in both hands (Plate III, facing page 32). This is of about 500 B.C. nearly half a century later than the wooden life-size statue with inlaid enamelled eyes made by Endoios. Instead of the young doe in her hands, she was flanked by a pair of stags, made separately, of course; and these could be removed at will and a pair of does substituted.[2] Inspired by the Oriental custom of loading cult statues of the gods with rich metallic decoration, kings and merchant-princes gave, and the temple staff accepted, an ever-increasing panoply of gold and silver clothing for the goddess, who could never wear all her possessions at any one time. Mistresses of the Robes were appointed from among the wealthy and established Ephesian families, to dress and re-dress the image, of which only the original wooden face, hands, and feet were now visible, and these grew slowly black with age and with the constant application of preservative oil.

Two kinds of Things belonging to this image were very strange indeed. Coin-pictures and copies of the statue depict her with what at first sight seem to be many udder-like breasts, hanging sometimes well below the waist. But these were no part of the old black wooden statue, for they were put on apron-like above the clothing, and there were many sets of them with protuberances varying in number from eleven up to forty-four. Since they were either gilt or, more probably, golden, they were the colour of ripening dates, and each set of the things represented a date-

[1] In the collection of Mrs Robert Emmet of Wilton, New Hampshire, U.S.A.
[2] For a full discussion of this statue and all its paraphernalia see Seltman, 'The Wardrobe of Artemis', in *Numismatic Chronicle*, 1951, Part II.

cluster with large (but not unnaturally large) fruits. In Ephesus the date-palm was definitely sacred to the goddess. The other strange appurtenance of the image was a small temple-like shrine open on three sides and worn instead of a hat on top of the head. It seems probable that this contained the *diopet*, which represented mystically the infant Artemis herself, and which was thus kept in close contact with the overdressed statue, being both the most ancient and the most holy thing in the Sanctuary. This was not a 'godhead like unto gold, or silver, or stone graven by art and man's device',[1] but a heavenly supernatural creation.

Paul of Tarsus lived for three years in Ephesus, A.D. 52–54, long enough to make a considerable number of converts, including members of the middle class as well as proletarians, to what was then called 'The Way'. Towards the end of his stay trouble started under the leadership of a prosperous silversmith Demetrios, who 'made silver shrines of Artemis,'[2] probably silver replicas of the miniature shrine worn on the head of the goddess. A riot ensued, and when a high official had quietened the people he said:

Men of Ephesus, what man is there that knoweth not how that the city of the Ephesians is Temple-Warden of the great Goddess Artemis and of the 'Zeus-fallen THING'? [3]

Two cult-objects are kept distinct in this speech: the statue of the great goddess Artemis and the *diopet* itself. The former was to be destroyed; the latter perhaps survives.

Despite all this oddity, the Greeks still imagined the actual goddess as a young athletic huntress, and the young girls who served as her priestesses in Ephesus were dressed as Artemis with skirts girt up to show half the thigh, the right breast sometimes bared, a quiver hanging at the shoulder, high hunting-boots, and a bow in hand.

The great temple of Artemis Ephesia was the richest and most trusted safe-deposit bank in the whole Greek world. Crœsus had honoured it; so did Persian kings and satraps, as well as powerful city-states. Alexander the Great contributed to the reconstruction of the temple after a fire. All the Hellenistic kings,

[1] *Acts*, XVII, 29.   [2] *Acts*, XIX, 24.   [3] *Ibid.*, XIX, 35.

Roman proconsuls and emperors respected and often enriched the place. From the time about 650 B.C. when barbaric Cimmerians had destroyed the old Amazonian shrine to A.D. 250 the temple remained unmolested and unrobbed – a record of some nine hundred years, unparalleled elsewhere. Finally, about A.D. 406 the famous statue was smashed by a deranged Christian named Demeas, who carved a stone inscription to say he had torn down 'the demon Artemis'.

Three great cities looked to Artemis – usually a goddess of the countryside – as their chief deity. The second of them was Marseilles. Founded about 600 B.C. by men of Phocæa, an Ionian city of Asia Minor, it was strengthened by a fresh body of colonists who travelled west in 540 B.C. These men took with them a replica of the newly carved wooden statue of Ephesian Artemis, and it seems likely that it, too, was the work of Endoios himself, or of one of his colleagues, for coin-pictures of the figure in Marseilles prove it to have had the closest resemblance to the Ephesian type. But the replica which went to Marseilles retained its old simplicity unencumbered by orientalising metallic trappings. The colonists also took with them the olive-tree, which from then to the present day has been of importance in the south of France; and therefore in Marseilles it was the olive-tree, not the palm, which became the special tree of Artemis. In the fourth century B.C. the goddess was thought of as a very young girl, for there are charming coins of the place with her olive-crowned head based on Syracusan models.

In the third great city in which her deity was dominant, Syracuse, she was known by the double name Artemis Arethusa, even as the goddess of Athens was frequently called Pallas Athene. It was said that the nymph Arethusa roaming in the land of Elis went to bathe in the River Alpheus, which flows past Olympia. The river-god of that big stream sought to violate her, and she dived into the sea, nor did she come up to breathe again until she was within the harbour of Syracuse, wherefore there exists, even today, a spring of fresh water surrounded by the briny sea. But this Arethusa was but another name for Artemis, and her importance in the city is proved by the fact that her head, surrounded

by dolphins, became the principal type of the splendid coinage of
Syracuse. The people of that brilliant and wealthy city were often
able to employ some of the most gifted engravers and metal-
workers in the world to make their coins, still justly famed
today.

Besides the three great cities where her worship was all-impor-
tant, there were other townships and large villages where a like
cult existed. Zeus, a poet said, was so devoted to his daughter that
he wished to give her thirty cities. But her happiness was ever in
the meadows and mountains.

Mythology embraced Leto and her twin children Artemis and
Apollo as a single holy family, but this doctrine was really centred
in Delos, which, though essentially an Ionian islet, had adopted
stories of a somewhat Eastern character. It has already been
noted[1] that Apollo may have had a half-Dorian origin as *Apellon*,
and a half-Hittite derivation from *Apulunas*, a Central Anatolian
deity; while his name *Lykios* refers to his worship in Lycia, a land
early affected by the Hittites. Yet by the time his worship in Delos
comes within our knowledge he is a perfectly Greek god, for he
is ancestor of the Attic nobility and of the Ionians. Zeus, the story
said, was greatly enamoured of Leto; but Hera – madly jealous –
determined to make her confinement as difficult as possible. First
Leto bore Artemis under a palm-tree at Ortygia close to Ephesus;[2]
and then, after much suffering, Apollo beside a palm-tree on the
island of Delos. The story is told in one of the oldest Homeric
Hymns, written perhaps as early as 700 B.C. – the Delian Hymn –
which is exclusively Ionian and insular in style and in sympathy,
for Delos and no other is Apollo's chosen seat.

I will remember and not be unmindful of Apollo who shoots afar. As
he goes through the house of Zeus the gods tremble before him and all
spring up from their seats when he draws near, as he bends his bright
bow. But Leto alone stays by the side of Zeus who delights in thunder;
and then she unstrings his bow, and closes his quiver, and takes his
archery from his strong shoulders in her hands and hangs them on a
golden peg against a pillar of his father's house. Then she leads him to a

[1] See p. 109. [2] But the island of Rheneia near Delos and the citadel of Syracuse
were also named Ortygia.

seat and makes him sit: and the Father gives him nectar in a golden cup
welcoming his dear son, while the other gods make him sit down there,
and queenly Leto rejoices because she bare a mighty son and an archer.
Rejoice, blessed Leto, for you bare glorious children, the lord Apollo
and Artemis who delights in arrows; her in Ortygia, and him in rocky
Delos, as you rested against the great mass of the Cynthian hill hard by
a palm-tree by the streams of Inopus.

Far roamed Leto in travail with the god who shoots afar, to see if
any land would be willing to make a dwelling for her son. But they
greatly trembled and feared, and none, not even the richest of them,
dared receive Phoibos, until queenly Leto set foot on Delos and uttered
winged words and asked the isle:

'Delos, would you be willing to be the abode of my son Apollo and
make him a rich temple? For no other will touch you, as you will find:
and I think you will never be rich in oxen and sheep, nor bear vintage
nor yet produce plants abundantly. But if you have the temple of far-
shooting Apollo, all men will bring you hecatombs and gather here,
and incessant savour of rich sacrifice will always arise, and you will
feed those who dwell in you from the hand of strangers: for truly your
own soil is not rich.'

Then the isle of Delos consented to receive the dread god, but
Leto was racked nine days and nights with pangs because Hera
was using her wiles to keep the birth-goddess away from the isle.
Yet at last Iris found her and brought her there, and

the pains of birth seized Leto, and she longed to bring forth; so she
cast her arms about a palm-tree and kneeled on the soft meadow while
the earth laughed for joy beneath. Then the child leaped forth to the
light, and all the goddesses raised a cry. Straightway, great Phoibos,
the goddesses washed you purely and cleanly with sweet water, and
swathed you in a white garment of fine texture, new-woven, and
fastened a golden band about you. . . .

And you, O lord Apollo, god of the silver bow, shooting afar, now
walked on craggy Cynthus, and now kept wandering among the
islands and the people in them. Many are your temples and wooded
groves, and all peaks and towering bluffs of lofty mountains and rivers
flowing to the sea are dear to you, Phoibos, yet in Delos do you most
delight your heart; for there the long-robed Ionians gather in your
honour with their children and gentle wives: mindful, they delight you

with boxing and dancing and song, so often as they hold their gathering. A man would say that they were deathless and unageing if he should then come upon the Ionians so met together. For he would see the graces of them all, and would be pleased in heart gazing at the men and well-girded women with their swift ships and great wealth. And there is this great wonder besides – and its renown shall never perish – the girls of Delos, handmaidens of the Far-shooter; for when they have praised Apollo first, and also Leto and Artemis who delights in arrows, they sing a strain telling of men and women of past days, and charm the tribes of men. Also they can imitate the tongues of all men and their clattering speech: each would say that he himself were singing, so close to truth is their sweet song.

And now may Apollo be favourable and Artemis; and farewell all you girls.[1]

Some four hundred years later Callimachus wrote his charming Hymn to Artemis. It was a scholarly work in imitation of the grand manner of the old Delian masterpiece; and for such an attempt it was not ill done.

Artemis we hymn – no light thing is it for singers to forget her – whose study is the bow and the shooting of hares and the spacious dance and sport upon the mountains; beginning with the time when sittiing on her father's knees – still a little maid – she spake these words to her sire: 'Give me to keep my girlhood liberty, Father, for ever: and give me to be of many names, that Phoibos may not vie with me. And give me arrows and a bow – stay, Father, I ask thee not for quiver or for mighty bow: for me the Cyclopes will straightway fashion arrows and fashion for me a well-bent bow. But give me to be the Bringer of Light and give me to gird me in a tunic with embroidered border reaching to the knee, that I may slay wild beasts. And give me sixty daughters of Oceanus for my choir – all nine years old, all maidens yet ungirdled; and give me for handmaidens twenty nymphs of Amnisus who shall tend well my buskins, and, when I shoot no more at lynx or stag, shall tend my swift hounds. And give to me all mountains; and for city, assign me any, even whatsoever thou wilt: for seldom is it that Artemis goes down to the town. On the mountains will I dwell and the cities of men I will visit only when women vexed by the sharp pangs of childbirth call me to their aid.'

So spake the child and would have touched her father's beard, but

[1] Translation by H. G. Evelyn-White.

many a hand did she reach forth in vain, that she might touch it. And
her father smiled and bowed assent. And as he caressed her, he said:
'When goddesses bear me children like this, little need I heed the wrath
of jealous Hera. Take, child, all that thou askest, heartily. Yea, and
other things therewith yet greater will thy father give thee.'

There follows a long account of how the child's wishes were fulfilled and of the places that found favour with her, until she is
brought to Ephesus.

For thee, too, the Amazons, whose mind is set on war, in Ephesus,
beside the sea established an image beneath an oak trunk, and Hippo
performed a holy rite for thee, and they themselves around the image
danced a war-dance – first in shields and in armour, and again in a
circle arraying a spacious choir.[1]

And so the hymn ends with four warnings: let none disparage
Artemis, nor let anyone vie with her in archery, neither let any
man woo the *parthenos*, nor let any person shun his part – or her
part – in the yearly dance.

Apart from the birth, childhood, and hunting stories there were
few myths about Artemis. She helped her brother to kill the giant
Tityos, who tried to rape their mother Leto, and to slay the children of Niobe because their mother vaunted her superior fecund-
ity over Leto. A giant hunter named Orion boasted that he was
about to kill all living creatures, and Artemis, as Mistress of
Animals, very properly slew him; whereupon he became the
famous constellation. Finally, there was Actæon, another keen
hunter, who came upon Artemis bathing. Offended at being seen
naked by a man, the goddess turned him into a stag, and he was
killed by his own hounds. Here was one of the most popular of all
themes for art, not only in ancient times but also in the Renaissance and for long after. The offence lay in seeing any deity naked
without her permission, and one remembers how a similar inci-
dent concerning Athene brought disaster on another youthful
hunter;[2] but only blindness, not death. A streak of cruelty was
imputed to Artemis, as it was to her brother in Greek Asiatic
legends. There was, after all, the Apollo and Marsyas story in

[1] Translation by A. W. Mair.   [2] See pp. 57f.

which the latter, beaten in a musical contest by the god, was flayed alive.

The worship of Artemis conceived as a living goddess lasted longer perhaps at Ephesus than it did elsewhere. Nevertheless, in that very city one *parthenos* was slowly eclipsed by another, and it happened in the following manner.

St John the Divine, presumed author of the *Apocalypse*, or Book of Revelation, was mistakenly identified with St John the Apostle, who received from the Cross instructions to cherish the mother of Jesus. Since the former St John is held by many scholars to have written his work at Ephesus – precisely as Christian legend maintained – one can understand that his confusion with the Apostle John led to the view that he must have brought the Virgin Mary to live there.[1] Hence her dormition and assumption were localised in the place, and when Artemis was finally annihilated the Virgin Mary took over much of her cult and kept the right of sanctuary, or of asylum, which had been so important a feature of the great shrine and sacred precinct of Artemis Ephesia.

Since the latter, by giving sanctuary, had been the especial favourite deity of outlaws and thieves, and since the Virgin Mary succeeded to all these rights and privileges, she automatically became in Ephesus, and afterwards in other places, Patroness of Thieves; and that may account for the evidence in Winchester Cathedral of her assistance to them.[2] Thus it may happen in religious belief and practice that one situation fraught with absurdity leads to another.

---

[1] On all this see especially C. Picard, *Éphèse et Claros*, pp. 709 ff. [2] See p. 64.

XI. POSEIDON

Analysis along critical and scientific lines of what is called belief-formation has at times been condemned by the devout as something hostile to ethics as well as to faith. Since they resent its application to current religion, they may regard such analysis as in itself undesirable. Yet, as beliefs take form in the minds of men, what comes to matter is the way in which they are held, for it is the *manner* of believing which determines the duration and value of belief. A survey of the different ideas and beliefs held over many centuries concerning Poseidon is certainly of great interest, and there is perhaps no other Olympian god whose arrival we can so clearly envisage and whose development we can so well observe.

Five or six thousand years ago a number of kindred peoples were living in a huge area of pasture-lands in that part of South-eastern Europe which is watered by the lower reaches of great rivers like the Danube, Dniester, Dnieper, and their tributaries. It is likely that they had remained for long self-contained, cut off from the rest of thinly-peopled Europe and Asia by mountains, by immense forests and, towards the sea, by wide belts of swamps and marsh. They had once had a common tongue, which gradually produced varied dialects, until each dialect in turn was so far altered as to become a language, which, at a certain point of maturity, began to spawn more dialects due in time themselves to become languages. The 'parent' – the common tongue – has long vanished, though its descendants are evidence that it once existed. The whole group of languages are what we call the Indo-European or Aryan group, of which the oldest known tongues are Sanskrit, Iranian, ancient Greek, Hittite, and the Latin-Celtic language blocs as well as the old Norse–Germanic tongues. Dwelling in an area of wide pasture-lands, these Aryan peoples succeeded in domesticating the wild horse of the Eurasian steppes and invented the wheel. Consequently, when ultimately they found themselves driven to migration because they were multiplying too quickly, they were able to break out of their confines and to overrun vast regions of the habitable globe at a speed far greater than had ever previously been possible to any wandering races and nations. Possessed of locomotive animals and wheeled transport, they became a wagon-dwelling culture which moved in search of pasture-lands;[1] and since they carried women, children, and chattels with them, they were enemies far more formidable than any body of brigands and pirates which the civilised Mediterranean communities had sometimes to fear. Theirs was the earliest big 'folk-wandering' for which we have historical evidence, and numerous others have occurred since, always bringing disaster to the occupants of the invaded lands, the latest example being one of the most romantic of recorded adventures, the movement of the covered wagons across the great plains of the American continent in the last century.

Co-ordination of archæological and historical evidence supplies a pattern of steady invasion and conquest by Aryan speakers of the Eastern Mediterranean and Middle Eastern lands over a period of two centuries from about 2000 to 1800 B.C. Aryan ruling castes established themselves among the Hittites of Anatolia and the Mitanni of East Syria, while cousins of the latter reached Northern India. Aryan Kassites first raided and finally conquered Babylonia, and a mass, led by a Northern chariot-owning nobility, effected the famous Hyksos conquest of Egypt. In every case the total success of the invaders was due to their tribal mobility in wagons and their battle mobility in chariots, for none of their victims had horses. Contemporary with these events was the first movement into Greece of the Greeks, for it appears that around 2000 B.C. Greek-speaking Aryan tribes, later referred to as Minyans and Ionians, came down into the peninsula, some of them presumably bringing their families. It is possible to say that they brought four things with them: wheeled vehicles, the art of producing wheel-made pottery, the horse, and their chief god – himself apt to be equine – Poseidon.

His name in its oldest known form was Poteidān, that is 'Potei Dān', and his mate (in classical times Demeter) was 'Dā Mater'.[2]

---

[1] Cf. *CAH*, I, pp. 84, 107 ff., 310 ff. [2] See p. 38 above; also Guthrie, *The Greeks and their Gods*, pp. 96 ff., for a discussion of the names.

Dān and Dā were the divine pair, and his title 'Potei' is to be interpreted as coming from some form like 'potis' or 'posis', a word
meaning 'lord, master, or husband'. So the simple Minyans referred to 'Lord Dān' and 'Mother Dā' – that much seems a reasonable deduction. Possibly they thought he was of the sky and she of
the earth, even as other divine successors of the pair were imagined. Dān was probably sometimes, somewhere, called 'sDān',
which can become 'Zān'. His Minyan worshippers, as they came
down into the Greek peninsula, left a big cousin-tribe behind to
settle among the pasture-lands in what is now Macedonia or
Thrace. These people – presently known as Achæans when they
came into Greece – worshipped what was at first the same divine
pair, Zeus and Diōne (or 'Di-Ōnē'); and it seems that after some
time no one really knew whether the name 'Zān' belonged to
the elder brother, Poseidon, or to the younger brother, King
Zeus.

Thus 'Potei-Dān', or 'Zān', if he was the sky was the producer
of thunder. And at times he was a horse – not any horse, but
'HORSE' – an untameable stallion whose hooves thunder across the
wide grass-land; one of the most dangerous of all creatures, and
great in strength. Do not we as good Aryans still use him as a
measure when we talk of 'horse-power'? And what can shake the
earth better than the wild herd of stallions, mares, and foals in a
stampede? When men have with infinite patience trained and
reined them, there may come one day the cavalry charge or the
massed onrush of battle-chariots, and once more the earth is
shaken.

In Homer, time and again, the favourite title given to Poseidon
is 'Earth-shaker', for, by way of the charging stallion and the wild
galloping herd, the divine 'Horse' had become the god that makes
earthquakes. No volcanic association existed for him, because the
early Greeks had no evidence of any link between volcanoes and
earthquakes. In general, Poseidon frequently had another title –
'Hippios', which meant 'Horsey-one'; and in art he appears beside a horse or riding on horseback, or with a little horse's head in
his hand as on an attractive bronze statuette in the British Museum (Plate XI, facing page 128). There was a story told in

several parts of Greece about Poseidon and his mate which is of signal importance as evidence for his origin.

In the heart of Bœotia there were ancient cities of Minyan origin with temples of Poseidon; and near one of these, named Haliartus, was a spring called Tilphusa, where a nymph or a goddess of Earth attracted the god's interest, and she in her fear changed herself into a mare, thinking to escape. But the god turned himself into a stallion, pursued and won her. At another place called Thelpusa, in Arcadia, the same tale was told, and there the goddess was specified; for it was Demeter who changed herself into a mare and was pursued by Poseidon in the guise of a horse. Of their union two children were born: a girl-goddess, Persephone, and a divine horse, Arion. In another Arcadian town there was a very primitive statue of Demeter with the head of a mare. Yet another legend mentions Poseidon as consort of the Gorgon Medusa, who in early art is a half-equine creature and whose name originally meant only 'bright-eyed queen', another epithet for Demeter. By Poseidon Medusa has two children, the young hero Chrysaor and the winged horse Pegasus. It is evident that the divine horses Poseidon and Demeter (or Medusa) had got down into Peloponnese with Minyan Greeks who had migrated from Bœotia; but they must have had these horse-gods long before. The observation has been made that there was close linguistic association between the early Greeks and the Sanskrit-speaking Aryans who moved into Northern India; and it is worthy of remark that the latter related the same kind of story. 'In ancient Indian mythology', as Sir James Frazer has pointed out, 'the goddess Varanyu turns herself into a mare; Vivasvat turns himself into a horse, follows her, and embraces her, and she gives birth to the two Asvins, who correspond somewhat to Castor and Pollux. . . . The Indian and Greek myths are identical, the Hindus and Greeks having inherited the myth from their common Aryan forefathers.'[1] It was in his earlier Minyan phase that Poseidon was the god of fresh-water springs, and his equine son the winged horse Pegasus was said to have produced the famous spring Peirene in Corinth with a blow of his hoof.

[1] J. G. Frazer, *Pausanias*, IV, p. 291.

With the arrival in Greece, perhaps about 1450 B.C., of the Achæan Zeus-worshippers, the second phase of Poseidon's cult began. He was recognised as the elder brother of Zeus, though the latter was ruler in Olympus, and one may observe that where grave dissension arising from a scandal within the Olympian family occurred, it was Poseidon as head of the family – not Zeus – who intervened to stop things from going too far. It will be remembered how the angry Hephaistos had made a net to ensnare Aphrodite and Ares in one another's arms,[1] and how he summoned the gods to see, and laughter fell upon them.

All but Poseidon himself; unsmiling he stood and entreaty
Made to Hephaistos the cunning to loosen the fetters of Ares.
Thus then raising his voice these swift-winged words he addressed him:
'Loose him, I pray! and I promise that whatsoever thou biddest,
All he shall pay that is held to be fair with the gods everlasting.'
'Nay but, Poseidon, Lord, Earth-shaker, thou shouldst not demand it!
Worthless is ever a pledge that is offered by one that is worthless.
How can I hold thee bound in the eyes of the blessed immortals
Should our Ares depart and escape both fetters and forfeit?'
Him then again gave answer the King Earth-shaking Poseidon:
'Nay, but Hephaistos, if ever it hap that avoiding the forfeit
Ares elude thee, I promise myself all dues to repay thee.'
Him then addressing again gave answer the famous Craftsman:
'Truly 'tis neither becoming nor possible this to refuse thee.'[2]

Obviously it is as head of the family that he is ready to pay the fine for adultery and to see the scandal averted. That episode defines his status, but the most remarkable fact is the change brought about in his cult by his becoming god of the sea. He did not abandon the care of horses, and the ancient 'horsey' families of Minyan ancestry still traced their descent from him. Earthquake was still ascribed to him; but his main concern now became the sea and all that belonged to it. When the Achæans came south they probably had little knowledge of ships, whereas the Minyans, who had been for generations in Greece, were already experienced sailors. From the earliest times, as far as we can perceive, the Greeks were accommodating in matters of religion, and no Greek

[1] See pp. 103 ff. above.   [2] After H. B. Cotterill's translation.

would ever have expressed the arrogant view that his god was the only true god and the other man's god a mere demon. His assumption would be that both gods required serious consideration and an enquiry how best to attribute to them vast and appropriate spheres of influence.

With his change of *métier* came a change of mate. On land he might still be thought of as spouse of Demeter. But an earth-mother does not readily take to ships; therefore Poseidon the sea-god wedded Amphitrite, the most important of all the Nereïds. Here, as so often, is a divine reflection of what went on in fact among the feudal nobility. The conquering stranger arrives, captures the palace, weds the daughter, and turns out the old man, or permits him to stay on in a subordinate position. Before Poseidon there had been another sea-god of the more primitive folk, having different names: Aigeus, or Triton, or – most commonly – Nereus, who had a host of lovely daughters, the sea-nymphs or Nereïds, all of whom now became companions of the new god and their own eldest sister, Amphitrite, Queen of the Sea. In the Homeric poems she has not yet attained this rank, but in those of Hesiod she has.

The trident which Poseidon regularly carried was a weapon of dual origin, for it is likely that its three-pronged head was at first a thunder-weapon, and an earthly form of the bolt of Zeus. Fitted on to a shaft it became the thing with which the earth-shaker smote the earth in order to cause earthquakes, and on the Acropolis of Athens there may be seen to this day in the bare rock beneath the north-porch floor of the Erechtheum three marks, where they said the trident smote the rock and a spring welled up close by. Yet when Poseidon became lord of the sea his trident seemed quite appropriate, because of its resemblance to a fish-spear such as men still use today in the Mediterranean. But there is this difference, that useful fish-spears have usually four, five, or more prongs, but Poseidon – the memory of his original thunder-bolt never quite lost – had always a three-pronged trident. Amphitrite and other members of this marine throng sometimes carried the trident too, and it gradually became, among Hellenistic kings and Roman emperors, a symbol of the dominion of the seas, for which reason it may still be observed upon the reverse of a British penny.

Perhaps Poseidon is among the gods whom nowadays it is not very easy to take seriously as a deity really receiving the devotion of sailors in the ancient world, yet there is a dignity and fineness in the short Homeric Hymn[1] written in his honour:

I begin to sing about Poseidon, the great god, mover of the earth and fruitless sea, god of the deep who is also lord of Helicon and wide Ægæ. A two-fold office the gods allotted you, O Shaker of the Earth, to be a tamer of horses and a saviour of ships!

Hail, Poseidon, Holder of the Earth, dark-haired lord! O blessed one, be kindly in heart and help those who voyage in ships!

In art he is generally depicted as of a well-developed athletic type, naked, very like Zeus but with more shaggy hair, suggesting a briny moisture. When the contacts with Rome became established he was identified with an Italian water-god, not of the sea, named Neptunus, who seems – perhaps because the Romans disliked and feared the sea – to become slightly ridiculous. Of all the popular symbolic figures who have come down from ancient mythology to the present day, there is only one who is something of a figure of fun: Father Neptune with his company of fish-tailed mermaids. There is a sense of magnificent incongruity in the juxtaposition of deity and fish as in Rupert Brooke's little poem *Heaven*:

> Fish (fly-replete, in depth of June,
> Dawdling away their wat'ry noon)
> Ponder deep wisdom; dark or clear,
> Each secret fishy hope or fear.
> Fish say, they have their Stream and Pond;
> But is there anything Beyond?
> This life cannot be All, they swear,
> For how unpleasant, if it were!
> One may not doubt that, somehow, Good
> Shall come of Water and of Mud;
> And, sure, the reverent eye must see
> A Purpose in Liquidity.

[1] Translation by H. G. Evelyn-White.

And the piscine deity:

> Immense, of fishy form and mind,
> Squamous, omnipotent, and kind;
> And under that Almighty Fin,
> The littlest fish may enter in.

Much of the myth about Poseidon has already been mentioned in the course of explaining his origins and development in time, but there still remain various details to record from the Homeric and later ages. His birth-story and that of his sister-wife, Demeter, can now be traced to the same grim oriental sources as the stories already recounted about Hera and Zeus,[1] for they were all children of the cannibal god Kronos, whose story is neither Greek nor Aryan, because it may trail back into some remote Mesopotamian creation-myth. The liking sometimes shown by Aryan mythology for trinitarian theology may explain the appearance in Homer of a third person, Hades, alongside the brothers Poseidon and Zeus. In the fifteenth book of the *Iliad* Poseidon, angered by a message from Zeus, makes his protest:

There are three of us Brothers, all Sons of Kronos and Rhea: Zeus, myself, and Hades the King of the Dead. Each of us was given his own domain when the world was divided into three parts. We cast lots and I received the grey sea as my inalienable realm. Hades drew the nether dark, while Zeus was allotted the broad sky and a home among the clouds in upper air. But the earth was left common to all of us, and high Olympus too. So I am not going to let Zeus have his way with me. Powerful as he is, let him stay quietly in his own third of the world.[2]

Within the grey sea, his inalienable realm, Poseidon had his own strange submarine palace described in the beginning of the thirteenth book of the *Iliad*:

Now up got Poseidon and came swinging down the rocky slope. The high hills and the forest lands trembled under the deathless feet of the descending god. He made three strides and with the fourth reached Ægæ, his goal, where his famous palace built of gleaming gold stands deep in the lagoon and will stand for ever. There he harnessed to his chariot his two swift horses, who had brazen hooves and flowing golden manes. He clothed himself in gold, picked up his well-made golden

[1] See pp. 31f., 50.   [2] Translation by E. V. Rieu.

whip, mounted his chariot and drove out across the waves. The monsters of the sea did not fail to recognise their King. On every side they issued from their caves and gambolled at his coming. The sea itself made way for him in its delight, so that his bounding horses flew along, and the bronze axle of his chariot remained dry below as they carried him towards the Achæan fleet.

Midway between Tenedos and rugged Imbros there is a large cavern, down in a deep sea-pool. Here Poseidon the Earth-shaker unyoked and left his horses, after throwing down some ambrosial fodder beside them and tying their legs with golden hobbles they could neither break nor shake off, to make sure of their staying there till their Master's return.[1]

The reason for his hostility to Troy was the fact that he had helped long ago to build the city's walls for an ancient king, Laomedon, who, having promised a fixed reward, cheated by refusing it once the walls were built, not knowing that his hireling was a god in disguise.

As a gallant god Poseidon fell short of the achievements of his brother Zeus, but was nevertheless philoprogenitive. The nymphs and mortal girls with whom he had love affairs included Tyro, Thoosa, Medusa, Scylla, and Aithra, of whom the third has already been mentioned above, while the last was mother of Theseus, greatest of all Attic heroes, only second in place to Herakles himself. The story told about Scylla is of interest, because Amphitrite, as wife of Poseidon, played a part such as might have been played by Hera, mate of Zeus. The sea-god's wife, made aware that her husband was consorting with the lovely nymph Scylla, was so filled with jealousy that she cast magical herbs into the well wherein her rival was accustomed to bathe. The painful effect of this sorcery was to transmute the girl into a monster with a fishy tail and bitches' bodies springing from her hips.

Among Poseidon's children were Minyas and, by Tyro, the twins Pelias and Neleus, as well as Theseus, the Horses, and Chrysaor and Persephone to whom reference has already been made. To this list of children one must add the cannibal giant

[1] Translation by E. V. Rieu.

Polyphemus, whom Odysseus blinded and thus incurred from Poseidon hostility which cost him dear. We should expect that one group of mythical creatures in particular would have been descended from Poseidon: the Centaurs. Their popularity in art and legend has made their mythology very confused, for the tales of their parentage are as contradictory as they are complicated. Yet according to one story these creatures, half-human and half-equine, were by Zeus (metamorphosed into a horse, and that means Poseidon) out of Dia (a variant, perhaps, of 'Mother Dā').

This strange god, so varied in his functions, was worshipped in many Greek lands. In Attica he was very important. He had competed against Athene for possession of the Acropolis and had lost; but a brilliant, venturesome, and maritime people like the Athenians paid him especial honour. On the island of Poros, off the north-east coast of Peloponnesus, there was his Kalaurian sanctuary, centre of an ancient maritime league; at Corinth the quadrennial Isthmian Games were held in his honour; and among the Western Greeks of Italy he was a deity of distinction at both Poseidonia (Pæstum) and Tarentum.

Though Poseidon-worship never developed into an ethically austere and monotheistic cult, as that of Zeus did, he remained to the Greeks an awe-inspiring but well-loved deity – a conception not altogether easy for us to apprehend. Foolish, bleary old 'Father Neptune' has for us contaminated the thought of divinity in Poseidon of the dark-blue hair, earth-shaking god of the sea. But Poseidon the HORSE! Every horseman, every lover of horseflesh, knows what it is to feel a good mount between the knees when rider and animal have become a single centaur-like unit raised up in power and authority over mere two-legged men, and when the physical contact between man and beast gives rise to a confidence that sometimes verges on love. Every horseman knows well that in the 'man-horse' relationship there can even be something numinous, and he will – unless blinded by prejudice – put up a prayer sometimes to Poseidon Hippios.

XII. DEMETER

PEOPLE of the great pasture-lands of South-eastern Europe, the speakers of Aryan tongues who began to wander south and eastward about 2000 B.C., with their wagons and horses, were not unacquainted with agriculture. The group known as Minyans had a pair of supreme deities, 'Lord Dān' and 'Mother Dā', as we have already observed in the preceding chapter. He was perhaps originally of the sky, she of the earth-grown corn. Both could become horses; and while he became the 'Earth-shaker' she became the 'Corn-mother'. Today in Central Europe there are peasants who will say, when the wind sweeps over wheat or rye, that the 'horses are in the corn'. The time came when he – 'Potei-Dān' – went to sea, became Poseidon, and took another wife, Amphitrite, child of Nereus, the Old Man of the Sea. Meanwhile 'Dā Mater', whose cult was spread widely in Greek lands, rose to special importance in one particular place – Eleusis, in Attica. Here, however, her worship was imposed upon and merged with a much older cult of the primæval mother-goddess of the pre-Hellenic peoples whose manner of life was founded on matriarchy and polyandry. The story of Hera as one aspect of the goddess has already been told;[1] Damater, or Demeter as the Athenians called her, was really the identical Great Goddess in another form but free from any such association of marriage as was so important a part of the dogma concerning Hera.

She was many times a mother; first among her children by Poseidon were the foals Arion and Pegasus, and a girl identified with Persephone; yet Hesiod said that the last was her child by Zeus. Furthermore, she was the mother of Ploutos, the god of wealth, according to a strange Homeric tale.[2]

Also with Iasion when the fair-tressed goddess Demeter,
Yielding herself to desire, was united in tender embracements,
While in a thrice-ploughed fallow they lay, right quickly perceived it
Zeus; and he cast with blinding bolt of his thunder and slew him.

[1] See pp. 31ff.   [2] *Odyssey*, Book V, pp. 125 ff., translation by Cotterill.

Ploutos is the wealth of corn in the grain still hidden under-ground, as well as wealth in a buried hoard of gold. It was his 'undergroundness' that caused him to be identified with Pluto, a name for Hades, King of the Underworld, who in the myth was to become son-in-law of Demeter when he wedded Persephone.

For Demeter it is obvious that there was no clear answer con-cerning her husband, and for any mortal like Iasion to consort with a goddess was exceeding dangerous.[1] The important thing for mother-goddesses is that they should be fertile, not that they should be wives.

The primæval mother-goddess and the Minyan corn-goddess were merged into one at Eleusis, where at the same time her daughter Persephone attained to a high divine status. The girl was in reality something like a double of her mother, and they were thought of as permanently together except during those sad months of solitude when the mother was alone. The story, incor-porated as a myth in the Homeric Hymn to Demeter, is most brilliantly told and deserves ample quotation, but with a few pre-liminary notes on some unexpected names and labels. Hades, brother of Poseidon and Zeus, was Lord of the Underworld, and was known by various names like Aïdoneus and Pluto, or by titles such as seek to avoid direct allusion to the dead, like 'Host of Many', 'Many-named', 'Ruler of Many', while Demeter herself is sometimes called 'Dēo' – an Attic form of 'Dāo' and a variant of 'Dā'. When Hades first saw Persephone he desired her for mate and queen and, with the consent of Zeus, planned to capture her.

She was playing with the deep-bosomed daughters of Okeanos and gathering flowers over a soft meadow, roses and crocuses and beautiful violets, irises also and hyacinths and the narcissus, which Earth made to grow at the will of Zeus and to please the Host of Many, to be a snare for the bloom-like girl – a marvellous, radiant flower. It was a thing of awe whether for deathless gods or mortal men to see: from its root grew a hundred blooms and it smelled most sweetly, so that all wide heaven above and the whole earth and the sea's salt swell laughed for joy. And the girl was amazed and reached out with both hands to take the lovely toy; but the wide-pathed earth yawned there in the plain of

[1] Compare Aphrodite and Anchises, pp. 87ff., above.

Nysa, and the lord, Host of Many, with his immortal horses sprang out upon her – the Son of Kronos, He who has many names.

He caught her up reluctant on his golden car and bare her away lamenting. Then she cried out shrilly with her voice, calling upon her father, the Son of Kronos, who is most high and excellent. But no one either of the deathless gods or of mortal men heard her voice.

Then bitter pain seized the heart of Demeter, who wandered over the earth seeking her lost child, and at last she found Helios, the sun god, who answered her enquiry:

'Queen Demeter, daughter of rich-haired Rhea, I will tell you the truth; for I greatly reverence and pity you in your grief for your trim-ankled daughter. None other of the deathless gods is to blame, but only cloud-gathering Zeus who gave her to Hades, her father's brother, to be called his buxom wife. And Hades seized her and took her loudly crying in his chariot down to his realm of mist and gloom. . . .'

But grief yet more terrible and savage came into the heart of Demeter, and thereafter she was so angered with the dark-clouded Son of Kronos that she avoided the gathering of the gods and high Olympus, and went to the towns and rich fields of men, disfiguring her form a long while. And no one of men or deep-bosomed women knew her when they saw her, until she came to the house of wise Keleos who then was lord of fragrant Eleusis. Vexed in her dear heart, she sat near the wayside by the Maiden Well, from which the women of the place were used to draw water, in a shady place over which grew an olive shrub. And she was like an ancient woman who is cut off from childbearing and the gifts of garland-loving Aphrodite, like the nurses of king's children who deal justice, or like the house-keepers in their echoing halls. There the daughters of Keleos, son of Eleusis, saw her, as they were coming for easy-drawn water, to carry it in pitchers of bronze to their dear father's house: four were they and like goddesses in the flower of their girlhood. . . . They knew her not – for the gods are not easily discerned by mortals – but standing near her spoke winged words.

'Old mother, whence and who are you of folk born long ago? Why are you gone away from the city and do not draw near the houses? For there in the shady halls are women of just such age as you, and others younger; and they would welcome you both by word and deed.'

Thus they said. And she, that queen among goddesses, answered them saying: 'Hail, dear children, whosoever you are of womankind. I will tell you my story; for it is not unseemly that I should tell you truly what you ask. Doso is my name, for my stately mother gave it me. And now I am come from Crete over the sea's wide back – not willingly; but pirates brought me thence by force of strength against my liking.'

Presently the girls left her to run home and get permission to bring her to the house of their father Keleos and led her through the portico to where their

queenly mother sat by a pillar of the close-fitted roof, holding her son, a tender scion, in her bosom. And the girls ran to her. But the goddess walked to the threshold: and her head reached the roof and she filled the doorway with a heavenly radiance. Then awe and reverence and pale fear took hold of Metaneira, and she rose up from her couch before Demeter, and bade her be seated. But Demeter, bringer of seasons and giver of perfect gifts, would not sit upon the couch, but stayed silent with lovely eyes cast down until careful Iambe placed a jointed seat for her and threw over it a silvery fleece. Then she sat down and held her veil in her hands before her face. A long time she sat upon the stool without speaking because of her sorrow, and greeted no one by word or by sign, but rested, never smiling, and tasting neither food nor drink, because she pined with longing for her deep-bosomed daughter, until careful Iambe – who pleased her moods in aftertime also – moved the Holy Lady with many a quip and jest to smile and laugh and cheer her heart. Then Metaneira filled a cup with sweet wine and offered it to her; but she refused it, for she said it was not lawful for her to drink red wine, but bade them mix meal and water with soft mint and give her to drink. And Metaneira mixed the draught and gave it to the goddess as she bade. So the great queen Deo received it to observe the sacrament.

This mint-julep made of sacred barley-water and mint was taken as an act of communion and was one of the most important pieces of ritual in the Eleusinian mysteries commemorating the sorrows of the 'Mater Dolorosa'. After this Metaneira, wife of Keleos, asked the stranger-woman to become nurse to her youngest infant Demophoön.

And the child grew like some immortal being, not fed with food nor nourished at the breast: for by day rich-crowned Demeter would anoint him with ambrosia as if he were the offspring of a god and breathe sweetly upon him as she held him in her bosom. But at night she would hide him like a brand in the heart of the fire, unknown to his dear parents. And it wrought great wonder in these that he grew beyond his age; for he was like the gods face to face. And she would have made him deathless and unageing had not well-girded Metaneira in her heedlessness kept watch by night from her sweet-smelling chamber and spied. But she wailed and smote her two hips, because she feared for her son and was greatly distraught in her heart; so she lamented and uttered winged words:

'Demophoön, my son, the strange woman buries you deep in fire and works grief and bitter sorrow for me.'

Thus she spoke, mourning. And the bright goddess, lovely-crowned Demeter, heard her, and was wroth with her. So with her divine hands she snatched from the fire the dear son whom Metaneira had borne unhoped-for in the palace, and cast him from her to the ground; for she was terribly angry in her heart. Forthwith she said to well-girded Metaneira:

'Witless are you mortals and dull to foresee your lot, whether of good or evil, that comes upon you. For now in your heedlessness you have wrought folly past healing; for – be witness the oath of the gods, the relentless water of Styx – I would have made your dear son deathless and unageing all his days and would have bestowed on him everlasting honour, but now he can in no way escape death and the fates. Yet shall unfailing honour always rest upon him, because he lay upon my knees and slept in my arms. But as the years move round and when he is in his prime, the sons of the Eleusinians shall ever wage war and dread strife with one another continually. Lo! I am that Demeter who has share of honour and is the greatest help and cause of joy to the undying gods and mortal men. But now, let all the people build me a great temple and an altar below it and beneath the city and its sheer wall upon a rising hillock above Kallichoros. And I myself will teach my rites, that hereafter you may reverently perform them and so win the favour of my heart.'

When she had so said, the goddess changed her stature and her looks, thrusting old age away from her: beauty spread round about her and a lovely fragrance was wafted from her sweet-smelling robes, and from the divine body of the goddess a light shone afar, while golden tresses spread down over her shoulders, so that the strong house was filled with brightness as well as with lightning. And so she went out from the palace.

The people of Eleusis built the goddess a temple and raised an altar; but still Demeter grieved for her lost daughter.

Then she caused a most dreadful and cruel year for mankind over the all-nourishing earth: the ground would not make the seed sprout, for rich-crowned Demeter kept it hid. In the fields the oxen drew many a curved plough in vain, and much white barley was cast upon the land without avail. So she would have destroyed the whole race of man with cruel famine and have robbed them who dwell on Olympus of their glorious right of gifts and sacrifices had not Zeus perceived and marked all this in his heart.

At last Zeus perceived that the only solution was to send Hermes down to the underworld with a command to bring Persephone up to earth again so that mother and daughter might be united once more in joy.

And all-seeing Zeus sent a messenger to them, rich-haired Rhea, to bring dark-cloaked Demeter to join the families of the gods: and he promised to give her what rights she should choose among the deathless gods and agreed that her daughter should go down for the third part of the circling year to darkness and gloom, but for the two parts should live with her mother and the other deathless gods. Thus he commanded. And the goddess rushed down from the peaks of Olympus and came to the plain of Rharos, rich, fertile, corn-land once, but then in nowise fruitful, for it lay idle and utterly leafless, because the white grain was hidden by design of trim-ankled Demeter. But afterwards, as spring-time waxed, it was soon to be waving with long ears of corn, and its rich furrows to be loaded with grain upon the ground, while others would already be bound in sheaves. There first she landed from the fruitless upper air: and glad were the goddesses to see each other and cheered in heart.

So Rhea besought her to increase once more the fruits of the earth.

And rich-crowned Demeter did not refuse but straightway made fruit to spring up from the rich lands, so that the whole wide earth was laden with leaves and flowers. Then she went and to the kings who deal

justice, Triptolemos and Diokles, the horse-driver, and to doughty
Eumolpos and Keleos, leader of the people, she showed the conduct of
her rites and taught them all her mysteries, to Triptolemos and Polyx-
einos and Diokles also – awful mysteries which no one may in any
way transgress or pry into or utter, for deep awe of the gods checks the
voice. Happy is he among men upon earth who has seen these mysteries; but he who is uninitiate and who has no part in them, never has
lot of like good things once he is dead, down in the darkness and gloom.

But when the bright goddesses had taught them all, they went to
Olympus to the gathering of the other gods. And there they dwell
beside Zeus who delights in thunder, awful and reverend goddesses.
Right blessed is he among men on earth whom they freely love: soon
they do send Ploutos as guest to his great house, Ploutos who gives
wealth to mortal men.[1]

In this great poem of the seventh century B.C., Persephone, or
– as she is often called – Korē, the Girl, stands for the life of the
crops, which for a third of the year when the fields are empty rest
beneath the earth. It was the Greek custom to store the ripe grain
for next year's sowing in large jars in underground chambers – a
kind of refrigeration. For the four months while this was hap-
pening Persephone dwelt beneath with Hades her husband.

Eleusis, which is about twelve miles by road from Athens, was
incorporated in the Attic state probably between 625 and 600 B.C.
Its cult and mysteries were thus taken over by a comparatively
large state rapidly rising in importance; and when by the fifth
century B.C. the culture of Athens began to dominate the whole
of Greece it came to pass that everything which Demeter in
Eleusis could give became as pan-Hellenic in value as that which
Zeus could give at Olympia and Apollo at Delphi or Delos. In
fact, the Eleusinian Mysteries soon became an Athenian affair
made to serve the glory of the city and the ends of Athenian
nationalism; for by the fifth century Athens claimed that the gods
had revealed to the people of Attica alone their two greatest gifts.
The first of these was agriculture, which made possible on earth a
civilised and happy life; the second was the assurance of a better
life after death. It was a token of their generous philanthropy,
said the Athenians, that they passed on to the rest of mankind these

[1] Translation by H. G. Evelyn-White.

precious revelations. Such claims as these were not diminished by time, for they were clearly set out in the fourth century B.C. by Isocrates, the most famous orator of his day; and even in 117 B.C. an inscription was set up in Delphi[1] in honour of the Athenian people who, it is declared,

converted men from the life of beasts to civilisation, and contributed to their mutual association by being first to impart the mysteries, and by their means proclaiming to all that the greatest good among men is mutual commerce and good faith. Athens imparted also what the gods have given concerning human laws and education; and likewise the gift of the fruits of the earth, though she had received it for herself alone, yet she granted the use of it to be common to all the Greeks.

It is an important point that initiation into the mysteries was open to every Greek, male or female, bond or free; and many a slave became a *mystes* with the promise of happiness after death. If a *barbaros* could not enter in, this was due to no racial barrier, but only to his inability to speak and understand Greek, for he could not have comprehended the terrifying oath of secrecy imposed on every candidate who came through to the end of initiation at the final rite of 'the Beholding'. Responses must be made and the oath taken in language 'understanded of the people'.

Indeed, plenty of distinguished people, Roman senators, governors and emperors, Oriental potentates and their subjects, were in later years accepted for initiation; but it was an absolute requisite that they spoke Greek, and were thus no longer *barbaroi*.

The Eleusinian Festival, and the celebrated procession which led up to it, most probably received its full official form in the reign of the great Peisistratus during the second half of the sixth century B.C. Its institution was perhaps nearly contemporary with the installation in Athens of the cult of Dionysos, which is to be considered in the next chapter. Certain Holy Things belonging to Demeter and to the Saviour Girl – as Persephone was often called – were deposited for a time in their joint shrine near the Acropolis in Athens; and at the right moment were carried with pomp and ceremony in the famous procession along the twelve-mile sacred way from Athens to Eleusis. The Dionysiac cult, with its emo-

[1] Quoted by Guthrie, *The Greeks and their Gods*, p. 287.

tional, orgiastic, and intensely mystical nature, had a kinship with the mystic emotions raised by the Mysteries of Demeter. He, the god of wine and milk and honey, and she, the goddess of corn and vegetables and fruit, had in common given blessings past estimation to mankind. And so it was thought that the god himself accompanied the votaries on the joyous journey along the sacred way. He was hailed not by his usual name of Bacchos, but by a variant title, 'Iacchos', and the cry of 'Iacche, Iacche' rose from the torchlight procession that wended its way through the lovely groves and flowered meadows which bordered the track that ran from Athens out by the Dipylon Gate, up through the rustic groves of Daphne, down to the Salaminian sea, in which all the neophytes, participants, and initiates bathed in the silver dawn, before the cheerful throng moved on to the great sanctuary at Eleusis.

Much of the ceremonial there was common knowledge, but the content of the final rite, 'the Beholding', will probably never be revealed. That celebrated renegade, Clement of Alexandria, who had once been himself an initiate at Eleusis, pretended in his *Exhortation to the Greeks* to betray the secret of the last act. Yet it is likely that he did nothing of the kind and merely substituted a cheap little piece of pornography for the ultimate vision. For the violence of his attack on paganism is significant of his secret belief therein, and so timid a creature as Clement could never have brought himself to break a terrible oath. For us it must suffice to recognise that every initiate into the Eleusinian Mysteries was a happy human being, confident in the assurance of a better life after death – of a place in Heaven.

Now, man is always interesting when busy designing his Heaven, because from his ideal structure for an after-life we can learn about that from which he most wants to escape. The secluded prophet or impecunious eremite longing for the glamour of the capital supplied his revelation of the divine city from the stock-in-trade of a grandiose jeweller's shop bursting with wealth; and the same vision had its ready appeal to many a mediæval mind vowed to a dingy life of poverty. Wandering barbarians of the bitter North, who never knew when the next meal could be thieved, nor whence, conceived a Valhalla in which their un-fathomed stomachs could absorb unmeasured food and drink. Sand-whipped and sex-starved Bedouin could find no comfort save in the thought of an all-potent after-life lived in a divine *seraglio* staffed by delectable *houris*. By contrast, the industrial revolution, engendering its slums for workers and clammy lodgings for poor students, produced a herd mentality whose greatest fear was solitude. The design for Heaven born of this social group conceives mankind shoaling herring-like at Blackpool or Coney Island, and living in boxed, hygienic tenements as indistinguishable as one sardine-tin from another, since there is no truer security than the inside of an unopened can. Here is that childish concept, the classless society, to which Marx hoped humanity might aspire.

If these are all escapes from the pressing realities, one may ask from what did the Greeks seek refuge? And the answer seems to be from the town, the *polis*, and those *political* things that go with it. No ancient town or city was really attractive. Fifth-century Athens, like 'Turkish' and like mediæval Athens, was a city of mean, narrow, dust-encumbered streets and dark little dwellings. In the midst was a great *agora* – a market wide and dignified – while over all towered the mighty, glittering, white temples of the gods cut out against a cobalt sky. 'The Athenian', as Théophile Gautier remarked, 'kept his body in a hovel and his soul on the Acropolis.' Aristotle defined man as a political animal, but such a one can find escape and happiness only in becoming a rural animal; and that is what every Greek most wished to be. He loved above all the glory of his countryside, his mountains and glens, his 'wine-dark' sea and icy silver fountains. And every traveller soon surfeited with Athens today, every modern man to whom fortune has given the supreme happiness to roam through the flowered landscape of Greece in springtime, will share that love and comprehend the longing for the asphodel meadows of Elysium and carpets of crocus, daffodil, iris, anemone, and thyme. Such was the meadow in which Persephone wandered when Hades, 'the Host of Many', swept her away; and the Athenian notion of Heaven as just such a place was exquisitely pictured by Aristophanes.

In 405 B.C. he produced one of his most famous comedies, *The Frogs*. Himself an initiate in the Eleusinian Mysteries, he gave to the play a chorus of initiates in that part where the scene is laid in Hades, to which Dionysos had gone down to bring back to earth a true poet; and this chorus describes for us what an Athenian *mystes* hoped the after-life held for him.

Here in thy home we await thy tread,
O come, Iacchos of high renown.
Dance o'er this meadow, shake on thy head
The berries that cluster thy myrtle crown.
And lead with the beat of thy tireless feet
The holy bands in the mystic rite,
The dance of wantonness and delight,
Where the Graces find their chiefest pleasure,
Thy hallowed worshippers' sacred measure.

Wake. For the blazing torch he wields,
Daystar of our nightlong festival.
He comes, Iacchos, ablaze are the fields;
See how the old man hears his call,
And all the tears and the long, long years,
As he moves his limbs, fall away and are gone.
Blest god, with thy fiery lamp, lead on
To the flowery marshy floor advancing,
Lead on the youths in the sacred dancing.

Onward! See ye nobly raise
High the Saviour Maiden's praise.

Queen of sacred ritual,
Save the choirs that praise thee;
Stand Demeter by us all,
Grant that safely all the day
I may dance and I may play.

Come hither, come hither, Iacchos renowned,
Who the loveliest tune for thy revels hast found,
To the home of the goddess come follow thy throng,
And show that untired, be it never so long,
Thou canst travel the road at the worshippers' side.
Thou lover of dances, O be thou my guide.

Yes, just now, when my eye to the side took a glance,
A sweet pretty girl I observed in the dance,
In her dear little tunic I noticed a tear
And the tip of her breast was just peeping out there
As this charming companion danced on by my side.
Thou lover of dances, O be thou my guide.

On to the fields of roses
The flowery meadow lands,
E'en as our will disposes
This loveliest of bands.
Beside us go the Muses blest
Uniting us in song and jest.

The sun to us is giving
Alone his gladsome ray,
For holy was our living,
And we have learnt the Way;
Did citizen or stranger call,
We had a welcome for them all.[1]

Aristophanes and countless Athenians and many other Greeks believed the next life held such existence in store, and it may be conceded that of the imagined Heavens we have enumerated, the Greek Elysium and the Moslem paradise are in better taste than the rest.

Demeter, of all the ancient deities, lived on longest in the hearts of the country-folk of Greece, for at the beginning of the last century an ancient statue in Eleusis was still venerated under the name of 'St Demetra' – a saint unknown to the Calendar – and was presented with garlands of flowers to secure good harvests. In the Fitzwilliam Museum at Cambridge is the upper half of a colossal statue of a girl basket-bearer made of Pentelic marble in the first century B.C. It was found at Eleusis in 1801 by E. D. Clarke and J. M. Cripps

on the side of the road, immediately before entering the village, and in the midst of a heap of dung, buried as high as the neck, a little beyond

[1] Translation by D. W. Lucas and F. J. A. Cruso.

the farther extremity of the pavement of the *Temple*. Yet even this de-grading situation had not been assigned to it wholly independent of its ancient history. The inhabitants of the small village which is now situate among the ruins of Eleusis, still regarded this Statue with a very high degree of superstitious veneration. They attributed to its presence the fertility of their land; and it was for this reason that they heaped around it the manure intended for their fields. They believed that the loss of it would be followed by no less calamity than the failure of their annual harvests; and they pointed to the *ears of bearded wheat*, among the sculptured ornaments, upon the head of the figure, as a never-failing indication of the produce of the soil. The Eleusinians, whose superstitions respecting it were so great that Dr Chandler paid a large sum for permission to dig near it, related that as often as foreigners came to remove the statue, some disaster ensued. They believed that the arm of any person who offered to touch it with violence would drop off; and said that once being taken from her station by the French, she returned back in the night to her former situation.[1]

On the evening preceding the removal of the statue an ox, loosed from its yoke, butted with its horns against the marble and then ran off, bellowing, into the plain of Eleusis. This roused all the terrors of the peasantry, whose scruples were not removed till the priest of Eleusis arrayed in his vestments struck the first blow with a pickaxe. Even then the people maintained that no ship would ever get safely to port with the statue on board. Curiously enough, the *Princessa*, a merchantman conveying it home from Smyrna, was wrecked and lost near Beachy Head, though the statue itself was recovered.[2]

Wherever in the Greek Mediterranean world there existed a few square miles of rich soil fitted for the growing of barley or wheat, there one would find the worship of Demeter and Perse-phone, for mother and daughter naturally co-existed. Their cult was of importance at Syracuse, and especially at Metapontum, in South Italy, perhaps the richest in corn of any Greek colony. In Asia Minor various states honoured Demeter, among them a

[1] E. D. Clarke, *Travels in various countries of Europe, Asia and Africa* (London), 1818, vi, 601: and the same, *Greek Marbles brought from the Shores of Euxine, Archipelago and Mediterranean* (Cambridge), 1809, pp. 32 ff.
[2] See Cook, *Zeus*, I, p. 173.

Carian city where her most famous surviving statue was discovered – the celebrated Demeter of Cnidus of about 330 B.C.[1] This has been called 'probably the finest single statue in the British Museum' (Plate VIII, facing page 81), an appraisal which some might consider a little rash. The goddess is seated swathed in a large cloak which discloses little of her matronly body; only head and forearms are uncovered, and these are of marble, while the rest is of a roughish stone. Contrasted materials can be very effective, as they are here; and one imagines that the famous Athenian sculptor Leochares, who carved the head, was a fervent believer in the goddess and surely an initiate, for no more emotional, no better figure of a 'Mater Dolorosa', mourning for a child that shall achieve resurrection, has been made since mankind took to statuary.

[1] Bernard Ashmole, 'Demeter of Cnidus', in *JHS*, 1951, pp. 13 ff.

WHEN Homer wrote, rather earlier than 700 B.C., there were twelve Olympian gods, and Dionysos was *not* of their number. Homer – bard of an ancient and magnificently feudal aristocracy – knew about the god and that he came from foreign parts, but did not attach much importance to a deity, even though reputedly Zeus-begotten, who was then a god of the lesser classes. At some time in the eighth century B.C. wandering bands, ecstatic devotees of this strange god, had moved from regions bordering upon both sides of Hellespont (now the Dardanelles) into Greece. The natives of those regions were called Thracians in Europe and Phrygians in Asia, but were one in kin and language, the tongue being related to Greek and easily learnt. There is some evidence that this cult was also brought by sea, since a Homeric hymn of the seventh century B.C. tells how Tyrsenian pirates – men of Lemnos off the coast of Thrace – were the unwilling means of bringing the god to Greece.

I will tell of Dionysos, the son of glorious Semele, how he appeared on a jutting headland by the shore of the fruitless sea, seeming like a stripling in the first flush of manhood: his rich, dark hair was waving about him, and on his strong shoulders he wore a purple robe. Presently there came swiftly over the sparkling sea Tyrsenian pirates on a·well-decked ship – a miserable doom led them on. When they saw him they made signs to one another and sprang out quickly and seizing him straightway put him on board their ship exultingly; for they thought him the son of heaven-nurtured kings. They sought to bind him with rude bonds, but the bonds would not hold him, and the withes fell far away from his hands and feet: and he sat with a smile in his dark eyes. Then the helmsman understood all and cried out at once to his fellows and said:

'Madmen! what god is this whom you have taken and bind, strong that he is? Not even the well-built ship can carry him. Surely this is either Zeus or Apollo who has the silver bow, or Poseidon, for he looks not like mortal men but like the gods who dwell on Olympus. Come, then, let us set him free upon the dark shore at once: do not lay hands on him, lest he grow angry, and stir up dangerous winds and heavy squalls.'

So said he: but the master chid him with taunting words: 'Madman, mark the wind and help us hoist sail on the ship: catch all the sheets. As for this fellow we men will see to him: I reckon he is bound for Egypt or for Cyprus or to the Hyperboreans or further still. But in the end he will speak out and tell us his friends and all his wealth and his brothers, now that providence has thrown him in our way.'

When he had said this, he had mast and sail hoisted on the ship, and the wind filled the sail and the crew hauled taut the sheets on either side. But soon strange things were seen among them. First of all sweet, fragrant wine ran streaming throughout all the black ship and a heavenly smell arose, so that all the seamen were seized with amazement when they saw it. And all at once a vine spread out both ways along the top of the sail with many clusters hanging down from it, and a dark ivy-plant twined about the mast, blossoming with flowers, and with rich berries growing on it; and all the thole-pins were covered with garlands. When the pirates saw all this, then at last they bade the helmsman to put the ship to land. But the god changed into a dreadful lion there on the ship, in the bows, and roared loudly: amidships also he showed his wonders and created a shaggy bear which stood up ravening, while on the forepeak was the lion glaring fiercely with scowling brows. And so the sailors fled into the stern and crowded bemused about the right-minded helmsman, until suddenly the lion sprang upon the master and seized him; and when the sailors saw it they leapt out overboard one and all into the bright sea, escaping from a miserable fate, and were changed into dolphins. But on the helmsman Dionysos had mercy and held him back and made him altogether happy, saying to him: 'Take courage, good friend; you have found favour with my heart. I am Boisterous Dionysos whom Cadmus' daughter Semele bare of union with Zeus.'[1]

The evidence that Dionysos' worship was brought down by wandering devotees through Macedon and Thessaly to Bœotia, Delphi, Athens, and beyond is based, however, on a very sound tradition. Now the cult which these wandering Thracian bands of men and women brought into Greece was utterly different from the quiet 'gentlemanly' cults of the old nobles who worshipped Zeus and the Olympian Family. First and foremost, the worship of Dionysos was intensely mystical, and therefore fraught with possibilities of benefit or of injury to mankind. So long as

[1] Translation by H. G. Evelyn White.

any part of humanity continues to believe in divinity, to investigate the meaning of deity, and to seek relation with the divine, there is bound to be mysticism, that indefinable thing which can lead men and women into unhealthy, dank, and masochistic actions, or which can involve men and women in the rush and *ecstasis* of union with nature and creation. The Greeks were very fortunate, since mysticism learnt through Dionysos was not comprehended by way of abnegation and mortification of the flesh, but by way of oblivion and abandonment to the body's clean desires. But in both forms mystical excess may bring disaster, and it seems likely that in the sixth century B.C. Dionysiac *orgia* bid fair to injure humanity as much as did monastic asceticism in the fifth century of our era.

A picture of what occurred in Greece is painted in a great drama – some think the greatest of all the plays which Euripides wrote – *The Bacchæ*. The chief characters are given names out of the old mythologies, but the theme, the action, the thoughts, words, and wild movements of the chorus of Bacchic women are all things of the poet's own day, of the fifth century B.C. Dionysos, the central figure – at times called Bromios, 'the Boisterous' – is also Bacchos, for that is another name for him. But each ecstatic, old man and young, each girl and woman, in that throng of his followers is also Bacchos; for this is the heart of the mystery, that when you have given yourself over to this 'madness', you are of the god, and the god is of you. He in you drives you to the woods and mountains; you containing the god perform acts that no normal mortal can do. But you are not alone the god, because the other members of the throng are also the god, for the men are Bacchoi and the women Bacchai. 'Mad ones', Mænads, is another name for the women; but in both Athens and Delphi they were called Thyiads, of whom more must presently be related. All this is remotely strange to us, but was utterly real in those days, and the chorus in Euripides' play expressed the mystic emotion that was known to thousands of women and girls in ancient Greece. They enter clad in fawn-skins over disordered robes and holding each in her hand a *thyrsos*, a long wand tipped with a bunch of leaves, ivy, or vine.

Who is abroad, who is abroad? Who is within? Let him withdraw, let each man keep his lips hallowed in silence; for I am about to sing to Dionysos the hymns that were ever customary.

Blessed is he who, having the good fortune to know the secret mysteries of the gods, consecrates his life and hath his soul filled with the spirit of Bacchos in the holy purification of his mountain revels; who brandishing the thyrsos aloft, his head crowned with ivy, serves Dionysos. On, on, ye Bacchai, ye who bring Bromios, the god born of a god, Dionysos, home from the Phrygian hills to the spacious cities of Greece, who bring Bromios. . . .

Soon shall the whole land go forth to dance as often as Bromios leads his revellers to the mountains, to the mountains; where abides that host of women driven out in madness by Dionysos from beside their looms and shuttles. . . .

Sweet upon the mountains is he who falls to the ground from among the hurrying bands of Bacchantes, clad in his holy garment of fawn-skin, as he pursues the blood of the slain goat. . . . The land is flowing with milk, flowing with wine, flowing with nectar of the bees, and there is a fragrance as of Syrian incense. And the Bacchant with a flaming torch of pinewood fixed to his wand brandishes it as he runs, rousing the straying bands and making them leap up with his cries as he shakes his delicate locks in the wind. And amid the cries of 'Evoe' he shouts, 'On, ye Bacchai, on, ye Bacchai, hymn Dionysos to the sound of the booming drums, honouring with happy shouts the happy god, with Phrygian cries and clamour, when the sacred melodious pipe sings with sacred sportive music and to its tune ye hurry to the mountains, to the mountains.' And the Bacchanal bounds with nimble feet, happy as a foal with its mother at pasture.[1]

These women, because they are Bacchai, carry the *thyrsos*, since it is the god's own mystical emblem, and wear his holy garment, the fawn-skin hair-shirt – raiment of mysticism. But the Greek mystics wore it with the hair side outward.

Folk who of a sudden impulse abandon the social routine – the looms and shuttles – of their group, deserting parents, spouses, or children in order to indulge any form of private, personal, emotionally religious practice, are quite certain to incur resentment, for they are being all too literally 'unpopular'. Periodic bouts of Dionysiac frenzy may have come to the Greek villages and tiny

[1] Translation by D. W. Lucas.

townships in the seventh century B.C. and caused not only resentment but possible persecution of the cult by conventional persons.
However, by the beginning of the sixth century some cities of
Greece were growing fairly large, and for such Dionysos Bromios, with his mysteries that drove the women wildly to the mountains, became a subject of the very gravest concern. There are
indications that the whole trouble was resolved during the first
half of the sixth century B.C. by the actions of three brilliant Greek
statesmen, and in characteristic Greek fashion. In important centres the cult of Dionysos was taken into the mechanism of the
State cults, and the buskin of Bacchos was saved from becoming a
sabot, poised to immobilise the machinery of government.

Periander, who ruled Corinth from about 625 to 585 B.C.,
deliberately introduced a Dionysiac festival into the richest Greek
city of the day. His neighbour Cleisthenes, Despot of Sicyon, dis-
placed the cult of an old local hero by the cult of Dionysos. More;
this powerful man, who, supporting the Delphians in a local war
with Crisa, and commanding the allied forces, founded the quadrennial Pythian Games in 582 B.C. at Delphi -- this ruler of Sicyon
may have been the man who introduced the actual worship of
Dionysos into Delphi; or, if he did not bring it in, he so strengthened and encouraged it as to give to Bacchos a status second
only to that of Pythian Apollo. The holy sepulchre of Dionysos
was placed in the secret, underground *adyton* of the temple beside
the navel-stone of 'Earth' and the sacred tripod of the Pythia.
Thus to combine the realms of the careful god of law and order
and of the mystical god of licence and abandon was one of the
most startling examples of Greek genius for adjustment. Law
could be redeemed from mechanistic rote by the natural human
contact of the anarchic god, while licence could be put under control by companying with the god of self-knowledge and moderation. Order could learn about disorder, and disorder about order.

Corinth, Sicyon, Delphi were three, and Athens the fourth
place where great skill was used to accommodate the Dionysiac
trouble. Peisistratus was ruler of Athens from 566 B.C.; and at
about the time when he founded the Panathenaic Games for
Athene he also instituted the Great Dionysia. That is to say he

brought into Athens and installed at the foot of the Acropolis the ancient wooden statue of Dionysos from Attic Eleutheræ, on the frontier of Bœotia, a village which was claiming to be the god's birthplace. With the statue came its priest and his little company of village mummers called 'goat-singers' – in Greek *tragōdoi* – country lads and devotees of the god who at times kept company with the local village Mænads, the god-possessed girls who wandered in the woods of Mount Cithæron. Under the walls of the Acropolis they ranged some wooden seats for spectators in a semicircle, and put up a little stage on to which the first mummer leapt to tell his tale, while the others answered back and sang short choruses. Here the *tragōdoi* created for a city audience 'tragedy', and the theatre was born. Presently 'revel-singers' – *kōmōdoi* – produced shows of another kind, and 'comedy' came into being. Yet it was all built round the cult of Dionysos; and it canalised a great flood of energy that would have found anarchical outlets elsewhere. It did this for the men – but not for the women. In their case Delphi had to help.

'Thyiads' was the name used both in Athens and at Delphi – but not, apparently, elsewhere – for 'Mænads', the women in *ecstasis*; and this formed so strong a link between the women and girls of both communities that they established a joint biennial enterprise for the impelling mysteries. No certain date can be given for the beginning of this union of Thyiads from two places far apart from one another, but it may well have started after the days of Peisistratus and at the time when the Athenian Alcmæonid family – whose close connection with Delphi has already been mentioned – were in control of Athens. That would be towards the end of the sixth century B.C. Late in summer or in the autumn of every second year the Chief Priest of Athens selected a troupe of women and girls from among the best Athenian families to be Thyiads for the State.[1] No certainty exists about their number; but as figures fourteen and sixteen have been suggested, it is not likely that there were more than a score of them in any year. There was doubtless a woman experienced, but like Lysistrata relatively young and active, who had made the

[1] On Thyiads see K. Preisendanz in Pauly-Wissowa, *RE* II, vi (1937).

expedition several times, and was therefore the leader. At Delphi such a one was 'Principal' – at least in later days – and Plutarch when priest at Delphi valued the Senior Thyiad, Klea, as an intimate friend. But the Athenian women and girls chosen to be Thyiads were committed to weeks of hard outdoor life; for, starting in late October, they had to make their way on foot from Athens, by way of Eleusis, Eleutheræ, Platæa, Thebes, Lebadeia, Panopeus, and Arachova, to Delphi. It was a route little short of a hundred miles, traversing rough, steep mountain-passes; and it may be reckoned today as about forty-five walking hours, or five walking days. There were, of course, rests on the pilgrimage; they stopped in towns where Dionysos was worshipped to perform their dances, as Pausanias, the traveller, learnt from personal conversation with some Thyiads as late as the second century of our era. Perhaps they were ten days or more on the way. Yet such a walk undertaken barefoot in early winter proves that the young women and girls of Athens were assuredly tough. The once-popular notion that Athenian females were dull, unenterprising creatures, as physically inadequate as though they had never stepped outside a convent or a *seraglio* and therefore held in disdain by the men, is now ceasing to be maintained with conviction. The Thyiads are one more example – if such be really needed – of some temporary independence and of audacious activity on the women's part.

It is November, and the news has come that the Athenians are near. The Delphian girls go out to meet them. An hour away – and the two throngs mingle happily. Together they pass below the crags of Hyampia, from which the great rocks had crashed down upon the greedy Medes. Together they enter the precinct gate and wind up the paved way past the east front of Apollo's temple and along its north side to that place which is the 'temple' of Dionysos – the theatre. Every theatre is a temple of Bromios; and the subconscious knowledge of its ineluctable consecration to the spirit of the god may explain why even to our own day 'ciphers to this great accompt on your imaginary forces work'.

The Delphic theatre, up at the highest corner of the sacred precinct, was at first a semicircular hollow scooped from the

mountain-side and only later built of solid stone. From this the
Thyiads pass into the township of Delphi to stay with their hosts,
whom one may assume to have been Thyiads too, or the parents
of Thyiad girls. If you have been to the place early in the winter
season you can more easily picture the setting and the view. To
the south and west the sea in the Gulf of Itea looks oddly like
quicksilver, and the mountains, half veiled in cloud, seem very
distant. From the gorge of the River Pleistos below, with its long,
dark-green mat of olive-trees joining the huge olive-tree carpet of
the Itean plain, mists lift and gather and build themselves into
clouds, which rise still higher, as though speeding to join the
towering mass that shrouds Parnassus. When the sun gets through
fitfully he still gives warmth, but shadows have winter's chill. In
that setting and climate imagination may picture what happens
after a few days of rest for the Athenians. Sunset; and the air is
tense with a knowledge that Mystery is soon to begin. The
Thyiads are gathered in the theatre's circular orchestra, fawn-
skins falling over their pleated robes. Each holds a *thyrsos*, some
have castanets or little drums, some hold young animals in their
arms. The evening draws in, and a few Bacchoi climb up the
steps holding lighted torches; someone touches a drum and a sigh
goes up. At the altar in the centre the priest of Dionysos cuts the
throat of a young he-goat – a sacrifice to Bromios, who is coming
to possess his votaries. Bacchos is not merely the wine-god, but
the god of all natural fluids: wine, and honey, milk, and such
others as betoken a god of fertility. The blood of the goat runs
out on to the altar, down on to the pavement. Strange that either
fasting *or* raw meat, the scourge *or* the *thyrsos*, the tolled bell *or* the
beaten drum, the body buried in the hooded habit *or* the naked
limbs dancing upon the mountain-top may equally produce a
sense of mystical union with God.

High up on the Bad Stair a shepherd youth, with a tail of horse-
hair tied on to make one think him a satyr, puts his double flutes
to his lips. The thin, weird notes are magnified and repeated by
echoes. A girl in the theatre screams and flings back her head.
'Evoe, Evoe! He comes!' Drum, and another drum; rhythm, and
the castanets begin to clapper. It has grown almost dark, for the

torches seem brighter now. They are moving up through the gangways between the rows of seats and out to the highest corner, where the path leads straight to the Bad Stair. The whole throng of Thyiads follows the torch-bearers, for 'Bromios leads his revellers to the mountains, to the mountains'.

You, the barbarian from another land, may sit there alone in the theatre, wrapped in your warmest cloak, and look up to the mountain-side to see the torch-lights slowly rising in zigzags up that wild track while snatches of the music of Bromios the Boisterous come drifting down. For nearly two hours you may still see those lights before they vanish four thousand feet up. And then, what happened then?

Part of the answer is in *The Bacchæ* of Euripides, but not all. For that play is not set in the chill of creeping winter which these Athenian girls and women had to face in company with the Delphian Thyiads. The Corycian Cave, dedicated to Pan and the Nymphs, to which they climbed, is not easy of access nowadays – it is about three hours on foot from Delphi – but it is very large and a warm shelter in a storm. Once upon a time news came to Delphi that before the Thyiads could reach the cave they had been overwhelmed in a great snow blizzard, and the rescue-party which climbed up to look for them had all their clothing frozen stiff. Another time Thyiads lost their way one night after they had been ranging the mountain, and came down unwittingly to the township of Amphissa, where the citizens found them next morning asleep from sheer exhaustion in the market-place.

Such is the picture, as far as we can draw it, of the winter *orgia* in all their dire austerity, and the Athenian Thyiads knew only these; but there is other evidence for springtime *orgia* on the Corycian plain and round the sacred cave when the Delphian Thyiads climbed the mountain without their Athenian sisters. Then there were goats to be milked in the flowered meadows, and the male participants with tied-on satyr-tails carried skins of wine. No doubt exists that at this season there was sexual freedom. Euripides in another play, the *Ion* – the scene of which is laid in Delphi – held it to be natural. The hero, Ion, considers it to be a convincing account of his birth that his reputed father Xuthos came as a visitor to Delphi and took part with a throng of Thyiads in the Bacchic festival there.

Ion	Did you stay in a hostel?
Xuthos	Yes, and with Delphian girls.
Ion	Do you mean you were one of their throng?
Xuthos	They were Mænad girls of Bacchos.
Ion	Were you sober or wined?
Xuthos	Under the pleasant influence of Bacchos.
Ion	That indeed was my begetting!

But along with this one must ponder another passage from Euripides' *Bacchæ*: 'Dionysos compels no woman to be chaste. Chastity is a matter of character, and she who is naturally chaste will partake of Bacchic rites without being touched.' Their state of *ecstasis* left the Bacchai free to follow either the instincts or the restraints of Nature. No inhibitions stopped the satisfaction of desire; no exhibitionist urge drove them towards promiscuous folly.

Even to the end the cult of Dionysos was something of a mystical and terrifying incursion from the outside invisible world – an incursion from the dizzy heights beyond the limits of conscious personal men, and when this cult, reaching out to Central Italy, was suddenly discovered to exist underground in Rome, it was suppressed by a horrified Senate, which promulgated in 187 B.C. its famous 'Decree about Bacchanals'. But the Greeks had done better by the well-devised partnership of the brother-gods Apollo and Dionysos. In 432 B.C., when the Parthenon was complete, the latter had become the twelfth Olympian god, replacing Hestia, a gentle and self-effacing goddess.

In the myths about Dionysos the most important is the tale of his birth. His mother was Semele, a name almost certainly taken from Thraco-Phrygian religion, because in the language of that region the word 'Zemelo' meant Earth. In fact, she was an earth-goddess whose cult must have come to Bœotian Thebes with that of her son, and there been built into local legend. The usual form of the story is that Zeus loved Semele and consorted with her, but that Hera discovered the intrigue. Jealous, as was her wont, the goddess disguised herself as Semele's old nurse and urged her to obtain from her lover a promise to reveal himself to her in the fullness of his godhead. And so one night she got him to swear by the River Styx – that oath which no god or mortal dare break – to grant her one request, and when he had sworn she asked to see him. Stories have already been told about young hunters of whom one saw Athene, the other Artemis bathing, and about the evils that befell them. It is fatal to look upon a deity against his will; and even so heroic a leader as Moses could be vouchsafed no more than a glimpse.

And he [Moses] said, 'I beseech thee, show me thy glory.'

And He [the Lord] said, 'I will make all my goodness pass before thee, and I will proclaim the name of the Lord before thee; and will be gracious to whom I will be gracious, and will show mercy on whom I will show mercy.'

And He said, 'Thou canst not see my face: for there shall no man see me, and live.'

And the Lord said, 'Behold there is a place by me, and thou shalt stand upon a rock:

And it shall come to pass, while my glory passeth by, that I will put thee in a clift of the rock, and will cover thee with my hand while I pass by:

And I will take away mine hand, and thou shalt see my back parts; but my face shall not be seen.'[1]

Semele saw Zeus the all-terrible, even as he was; but that meant massed thunderbolts, which are inseparable from Zeus. Here in this legend was the shock and shudder of an ineffable occasion, which comprehended the majesty of deadly violet lightning and presaged the efficiency of atomic fission. At the very moment when the mother was destroyed by the levin bolt, Zeus snatched the unborn infant from her womb, cut open his own thigh, hid the child therein, and sewed it up, until, after the nine months were accomplished, Dionysos was born from the thigh of his divine father. It was this story that gave Dionysos a strange title, 'Insewn', by which he was sometimes addressed. His title of 'Iacchos', specially associated with his part in the Eleusinian

[1] *Exodus*, XXXIII, 18 ff.

Mysteries, has already been mentioned in the last chapter,[1] in which it was made clear that he was pre-eminently a god of the open air, meadow and woodland, glen and mountain.

No divine type shows more diversity in art than does Dionysos. At first he was depicted as bearded and wearing flowing garments; but already in the fifth century B.C. another type is coming in, youthful, beardless, his thick hair confined by a band, naked but for a pair of hunting-boots; a fine athletic type, as we see him on a bronze made about 470 B.C. and found at Olympia (Plate XI, facing page 128). This delightful figure, now in the Louvre in Paris, is one of the very earliest youthful and naked versions of the god; but by the Hellenistic age this type was destined to undergo deterioration, and many a museum now contains marble statues of a deity soft, degenerate, and weak with effeminacy, which are a token of queer tastes in the Græco-Roman age. Despite this, however, the bearded, long-robed Dionysos was still represented, and even the young athletic type was sometimes retained, especially when Dionysos was equated with Alexander the Great. Euripides knew stories of a triumphant procession of the Giver of Wine through the East. The god himself speaks in the opening lines of *The Bacchæ*:

I left the golden lands of the Lydians and Phrygians and traversing the sun-baked plains of the Persians, the towns of Bactria, the wintry country of the Medes, happy Arabia and all Asia that lies beside the salt sea, with her towered cities full of mingled Greeks and barbarians, I have come to this city first among the Greeks; there too have I set up my dances and established my mysteries, that I might be a god manifest to mortals.

With this in mind it is easy to see how Alexander, and his triumphant sweep through Asia deep into India, bringing civilisation to the lands of strangers, seemed to parallel the adventures of Dionysos. Did not Alexander also become a god? And were not both these divine creatures sons of Zeus?

[1] See p. 156.

A FEW men of exceptional talents and gifts, men who have impressed themselves profoundly on their contemporaries, have seemed to their followers to be superhuman and therefore nearly gods. On their deaths stories of their assumption have come into being. Moses, who led Israel out of Egypt, disappeared on Mount Nebo in the land of Moab, 'but no man knoweth of his sepulchre unto this day'. As for the prophet Elijah, 'there appeared a chariot of fire, and horses of fire, and Elijah went up by a whirlwind into heaven'.

HERAKLES, a mortal like the two Hebrews, likewise went up to heaven in fire. But he was not a mere myth, for it can hardly be doubted that he was Greek-Mycenæan, of princely rank, having an elder brother named Eurystheus who was King of Argos or Mycenæ, and Herakles was perhaps established himself in the castle of Tiryns. Owing to his fabulous labours he became a hero – the most famous of them all. Yet he was not a god because his name is derived from a divinity; and no ancient deity was ever named from another deity. Herakles means 'Hera's Glory', a human name which fits his origin in Argos, in which land the worship of Hera was more important than in any other region of Greece.

The Labours of Herakles were always a favourite subject among Greeks of widely-scattered states, and, though more than the standard 'twelve' got into story and legend, the designers of the Temple of Zeus at Olympia established the canonical twelve labours. Half of them were said to have been performed in Peloponnesus, which is natural in view of the hero's Argive birth, and were listed as follows: (1) While still a youth he strangled the lion of Nemea which had been ravaging the region round that city. Having flayed the dead lion he acquired his chief accoutrement – the lion's skin – which he wore cloak-wise with the creature's scalp as a hood, or which he carried over his left arm as one might port a light overcoat. (2) At Lerna, south of Argos, a serpent-dragon, many-headed, gave much trouble to mankind, and when Herakles sliced off one head two fresh ones sprouted in its place. Here his henchman, Iolaos, helped by building a fire, heating a weapon and searing each stump as the head came off. (3) West of Argos on Mount Erymanthos, a great wild boar was picked up alive by the hero and brought along to frighten king Eurystheus. (4) Not far from the same mount a huge deer was giving trouble at Keryneia, devouring the crops until Herakles slew it. (5) Birds of evil aspect, bronze of claw and spreading the stench of carrion, haunted the Stymphalian lake south of the north Peloponnesian mountains. Herakles shot them all down with his great bow and arrows. (6) Augeas, a king in the land of Elis, kept his animals in filthy stables which Herakles cleaned in one day by diverting the course of the local river so that it ran through the byres.

It was the goddess Athene who was his continual adviser in all these exploits which he was impelled to undertake by Hera, who, in one version of the legend, was hostile to him because she learnt that he was a son of Zeus. But it remains to catalogue the other six official Labours which happened outside Peloponnesus: (7) the capture of a huge bull in Crete; (8) the seizure of savage horses belonging to Diomedes in Thrace; (9) the defeat of the Amazon queen, whose girdle he brought back home. Finally there were three other-worldly adventures, which were perhaps reflections of the story that Herakles once met Hades, god of the Underworld, and got the better of him: (10) in a 'sun-set isle' of the far West, Erytheia, he overcame a triple-bodied giant and took his cattle; (11) descending to the House of Hades, he brought up to the light of day the monstrous watch-dog Kerberos; (12) far in the West once more, on the Atlas mountains of North Africa, he had to pluck golden apples (were they perhaps oranges?) from a tree guarded by a dragon. It was on this occasion that he relieved for a while the giant Atlas of his load and took upon his own huge shoulders the whole weight of the firmament of heaven.

There was another hero, Bœotian in origin, who may have belonged to a later generation than the great Argive, and who also performed certain Labours and had numerous adventures in the central Greek region. Because he was an inordinately strong man he became merged in legend with the older hero. The Greeks of the sixth and fifth centuries B.C. apparently thought of Herakles as a single personality, though scepticism was to grow up. Even to a fit and athletic people like the Greeks there was a strange fascination in imagining the invincible bag of muscle, like the figures of films and 'comic strips' today with their Tarzan or their Garth. The Theban Herakles, however, was not 'Hera's glory' but 'Hera's pain', and she tried to compass his destruction, even from babyhood when she sent two large snakes into his cradle; but the infant prodigy strangled them both with his bare hands. In this story Zeus had loved Alkmene and begotten Herakles, and it was the discovery of this that stirred the wrath of Hera, who later on drove him mad.

Labours and adventures are rather mixed in the legends from central Greece. A lion killed on Mount Cithæron is a duplication of the Nemean deed. He fought with the river-bull god Acheloos, and he subjugated the city of Orchomenos, suzerain of Thebes. Yet not the least of his achievements occurred when he was guest of the laird of Thespiæ named Thespios, who had fifty daughters by a number of different wives. His host introduced the girls to Herakles, who enjoyed – some said in a single night – forty-nine of them, and became the father of fifty-one coeval sons. Only one girl refused him: two gave birth to twins.

Brief note must be taken of certain non-Greek associations. After a murder he had committed, Herakles had to expiate the deed by serving someone for three whole years, so he allowed Hermes to sell him as a menial to a Lydian queen named Omphale. A symbolic transvestism ensued, and the theme was popular among Hellenistic artists who represented a youthful Omphale, naked but for the lion-skin of the hero, and a bearded Herakles dressed in a thin chiton and holding spindle and distaff. Behind this tale there lay, perhaps, the myth of an Eastern goddess and an insignificant consort.[1] None the less, in the accepted version he had several children by Omphale.

Far more important – almost as soon as Greeks and Phœnicians began to meet – was the identification which occurred of Herakles with the Semitic god Ba'al Melqart. In ancient Spain at Cadiz,

[1] See Chapter II above on Hera.

HERAKLES holding a club and the broken horn of the river-bull Acheloos. Bronze statuette, made about 450 B.C.

ASKLEPIOS, the 'blameless physician', originator of the scientific attitude towards the art of healing. Life-size copy after a marble statue made about 450 B.C.

Silver coin of Camarina, Sicily, with the head of Herakles in a lion scalp, struck about 450 B.C.

PLATE XIII

ALEXANDER: the peoples of his realms felt that a god had been among them. Life-size head of a contemporary marble statue made by the sculptor Leochares.

(TOP, LEFT) Silver coin with head of Alexander the Great as Herakles, struck in 326 B.C. at Alexandria by Egypt.

Silver coin issued by Lysimachus, King of Thrace, with portrait head of the divine Alexander, struck about 300 B.C.

Large gold medallion (diameter 2½ ins.), with portrait of Alexander copied from the coin above, struck in Alexandria about A.D. 230.

PLATE XIV

which the Greeks called Gadeira, was a celebrated temple of
Herakles – the Greeks declared. But it had a tabu on swine, and
was clearly Semitic; so the deity in the temple was assuredly Melqart in a region controlled by Carthage. Yet on Carthaginian
coins the god appears as a replica of the Greek hero. It is a com-
posite story, even concerning the two princes, Argive and Theban,
who became Herakles, and in so brief an account many details –
especially concerning his many concubines – have been omitted.[1]
The final tragedy of his death is movingly told by Sophocles in the
Women of Trachis, written somewhere between 430 and 420 B.C.

Deianeira was the reputed daughter of Oineus, meaning 'wine-
man' or vintner, a local ruler in Calydon beside the river Acheloos, but was probably thought to be the child of Dionysos. Both
Herakles and the river bull-god wooed the girl, fought for her,
and Herakles won after breaking off one of the creature's horns
(Plate XIII, facing page 176). On the way home to Trachis, where
they were to settle, Herakles allowed the centaur Nessos to carry
his bride across a river, and when the savage man-horse tried to
assault her, Herakles killed him with a poisoned arrow. But the
dying Nessos gave Deianeira some of his blood in a phial telling
her it was a certain charm to regain lost love. She had several
children by the hero, until years later he brought back a young
and lovely girl-captive named Iole to be his mate. The full understanding of a woman's feelings, which is a vital part of Sophocles'
greatness as a poet, comes out in the character of Deianeira and in
words which she speaks when she has learnt the truth that she
must share Herakles with this young girl:

> I see how it is: the one with youthful beauty
> Ripening to its prime, the other falling away.
> The eye must ever enjoy the flower, the feet
> Turn from the withered stalk. This is my fear,
> Herakles to be called my *husband*, but her *man* . . .
> But there, as I said, a woman must have more sense
> Than to cherish anger. . . . Let me tell you, my friends,

[1] There is a full 'life' of Herakles in Robert Graves, *The Greek Myths*, II,
sections 118–146. While admiring the author's scholarship and industry, I am
not entirely in agreement with his interpretations.

Of the means by which I hope to find relief
And remedy for this affliction.

Deianeira must have our compassion, and we know her counterpart was there in any little street in ancient Athens as she is now in every modern city or township anywhere.

It was at this point that she decided to apply the blood of Nessos to a garment which was given to Herakles to wear, and the fearful venom began to burn his flesh and torture his whole frame, so that at last he made his henchmen build him on Mount Oeta a great funeral pyre on which he was laid. As the flames rose round him his father Zeus, moved at last to pity, sent thunderbolts to reduce the great pyre to ashes from which the soul – the divine part of the hero – rose up into the *aither*. There his guardian Athene met him and herself conducted him into the citadel of Olympus, where for the first time he met God his Father face to face. The topic was a favourite one with the vase-painters from an early date, and is often very lively, as on an Athenian cup made about 550 B.C. (Plate XII, facing page 129) on which Zeus himself seems a little perturbed by the eager enthusiasm of his armed daughter and his lion-skin-clad son. Reconciled to Hera, Herakles was given her child Hebe, goddess of eternal youth, to wife.

Perhaps enough has now been told to explain why Herakles had so wide an appeal to all Greeks, and why he seemed to them a very god. Herakles gave a pattern that humanity wants to see: son of Zeus almighty, born of a virgin princess, doer from birth of miraculous deeds, suffering that he might save others from fears that beset them, ascending into heaven. In Arcadia he was even worshipped as Herakles the Saviour. Yet his divinity was offset by many of the follies common to humanity, and he could therefore appear in ancient Comedy as the gluttonous buffoon, or as a kind of grown-up baby, unaware of its full strength, having a great appeal to the mother instinct in women. This, of course, offset what men so much admired – his inexhaustible sexual proficiency. The soft-hearted superman simply had to become a god.

ASKLEPIOS appears to have developed towards godhead partly by the confluence of two different persons, exactly as Herakles did.

In the Mycenæan age as it appears in the *Iliad* he was a princely personage like the other Homeric heroes and a mortal, though son of a god. Cheiron, the good centaur, wisest and most skilled of all his kind, had taught him the art of healing and his regular epithet is 'the blameless physician'. His two sons, described as 'Podaleirios and blameless Machaon', took part in the Trojan expedition, and by a remarkable anticipation of modern usage, we find Medical Officers holding Field Rank. Asklepios was a son of Apollo, who fell in love with the girl Coronis, daughter of a king of the Lapiths, living on the shores of a large lake in Thessaly. She gave herself gladly to the god, but was, while pregnant, unfaithful to him, and Artemis in anger slew her and her paramour.[1] But Apollo snatched the still living child from her dead body and handed him over to Cheiron's care. That is the basis of the Thessalian story.

In Argive Epidauros, which became the greatest centre of his cult, a rather different tale was told; so different that it looks as though we had the saga of another personage given to the art of healing, who became identified with the northern hero. The Lapith king, father of Coronis, came to Epidauros to spy out the land, bringing with him his daughter who was, without his knowledge, bearing the child of Apollo. The girl gave birth in Apollo's temple there, but in fear of her father's anger, exposed the infant on Mount Titthion, which in Greek means 'nipple'. A goatherd who frequented the mountain lost one of his goats as well as a bitch who helped to guard his herd, but presently found both animals busily taking turns to suckle a child. As he was about to pick up the little infant, it was suffused in a brilliant light which stopped the poor peasant from interfering with that which was obviously a divine mystery. Asklepios was therefore left to the care of his father, Apollo, who, as in the Thessalian story, handed him over to Cheiron. It is noteworthy that while the Thessalian Asklepios begat sons, the Argive Asklepios produced daughters who were given names that suggest a kind of personification. The eldest was Hygieia, the second Panaceia, and the third Iaso; their names meaning Health, Cure-all, and Healing. Epione was the

[1] See p. 124 above.

name of his wife, and we have the picture of a stable, well-integrated family.

Apollo and Athene between them taught Asklepios the arts of surgery and the use of drugs so that he became the founder of medicine. He began to raise people from the dead, until Hades complained that his victims were being stolen from him, whereupon Zeus killed the hero with a thunderbolt. But Zeus repented him of the deed and restored Asklepios to life, therefore his special symbol became the serpent which, when it sloughs its skin, seems to die and to rise from its own dead self. In art he appears as the dignified physician with a staff round which a serpent coils (Plate XIII, facing page 176). Later there were two serpents, as on the R.A.M.C. badges of today. At the main site of his cult, the great Epidaurian sanctuary at the foot of Mount Titthion, a clinic and sanatorium were well established by the fifth century B.C. Incubation – or sleeping on the ground – remembering your dreams, and reporting them to the ministering psychiatrist, was all part of the treatment. The second most important centre of cult and healing was in the island of Cos, which was the home in the fifth century B.C. of Hippocrates, whose medical practice reached so very high a level. It was Galen, A.D. 129–199, who was the last and most voluminous medical writer of antiquity. The legend of Asklepios tells of his second and final earthly death whereafter, because he had died once already, he was taken up to the *aither* to become a god and a permanent guest of the twelve Olympians.

Asklepios the hero appears at first hardly to merit the degree of admiration such as Herakles received. Canonisation seems understandable, but apotheosis calls for some explanation. Why did Asklepios actually become a god with temples, cult-statues and priestly ministrants? Something in the acute Greek mind appears to have made people aware that the beginning, small though it was, of a scientific attitude to phenomena started as early as the Homeric age, and that its first interpreter was Asklepios, father of Podaleirios and Machaon. All the same, all through the ancient world other and inferior types of medical notions existed. Superstitious and unreasonable beliefs about disease are more easily transmitted from generation to generation than any other body of

ideas. In classical antiquity there are literary references to practices based on low, and sometimes degraded, forms of magic;
sympathetic, contagious, and magic grounded in sorcery. Such
notions were complicated by a belief in demonic possession
which plays so large a part in the medicine of the New Testament.
It has been pointed out[1] that since there is little sign of demonism
in the Old Testament, it may derive from Persian contacts and
its main source may be Mesopotamia. However, faith in
demonism was greatly increased in the Christian era from the
Apostolic missionary age until comparatively modern times.

There was absolutely no reason why any ancient god – especially one of the twelve Olympians – should not be a god of healing.
Apollo himself was pre-eminently so, likewise Athene, Hermes
and Demeter. And the other gods such as Artemis, Dionysos,
Zeus himself and golden Aphrodite, all of whom might destroy,
were none-the-less capable of healing mankind. Thus the question
'why pick on Asklepios as the special god of healing?' becomes
more acute than ever; and it seems that the only possible answer is
the one just suggested, that there was a feeling that scientific medicine, separate from mere superstitious practice, originated with
him. There was one cult which had a 'general relation to the practice, if not to the theory, of Medicine. It was by no accident that
Asklepios became the god of doctors as well as of patients. His
worship, in its best presentation, stood for rational religion in
opposition to demonic and magical rites and purifications. It contained, moreover, a psychological element that was of great value
to rational practice. The physician's attitude to Asklepios, and that
of Asklepios to Medicine, is indicated in the famous Hippocratic
Oath':[2]

I swear by Apollo the physician, and Asklepios, and Hygieia, and
Panaceia, and all the gods and goddesses, calling them to witness that I
will fulfil, according to the best of my power and judgement, this oath
and written bond: to honour as my parent the master who has taught me
this art, and to share my substance with him, and to minister to all his
necessities; to consider his children as my own brothers, and to teach
them this art should they desire to follow it, without remuneration

[1] Charles Singer in the *Oxford Classical Dictionary*, p. 548.   [2] Singer, *loc. cit.*

or written bond; to admit to my lessons, my discourses, and all my other teaching, my own sons, and those of my tutor, and those who have been inscribed as pupils, and have taken the medical oath; but no one else. I will prescribe such regimen as may be for the benefit of my patients, according to the best of my power and judgement, and preserve them from anything hurtful and mischievous. I will never, if asked, administer poison, nor be the author of such advice; neither will I give to a woman a pessary to produce abortion. I will maintain the purity and integrity both of my conduct and of my art. I will not cut any one for the stone, but will leave the operation to those who cultivate it. Into whatever dwellings I may go, I will enter them for the benefit of the sick, abstaining from all mischief and corruption, especially from immodest action, towards women or men, freemen or slaves. If during my attendance, or even unprofessionally in common life, I happen to see or hear of anything which should not be revealed, I will consider it a secret not to be divulged. May I, if I observe this oath, and do not break it, enjoy good success in life, and in my art, and be esteemed for ever; should I transgress and become a perjurer, may the reverse be my lot.

ALEXANDER, son of Philip, King of Macedon, was born in 356 B.C. His mother, Olympias, was sister to the King of Epirus, lying to the west and being the most northerly region of mainland Greece. On his father's side the royal Macedonians claimed descent in direct line from the god Herakles, and the princes of the House of Epirus believed that their greatest ancestor was Achilles. It was an impressive pedigree. Olympias gave birth to a second child, a year after the first, who was named Cleopatra and was married in 335 B.C. to her first cousin, the new King of Epirus, the event coinciding with the death of Philip and the acclamation of Alexander as the new King of Macedon.

Obviously we are now in the realm of history; and yet, not quite. At the best Herakles and Asklepios, conceived as human beings, are shadowy persons to whose births and assumptions no fixed dates can be assigned; while, by contrast, Alexander and Augustus are persons of absolute historical reality whose indelible achievements have stamped themselves on the world for as long as any form of civilised and intelligent life may endure. None the less the stories and anecdotes told about these mighty men and the motives attributed to them must be studied by the historian with the utmost care. There have always been men to hate, even more than to fear, those who are very great. Indeed one of the easy roads available for the achievement of a reputation for cleverness is the road of denigration. To 'debunk' either an historical character or a work of art is a sure way of winning approval and some vocal praise from any body of disgruntled contemporaries. In all history perhaps the most malicious and most vicious of denigrators was the Macedonian Cassander, the Macbeth of the ancient world.

Three groups of stories about the life and deeds of Alexander became current after his death. There was a general tradition, referred to as 'the Vulgate', mixed in ideas, partly appreciative, but sometimes derogatory. There was the sober factual tradition, based largely on a journal kept by one of Alexander's greatest companions and successors, Ptolemy, which provides the richest information. And, in the last place, there was the profoundly derogatory story fostered by Cassander who, while he controlled Macedon and Greece, ordered the destruction of any document that favoured Alexander. Consequently for close on a generation the Greeks of Europe were deceived about his quality and genius, although the Greeks of Asia and Africa were fully alive to the story of one who had been the greatest man on earth. Cassander, aiming at the throne of Macedon, had procured the murder, one by one, of all Alexander's family: his mother Olympias, his wife Roxane, his young son Alexander IV, his sister Cleopatra. This accomplished, the arch-villain set about smearing the very memory of Alexander. These facts have been mentioned briefly in order to point out that anything, having a malicious hostility to the greatest of men, found nowadays in modern histories is undoubtedly derived from the late fourth-century anti-Alexander batteries which Cassander set to work. Yet these malignancies add a certain veil of obscurity comparable to the blanket of myth and legend which grew up around the more ancient heroes who became gods.

The briefest outline of Alexander's actions follows, just to remind the reader of how much he may enjoy from modern his-

torical books[1] where the adventures can be read in full. History
has placed its emphasis on Alexander the Conqueror, the military
genius. He was both; and yet these aspects were almost incidental
and of far less importance than his achievements as explorer, civi-
liser, humaniser, and unifier of mankind. In 334 B.C., when he
crossed into Asia, he fought one battle in which he defeated the
Persian satraps. Thereafter his road from Hellespont to Lebanon
was the route of a liberator, and all the rulers of Cyprus hastened
to join him. In Phœnicia he was obliged to exert force against
Tyre because he was championing the Greek cause against the age-
old rivals of Hellas. To Egypt he came as a liberator and uniter of
two great civilisations. When the empire of Darius was ended by
Alexander's victory at Gaugamela, and after the occupation of
the four capitals – Susa, Persepolis, Pasargadæ, Ecbatana – the
Græco-Macedonian simply replaced the Persian dynasty; and in
the event, this new and more enlightened rule was wholly benefi-
cent to the native population, among whom there was to grow
through the centuries the legend of 'Iskander of the Two Horns',
divinely good like the archangels of Allah. From Persia onwards
Alexander's expedition to the East, terminating in North-west
India and the Punjab, was a scientific exploration of a character-
istically Greek type, bent on the accumulation and recording of
knowledge. In this long expedition, only twice was opposition
encountered, since he and his Greeks and Macedonians were
almost everywhere welcome. The opposition, indeed, brought
reconciliation and union; for the campaign against the Sogdians
culminated in the romance of a love-marriage between Alexander
and Roxane, and the struggle against the Indian Porus, famed for
his brigade of elephants, ended in pledges of enduring friendship.

Especially characteristic of Alexander were his complete in-
difference to his own well-being and his devotion to the service of
mankind. These are the central factors that dominated his life.

A favourite method in the Hellenistic age was for traducers to
attack an enemy with lies about his private life, intending to rouse
either the jealousy or scorn of other men. Many Peripatetics and
Stoics thought to discredit Alexander's memory by accusations of

[1] The best are mentioned in the Bibliography on p. 11.

promiscuous excess either with one sex or the other. Some among Alexander's detractors raised another accusation – continence akin to neurotic impotence – surely in the ancient world the most unkindest cut of all! But Plutarch in his *Life of Alexander* carries evidence to refute so odd a notion. His attitude to women was indeed remarkable, especially in an age when – though philosophers and gentry might observe the decencies – the soldiery felt entitled to be brutal and licentious. Alexander as Commander in Chief made the rape of captured women a capital offence, and by way of an example, executed two of his Macedonians found guilty. That reveals a respect for womankind and a sense of the extreme delicacy of sex which is the privilege of moderate men given to temperate humanism. It is as distinct from the superciliousness of the homosexual approach as it is from the salacity of the lustful attack. Alexander, whose terrible temper might at times get the better of him, never failed in his regard for the female half of humanity.

He was blamed for encouraging, or allowing, his friends in Greek cities to have him declared a god. But this was a religio-political manœuvre to give the King of Macedon status in any Greek city whereof he was not a citizen, and it amounted to no more than a kind of 'naturalisation from above'. Even in Athens, the most brilliant of them all, this caused little resentment, except among an embittered minority, and the Athenians set up on the Acropolis a marble statue by the celebrated sculptor Leochares, one of the finest works of the time (Plate XIV, facing page 177). The head of this statue – the only extant contemporary life-size portrait of Alexander – survives.

At Opis in the Mesopotamian plain, well to the north of Babylon, Alexander arranged, in the last year of his life, a great festival of reconciliation between his diverse subjects; Greeks, Macedonians and Persians. The thousands of guests all made libation together with wine from loving-cups, and this was followed by the planned climax of the famous Prayer at Opis. The actual words are lost though there are fragments of reported speech which can be put together. Directly he must have said something as follows:

All men are sons of one Father and for myself I believe that I have a duty to be the Reconciler of the World. I pray for peace, and that Macedonians and Persians and all peoples of my empire may be alike partners in the commonwealth, and that the peoples of the world may live together in harmony and in that unity of heart and mind which we call *Homonoia*.

This indeed was to become the expression of the world's longing for something better than everlasting wars. Not long after, on the evening of a day that would correspond to June 13th in the year we call 323 B.C., Alexander died of malaria in Babylon, in his thirty-third year. He did not assume that he was a god; but, believing in some mystical revelation – vouchsafed at the desert sanctuary of Siwa and in the words of the Oracle there – he thought that he was a Son of God, that is of the Libyan god Ammon whom the Greeks identified with Zeus. Yet the peoples of his empire felt that a god had been among them and had ruled them; and half a century later Theocritus, in a poem honouring a Ptolemaïc king, wrote of Alexander as dwelling on Olympus among the eternal gods.

AUGUSTUS is not a name but a religious epithet. In the Greek half of the Empire the equivalent was SEBASTOS. Both words can best be translated as 'His Sacred Majesty'. The actual names of the first Augustus, who was born in 63 B.C., were at first Gaius Octavius, but after he had been recognised as the adopted son of his grand-uncle, the great Julius Cæsar, he became *Gaius Julius Cæsar Octavianus Divi Filius*. It was only in the January of 27 B.C. that he received from the Roman Senate the epithet of 'Augustus' by which name history knows him. That a fair-haired little man, only five foot six in height – diffident, shy, but with keen and brilliant eyes, should have become an Olympian god always was, and still remains, a matter for some astonishment. The main reason probably is that he saved Rome and its empire from disintegration and collapse. As one Mediterranean nation after another, seeking Rome's protection or provoking her resentment, became incorporated, the Roman Republic had slowly, unwittingly, and unwillingly acquired an Empire. Never in history except perhaps during the Spanish conquest of South America was there such opportunity for oppression, rapine, enrichment and corruption. By 70 B.C. the situation was appalling, and beyond cure even by men of comparative integrity like Cicero. Then came the clash of Civil War; Cæsar against Pompey, Cæsar against the Senate, followed by a breathing-space of peace under the great *Julius Cæsar Dictator Perpetuus Pontifex Maximus Parens Patriæ*. Salvation for harassed humanity was in sight, and the force of circumstance was thrusting upon Cæsar, not Ruler-Cult, but divine kingship, the claim to which lay in his direct descent from Iulus, Æneas, and thus from Aphrodite herself. Then came Cæsar's murder on the fatal Ides of March, and the returning horrors of yet more desperate Civil War: Octavian – Cæsar's grand-nephew and adopted son – against Antony and Cleopatra. Even the propaganda coinage struck by both sides helps to give a picture of the agony of the civilised world; for, amid this long-enduring turmoil in Rome, as formerly in Greece, the foundations of belief had given way. At last, in 31 B.C., came the sea-fight at Actium which ushered in a peace that saved the world. It was after this victory that Octavian devoted his life to the restoration of the State and the Empire, to the complete reform of religion and sexual conduct, to the administration and the law, and to the service of humanity. He had long been known as *Princeps*, or temporal head of the State, when in 12 B.C. he also became the Supreme Pontiff, the spiritual head; and it is as such that he figures, wearing a short-sleeved Greek *chiton* under his voluminous toga, in a marble statue found in 1910 by Roman archæologists (Plate XV, facing page 192). For the Greek half of the empire, however, upon gold coins struck somewhere in Greece or Ionia, he was presented after another fashion – in the guise of a Hellenistic Ruler, as remarkable in his own way for good looks as had been Alexander (Plate XV). From Spain to Syria, and from the Rhine to the Nile, the peoples of that huge empire gave him gratitude and love, expressed through a well-established Cult of the Ruler. It is true enough that

the assemblage of qualities and capacities that made up his personality are not such as to strike the imagination of the world. In the sense that

Alexander, Cæsar or Napoleon surpassed other men in intellectual equipment, Augustus cannot be counted a man of genius. That he was not: he was the man the world needed, and may claim to have been one of the greatest servants of the human race. [1]

The personality and character of Augustus is much more clear to us than that of Alexander because it is only slightly befogged by hostile propaganda; for Augustus was given a 'good press' by a biographer of learning and distinction, Gaius Suetonius Tranquillinus, born about A.D. 69, who was for a time private secretary to the Emperor Hadrian about A.D. 120. Suetonius[2] had evidently full access to a great many of the Imperial records and to letters preserved in the archives of Augustus. To the information in that biography much can be added from inscriptions and coins, as well as the many allusions in the works of Virgil and other contemporaries. For the Greeks, indeed, 'Sebastos' was a Greek, just as 'Augustus' was a Roman for the Romans. In his lifetime he really became a god manifest on earth; that is to say, such an individual as Augustus might be called a god, either unreservedly or with reference to yourself, a *god to you*. If you recognised in him the essential characteristics of a particular god, you might call him that god, again either unreservedly or with reference to yourself.[3]

Such an attitude explains why Augustus was actually worshipped while still on earth, and frequently in company with the goddess Roma, whose resemblance in religious art to the Greek Athene was so very close that one might think of Roma as personated by Athene, and therefore an Olympian.

There was a great altar at Lugdunum in Gaul (Lyons) to Roma and Augustus, a fine temple to the same pair at Pergamum in Asia Minor, and elsewhere. Furthermore, these two 'deities' appear enthroned side by side on the celebrated *gemma Augustea* of about A.D. 15 (Plate XV, facing page 192), a sardonyx cameo now in Vienna, showing Augustus as Zeus-Jupiter beside Dea Roma as Athene. Above is 'Capricorn', his natal constellation; a goddess

[1] Sir Frank Adcock in *Cambridge Ancient History*, vol. viii.   [2] An excellent translation of his *Lives of the Caesars* exists in the Loeb Classical Library.
[3] A. D. Nock in *JHS*, 48 (1928).

like the Greek Tyche, or Fortune, sets a wreath on his head. To
the right one sees Poseidon and Demeter. On the left an Apolline
figure steps down from a chariot driven by Nike, or Victory.
Work and conception alike are Greek.

Among the various bits of gossip which Suetonjus has preserved about Augustus is one which seems to imply a touch of
divine ruthlessness. A man of unusual kindness, he nevertheless
had a streak of cruelty for he cherished a passion, which his wife,
the Empress Livia encouraged, for possessing young virgins. This
may seem odd in the great reformer of sexual morals in Roman
society, but by that time he was securely established with altars
and temples to his name, and he was free to act outside all human
codes, for he was already an Olympian.

It remains beyond doubt that all the inhabitants of the ancient
civilised world loved Augustus. He could ask no higher praise
than the tribute he happened to receive shortly before his death
from the crew of a ship he met off Puteoli, when the sailors cried
out that it was through Him that they were alive, through Him
that they sailed the seas, through Him that they enjoyed liberty
and fortune. After the Imperial funeral a person of distinction, an
ex-Praetor, took an oath to say that he had seen the form of the
Emperor, although his body had been reduced to ashes, rising on
its way to heaven.

From among the blessed company of 'the godlike' (not gods),
whom the Greeks called *Theioi* (not *Theoi*) and the Latins *Divi*
(not *Dei*), four have been chosen, with full consideration given to
the fact that there were many other candidates who thought
themselves suited for honorary membership of Olympus. Should
Pythagoras have ascended into heaven, and Ptolemy Saviour?
Antiochus IV, styled 'God Manifest', and Cleopatra VII, Queen of
Egypt? The great Julius Cæsar was counted a god by the Romans,
but he was in direct line from Aphrodite herself (see page 91); and
claims were made for other kings and other emperors. Paganism
did not draw so distinct a line between 'the god-like' and gods,
as did the Church between saints and the Holy Family, for no
dogma existed that could stop thoughts, musings and private

theories about divinity from running fancy-free. Yet the four who have here been chosen have clearly shared this: each one was thought of as a supreme benefactor of the human race.

In passing one may observe that the sagas about these four had one surprising thing in common – a definite association with serpents. In the Theban legend Hera sent two malignant serpents to the infant Herakles in his cradle, and he strangled them with his bare hands; while in the Argive legend his second labour involved the destruction of a monstrous many-headed serpent at Lerna. Asklepios, the Cretans said, restored a son of Minos to life by using a certain herb which was shown to him by a serpent, and in Sicyon he was honoured in the form of a serpent, the reptile being associated with him constantly. On the night before her marriage to Philip, King of Macedon, Olympias, the mother of Alexander, dreamed that Zeus impregnated her in the shape of a serpent and she probably believed in the symbolic conception of Alexander in that night. Finally, Suetonius has the following story which he quotes from an earlier Greek work wherein he had read that when Atia, the mother of Augustus, had come in the middle of the night to the solemn service of Apollo, she had her litter set down in the temple and fell asleep, while the rest of the matrons also slept. On a sudden a serpent glided up to her, and shortly went away. When she awoke, she purified herself, as if after the embraces of her husband, and at once there appeared on her body a mark in colours like a serpent, and she could never get rid of it.

Once upon a time, not so very long ago, it was customary to regard snakes as symbols of the gods beneath the earth, simply because serpents have the habit of creeping out from holes beneath rocks. In reality they appear to have been associated with apotheosis, not only in the religion of ancient Greece, but also in that of Egypt. The great Cleopatra held to the religions of both civilisations and knew that serpents were sacred. 'Of the manner of her death no doubt should now exist, for it is known why she used an asp; the creature deified whom it struck, for it was the divine minister of the Sun-god, which raised its head on the crown of Egypt to guard the line of Rē.'[1]

[1] *CAH*, **x**, page 110.

Belief in the old gods and reflection about the spiritual existence of the Twelve Olympians came to no sudden end, nor did it peter out when the Church, under the Constantinian dispensation, gained ascendancy over the old faith. In the Eastern Church, more than in the Western, a belief in the Greek gods as mystical symbols of one godhead lingered on, and has never altogether ceased, as anyone may discover in converse with learned bishops and abbots of the Greek Orthodox Church. The Western Church was, however, unbending, claiming to know all the right answers to everything. For many centuries our ancestors were enslaved to dogma, and it is therefore difficult for modern man or woman to imagine a state of affairs in which intelligent people could be truly religious without the supporting props of recited creeds and litanies, or without a professional executive priesthood to shepherd the faithful. But the ancient Greeks, though they had none of these things, and though they never thought to suppress sciences or scepticism, were nevertheless a profoundly religious people.

Hitherto familiar notions such as 'god', 'soul', 'sin', 'worship', being part of our traditions tied to a Christian ethic, have blocked our approach to the genuineness of Olympian religion. Having perceived the unique brilliance of the Greeks, the moderns have found their religion either childish or decoratively and coldly formal. Yet surviving Greek literature, almost all of it, was seriously preoccupied with religious faith. In Hellenism, it has been maintained,[1] the faculty which in other religions is constantly being thwarted and inhibited, flowers forth with the admirable assurance of genius – the faculty of seeing the world in the light of the divine, for the Olympian Pantheon was spiritually adequate for civilised men. Recusants were few, the best-known a sixth-century writer, Xenophanes, the first deistic rationalist, who denied the existence of the Olympians. His followers, however, were intellectually vanquished by Empedocles, and the Pythagoreans, adherents of Olympianism. Greeks never forgot the existence of

[1] Walter F. Otto, *The Homeric Gods*, 1954.

the older, sinister gods, but for them the victory of the Homeric gods over the dark ones seemed as definite as the victory of Christ over Satan. The old faith had been much constricted by the elemental, as ancient existence itself, in which earth, procreation, blood and death were the dominant realities. If towards the end of the Pagan dispensation, the gloomier spirits of earth enjoyed a revival of cult as against the happier Olympians, this was due to the ill-mixed and unsavoury pottage, brewed from a variety of oriental cults, practices, superstitions and beliefs, which was washed into the Græco-Roman melting-pot. Until that misfortune befell, the Homeric gods held continual sway in Greek minds and gave its spiritual significance to Greek religion.

On the material side there is also important evidence for the belief of the great majority in their gods. Coins which were issued in their millions by hundreds of Greek States and Cities, bore as types the heads or images or symbols of the great gods themselves. Coined money was put under divine protection – exactly as mediæval money was. Issuers and users alike believed in the efficacy of such protection, for they believed in those deities.

An attempt has been made to emphasise this important piece of evidence by a selection of ancient Greek coins, mostly of great fineness and elegance, illustrated on our plates.

Olympia and its mints are represented by two silver coins,[1] the first with a severe head of Zeus, struck about 420 B.C. and depicting an early conception of the Father of Gods and Men (Plate II, facing page 17); the second, of about 380 B.C., has a queenly head of Hera (Plate III, facing page 32); and both coins carry the signatures of their engravers. Another coin with a head of the God (Plate II) is much later, minted at Antioch about 167 B.C. by a great Greek king of Syria, 'Antiochus IV God Manifest', as he was styled. The head of Zeus is under the influence of the famous gold and ivory figure which Pheidias, the sculptor, made for the temple of Zeus at Olympia about 430 B.C., but the features are those of King Antiochus.[2]

---

[1] All the coins briefly described are of silver unless exceptionally described as of gold or bronze. Some are shown a little larger than their true size.
[2] See above.

Gold coin with head of Augustus, as a young Greek hero, struck about 20 B.C. in Greek Asia Minor.

AUGUSTUS as Supreme Pontiff. Life-size marble portrait statue found in Rome, and made after 12 B.C.

Large cameo, the 'Gemma Augustea', showing Augustus as Zeus, beside Dea Roma and other gods. Made about A.D. 15.

PLATE XV

Intaglio black sard (and plaster impression) with bust of Antinoos, Hadrian's favourite, as a god. Made after A.D. 130 by Antonianos of Aphrodisias.

Gold medallion with head of the Emperor Diocletian, self-styled 'Jovius'. On the reverse he appears as Jupiter. Struck about A.D. 295 at Nicomedia.

Gold medallion with head of Maximian ('Herculius'), in the lion scalp of Herakles. On reverse, two Cæsars. Struck in A.D. 293 at Ticinum.

Gold medallion with head of Constantine the Great posing as Alexander (compare the two lowest coins in Plate XIV, facing p. 177). Struck about A.D. 320 at Siscia.

PLATE XVI

Artemis on coins appeared in various presentations. Two here shown are on a coin of the Achæan League of about 366 B.C. (Plate III, facing page 32) and on a brilliant coin of Syracuse made about 405 B.C. (Plate XII, facing page 129). On the former she is the Huntress, her hair gathered high on her head; on the latter she is Artemis-Arethusa, goddess and water-nymph combined, patroness of Syracuse. Her brother Apollo may be seen on the coins of very many Greek states. Here we observe one from the west struck about 424 B.C. in Sicilian Leontini (Plate VI, facing page 65); one from the east minted at Clazomenæ in Ionia about 370 B.C. (Plate VI) with a splendid facing head of the god. Both these masterpieces bear artists' signatures.

For Athene we have two contrasting coins: one from her greatest city, Athens, and made about 520 B.C., still quite archaic in style (Plate IV, facing page 33); and one from a Corinthian city on the west coast of Greece, dated to about 440 B.C. (Plate IV), which shows the goddess as a young girl. A similar contrast appears on two coins having heads of Hermes: the former stern and formal, minted at Ænus about 470 B.C. (Plate V, facing page 64); the latter made a century later at Sybrita in Crete, with a more realistic but admirable head of the young god (Plate V).

Aphrodite is best presented on two contrasting pieces, both from the south-western corner of Asia Minor. One (Plate VII, facing page 80) depicts her as a girlish goddess, Dorian in her simplicity, for it was struck about 470 B.C. at Dorian Cnidus. By contrast the other coin, made in Lycia about the same time (Plate VII), shows her in the guise of a lady of fashion, turned out to perfection.

Demeter, a favourite on ancient coins, appears in youthful form, corn-crowned, on a coin struck in South Italian Metapontum (Plate VIII, facing page 81) about 340 B.C. She is the mourning goddess, veiled as on the marble by Leochares, upon a Delphian coin of 335 B.C. (Plate VIII). No head of Dionysos was made by any artist more impressive than the one which the Ætna Master engraved about 460 B.C. for the people of Naxos in Sicily (Plate XI, facing page 128). With this firm, splendid, frightening god, one may contrast a soft, watery Poseidon on a coin made for a Macedonian king about 258 B.C. (Plate XI).

Two of the Twelve Olympians remain to be illustrated from Greek coins. Of Ares there is a very early picture, of about 540 B.C., pop-eyed and helmeted (Plate IX, facing page 112), from the island of Calymna. For Hephaistos we have to turn west and move to the volcanic island of Lipara off Sicily, to find a presentation of the god of about 350 B.C. (Plate IX), on a coin made of copper. Those are the goddesses and gods that the Greeks believed in as truly as any mediæval European believed in the Holy Trinity, the Blessed Virgin and the Saints. Had the Greeks not believed, they would not have employed their intense gifts for fineness, their love of human beauty manifest in godhead, to put so grand an array of small masterpieces upon the current coin.

And what of the honorary Olympians – those who were thought of as guests of the gods, and so, by association, gods themselves? Two dominated the scene – Herakles and Alexander. The former, already met with heavily-bearded on money of the sixth century B.C., was first shown as a young beardless god on a coin of Sicilian Camarina (Plate XIII, facing page 176) made about 415 B.C., and this became a prototype for coins of the Macedonian kingdom. The head of young Herakles wearing the lion's scalp was the obverse type of all the millions of silver pieces issued for Alexander's empire, the finest of them being the first coin of Alexandria by Egypt (Plate XIV, facing page 177) struck in 326 B.C. On this, the face of the god Herakles was the face of the god Alexander. A new type came into existence about 300 B.C. (Plate XIV) when Lysimachus, once a general under Alexander and now King of Thrace, set upon the coinage a head of the divine Alexander, the horn of the god Ammon shown in his hair. The strong neck and the lifted chin that gives the inspired and god-like look for which he was famous are there on this coin. Nearly five and a half centuries later, when the worship of Alexander the Great received a new and intense revival under the Roman imperial Severan dynasty, the same design was used again; this time for a great gold prize-medal (Plate XIV), issued in the reign of the Emperor Severus Alexander. The world conqueror and benefactor of mankind was thought of as a god who might yet return to save the civilised world.

Augustus, as has been noted, was treated in his lifetime as a personification on earth of more than one Olympian. Upon the 'Gemma Augustea' he figured as Zeus (Plate XV, facing p. 192);[1] on some coins he appeared in the guise of Hermes or Apollo, and where he resembled the latter (Plate XV), he posed as a kind of young Greek heroic figure with an aura of divinity about him. One hundred and fifty years after that little gold coin of Augustus was made by a Greek engraver, there occurred a strange attempt to place one more guest in the company of the Olympian gods. The emperor Hadrian, stricken with grief at the loss of his beloved favourite, the young Antinoos drowned in the Nile, asked the empire to treat the youth as a god risen to Olympus. All the skill of Greek artists of the day was lavished on creating statues, reliefs, medals and gems, the finest surviving a black sard (Plate XVI, facing p. 193) which ranks as a masterpiece. But this was all of no avail and Antinoos was soon forgotten after Hadrian's death, for the youth was no benefactor of the human race.

Towards the end of the ancient civilisation there occurred other interesting attempts to assume godhead, notably on the part of two co-emperors, Diocletian and Maximian. Uncouth in appearance, this pair of Dalmatian and Pannonian soldier-men, sprung from recent peasant stock, shared the Empire between them, propped its tottering frame and reconstructed its administration. Seeking to be recognised as gods rather than as men, Diocletian took the title 'Jovius', and Maximian called himself 'Herculius'. The rugged features of these self-made Olympians were emphasised on their coins and medals (Plate XVI), Maximian appearing in a lion's scalp. Upon the reverses on a number of these fine medallions the senior emperor appeared naked as Jupiter-Zeus, with sceptre and eagle; while his colleague figured as Herakles. For the last time in the ancient world a ruler was represented in heroic nudity, for the new faith which Constantine was about to establish looked upon the unclothed body as a shameful thing.

With Constantine, who recognised the Christian Church as the

[1] See p. 187.

official source of his religion in A.D. 313, our survey of divinity proclaimed on coinage comes to an end. 'According to the strictness of ecclesiastic language', wrote Gibbon, 'the first of the Christian emperors was unworthy of that name till the moment of his death; since it was only during his last illness that he received the imposition of hands, and was afterwards admitted, by the initiatory rites of baptism, into the number of the Faithful.' While a grateful Church raised him before long to sainthood among the Company of the Blessed in Heaven, he would have been more at home on Olympus as the companion of Alexander and Augustus.

Christian monograms appear discretely, but very rarely, on Constantine's money, which in general follows the pagan imperial tradition. As a symbolic piece one may note a handsome gold medallion struck in Siscia. On the obverse is a formalised portrait of Constantine as Alexander, for the strong neck and uplifted chin are unmistakable, and the suggestion is that the divine Alexander has achieved his 'second coming'. The reverse of the medallion is less pleasing in its symbolism. The emperor, in full armour, holding a spear and a trophy, marches to the right, and, in his stride, delivers a sharp kick on the buttock of a prostrate female figure who symbolises some vanquished State or Province. There comes to mind a twelfth-century carved capital at Clermont-Ferrand on which Adam punishes the temptress Eve in like fashion.[1] Apart from that one may take the picture on this coin as an omen that boded ill for womankind, destined to suffer many centuries of humiliation until the Renaissance should restore a measure of happiness and justice.[2]

When a historian attains a certain age he may be permitted, as a rare treat, to take a wide sweep across the centuries, especially if that which he has been describing appears to him to have some relevance for our own day. Readers who have read as far as these words have perhaps wondered whether I could seriously approve a going back to earlier ways in religious practice. Advocacy of such a thing must be sheer folly, for modern man would fit ill

[1] Seltman, *The Studio*, April 1953, p. 104, fig. 9.
[2] See Seltman, *Women in Antiquity*, 1956, Chapters XI and XII.

into any cultus pattern of the past. He would be as uncomfortable in God-denying revolutionary Paris as among God-fearing Tudor Protestants; under Peter the Great as under Pope Boniface VIII. The moderation of mediæval Manichees in France or the fanaticism of malodorous monks in fourth-century Alexandria, the grossness of Inquisitors or the obscurities of Gnostics, would all be equally difficult for him to stomach.

Neither could he return to paganism with its oracles, animal sacrifices, and multiplicity of gods.

But there remains a question of great moment to be asked. Has the study of paganism anything to offer that may help us now, at the present time, within the framework of our society built upon a Christian basis? In the early days of the Church the contribution which pagan thought made to it was tremendous, for it was this which transmuted a Jewish sectarian Christianity into a Hellenised form capable of becoming a world-religion. Yet to some historians it appears that Christianity unlearnt not all, but many, of its Greek lessons; and that even before Constantine there was a real slipping away from the teaching of Christ. The Western Pontifical experiment which overshadowed mediæval Europe was from the Christian angle not so much a wrong tendency as a false emphasis, which placed obedience to authority and conformity above the salvation of humanity and happiness. The Renaissance restored much of the goodness of the ancient world, while the Protestant Reformation – of which, in its purity, Erasmus was unwittingly the true begetter – brought back much more of goodness, only to stray away again into too many follies akin to those that had beset the early Church.

For twenty years I lived in the rooms which were once occupied by Erasmus, the prince of Northern humanists, who devoted himself with equal zeal to pagan and to Christian letters. His example is adequate to justify the view that a study of Greek paganism has still plenty to teach us about the value of a group of principles that make for humanism.

First, mankind must recapture a zeal for the Truth, even though Truth discovered often shocks the seeker. There are today far too many professing adherents to Christian form who echo the words of a certain Procurator of Judæa. Pilate put the question 'What is Truth?' in a mood of cynicism; his modern imitators put it in a mood of fear. And they think they can evade it by way of a wry smile, a deprecating gesture, and a vague reference to Faith as superior to Reason or Knowledge. At times fear of Truth produces a swift, impatient thrust of the ostrich-head into the sands of mortified mysticism. No Greek ever allowed religious prohibitions to curtail his passionate search for knowledge and for truth, come what may.

Second, humility, which the Church too often demands from men, would better become the Church herself. As a famous Anglican bishop once said, 'The assertion that any Church is infallible is both impudent and dangerous.' Especially is this true for the last four centuries and more, because since the Renaissance the greatest thinkers, writers and poets, including those of a religious bent, and all the great scientists have not accepted such of the Church's dogmas as demand a blind faith which is an offence against intellectual integrity.

Third, let all active proselytism and all patronising attitudes towards men of other faiths be for ever abandoned.

Fourth, let the all-out emphasis on sin be modified, and let the early Christian and Erasmian transmutation of the concept into 'folly' become the new Christian one. The word in the Greek New Testament means no more than 'fault' or 'error of judgment'. That is a tremendous lesson to be learnt from the ancient Greeks.

Fifth, there should be more trust in the frequent good intentions of mankind which do sometimes get implemented. There is no more vicious proverb than the one which asserts that the road to Hell is paved with good intentions.

Sixth, toleration – and honest toleration – must abound. Not that dubious toleration which is patronising, conditional, and permissive; but a mentally unreserved and total toleration of views that seem utterly wrong. To exchange this with Jews, Moslems, and Buddhists is apparently easy; but the Catholic must tolerate the Protestant gladly, and the Protestant must tolerate the Catholic gladly, even as Paul suffered fools gladly. Pythian Apollo was happy and proud to tolerate Delian Apollo; Delian Apollo showed enthusiastic toleration for one whom he looked upon as his other self, Pythian Apollo.

This is where ancient Greek paganism can supply the best, the finest, and the most valuable lesson of all.

The study of the beliefs of the Greeks, of their cults, and of their genial, healthy way of life is something that gives us confidence in humanity within the framework of history. It is something which can knock the frightened mood of self-depreciation out of mankind – a mood that would have repelled self-respecting Greeks, whose code of conduct was summed up in 'Know thyself', 'Don't exceed' – precepts conducive to the practice of good manners. Indeed, few will deny that our present civilisation's gravest fault is a shortage of these; for good manners are a trouble to acquire and, like toleration, difficult to keep. One maxim has been invented within the Christian dispensation which Apollo would gladly have added to the others inscribed in his temple at Delphi:

MANNERS MAKETH MAN.

INDEX

101201